Spanish Grammar For Beginners + Audio

The most complete textbook and workbook
For Latin American Spanish Learners

MyDailySpanish.com

No part of this book including the audio material may be copied, reproduced, transmitted or distributed in any form without the prior written permission of the author. For permission requests, write to: contact@mydailyspanish.com.

Also available:

<u>Spanish Stories for Beginners</u>

Table of Contents

Introduction

When learning any language, grammar definitely comes up as the most challenging–and boring–part. Spanish is no different. Unfortunately, grammar is not something that can just be relegated to the sidelines.

You simply cannot skip learning grammar if you truly want to become proficient. It doesn't work that way, and there are no shortcuts. If you want to be able to express yourself in Chinese using clear and precise language, you need to build a strong and solid foundation in Chinese grammar.

This book is here to help you. In the lessons in this book, we will lay down the rules in Chinese grammar and provide you with lots of examples, clarifications, and exercises.

Practice Your Spanish Listening Skills and Pronunciation

A key to succeed in language learning is to get a good grasp of pronunciation at the beginning of your lessons. This requires constant listening practice. With this book's audio accompaniment, you will get a head start in your listening comprehension as well as hone your pronunciation straight off the bat.

Each lesson and exercise contain audio narrated by a native Spanish speaker from Mexico. By listening to the audio and reading the written text at the same time, you will be able to connect how the Spanish words and sentences appear versus how it sounds when spoken in actual Spanish conversations.

Embedded Grammar Workbook

There is no need to buy a separate workbook to help you practice the grammar points you learn. We have integrated hundreds of different types of exercises into the book. This way, you will be able to cement your learning through taking the quizzes after each grammar lesson and you will be able to assess your progress as you go along.

Build a Learning Habit

This book also aims to help you build a learning habit that will help you sustain learning Chinese even if your motivation wanes as you go along. You'll find that the book is divided into 30 lessons with each lesson meant to be tackled each day. After 30 days of studying consistently every day, you will be able to form a learning habit that will ultimately help you achieve your learning goals.

Spanish Grammar, Simplified

Spanish grammar is already complicated, we don't need to make it even more complex. So in this book, you'll notice that we use the simplest yet thorough explanations. We do not want to burden you with wordy explanations and unnecessary jargons, and instead, in this book we explain Spanish grammar in a way that makes it easily digestible and easy to grasp.

We have put a lot of effort in this book so it will come out in a way that will be most useful to your Spanish language learning journey. We certainly hope that it will help you build the strong grammar foundation you need to eventually reach fluency in Spanish.

Thank you very much and good luck.

My Daily Spanish team

Advice on how to use this book effectively

This book is divided into 25 lessons and one lesson is meant to be followed each day for around 30 minutes to an hour.

If a lesson seems too long for you, you can split the lesson into two days. The important thing is that you work on it every day for 25 days (or more) so that it helps you build an effective learning habit.

HOW CAN YOU DOWNLOAD THE AUDIO?

On the last page of this book, you will find the link which enables you to download the Audio files that accompany this book. Save the files onto any device and listen to the stories anywhere.

Lesson 1. Greetings

The first thing you need to know about a new language is how to greet people. For our first lesson today, we'll take it easy and talk about how to say hello as well as other greetings in Spanish.

Let's start!

Listen to Track 1 (Reminder: <u>you can download the audio from the link available page 214</u>)

Basic Spanish Greetings

¡Hola!	Hello!
Buenos días	Good morning
Buenas tardes	Good afternoon
Buenas noches	Good evening
¿Cómo está?	How are you? (formal)
¿Cómo está usted?	How are you? (formal)
¿Cómo estás?	How are you? (informal)
¿Cómo están?	How are you (informal/formal plural)
Buenas.	Hello (something you'll hear a lot on the streets, or when you walk into shops, etc.)
¿Qué tal?	How are you doing?/ What's up? (very informal)
¿Cómo andas?	
¿Qué hay?	(Loosely translated) What's up? (Also very informal–use only with friends, family, etc.)
¿Qué onda?	(Loosely translated) What's up? (Also very informal–use only with friends, family, etc.)

Common Response

Listen to Track 2

You can reply with:

Bien, gracias	I'm good, thank you
Bien, gracias, ¿y usted?	Good, thanks, and you? (formal)
Bien, gracias, ¿y tú?	Good, thanks, and you? (informal)
Más o menos	More or less/Not so good
Como siempre	As always
Todo bien	Everything's good

Muy bien	Very good
Aquí estamos	Here we are (like saying, "still here, alive and kicking")
Estoy de maravilla	I´m great!

The other side of saying hello is saying goodbye. Let's have a look at the different ways to say this in Spanish.

Saying Goodbye in Spanish

Listen to Track 3

Adiós	Goodbye
Bye	Goodbye
Chao	Bye (informal)
Nos vemos	See you (informal)
Hasta mañana	See you tomorrow
Hasta luego	See you later
Hasta la próxima semana	See you next week
Que tengas un buen día	Have a nice day
Hasta pronto	See you soon

That was quite easy, huh? We're off to a great start! See you again tomorrow for a really long lesson on how to introduce yourself in Spanish. *¡Hasta la próxima!*

Workbook Lesson 1: Los Saludos – Greetings

Exercise 1: Tick the right answer.

1- Camila is a friend of Paula's. She would ask her:

a. *¿Cómo estás?*   b. *¿Cómo está usted?*

2- It's morning. Pedro wants to say good morning to Marcos. He would say:

a. Buenas tardes   b. Buenos días   c. Buenas noches

3- To wish someone a good night, you would say:

a. Buenos días   b. Buenas tardes   c. Buenas noches

4- To say goodbye, you should say:

a. Hola   b. *¿Cómo estás?*   c. Hasta luego

5- You want to ask your boss how he is. You say:

a. *¿Cómo estás?*   b. *¿Cómo está usted?*

Exercise 2: Translate from Spanish to English and vice versa.

Spanish	English
1- ¡Buenos días!	.... *Good morning*
2- ...... *Como estás*	How are you (informal)?
3- ...... *Bien, gracias*	Well, thank you.
4- No muy bien.	.... *Not very well*
5- ...... *Y tú?*	And you? (informal)
6- Nos vemos.	.... *See you*

Exercise 3: This is a conversation between you and a friend (informal). Make the necessary changes so that it becomes a conversation between you and your boss (formal).

Tú (you): ¡Hola! ¿Cómo estás?

You (you): Hello! How are you?

Tú amigo (your friend): Bien. ¿Y tú?

Your friend: Fine. And you?

Tú (you): Todo bien. ¡Hasta luego!

You (you): All good. See you then!

Tú (your friend): ¡Adiós!

Your friend: Goodbye!

Tú (you): _usted Hola como está_

Tu jefe (your boss): _Muy bien gracias_

Tu jefe (your boss): _Bien, y usted_

Tú (you): _?_

Tú (you): _____

Tú jefe (your boss): _____

Tú jefe (your boss): _____

Tú (you): _____

Exercise 4: Translate from Spanish to English and vice versa.

Spanish	English
1- ...... *Buenos tardes*	Good evening.
2- ...... *Como estás*	How are you? (informal)
3- Muy bien.	...... *very well*
4- ...... *Mas or menos*	Not so good.
5- ...... *Y usted*	And you? (formal)
6- ¡Hasta pronto!	...... *See you soon.*

Exercise 5: Translate this conversation from Spanish to English.

You: Good morning. How's it going?   *Buenos días como estás*

Your friend: Good . And you?   *Bien, y tú?*

You: Everything is going well. See you soon!   *Todo bien, hasta pronto!*

Your friend: Bye!   *Adiós*

Exercise 6: Tick the right answer.

1- Your friend asked you "¿Cómo estás?" You're not feeling very well, so you would say:

   a. Muy bien.   b. De maravilla.   c. No muy bien.

2- To wish someone a good day, you would say:

   a. Buenas tardes.   b. Buenas noches.   c. Buen día.

3- You've been talking to a friend and you want to say "See you soon" before going your separate ways. You would say:

   a. ¡Hasta pronto!   b. ¡Hasta luego!   c. ¡Hola!

4- You're talking to your boss. You say:

   a. Yo estoy bien, gracias. Y ¿tú?   b. Yo estoy bien, gracias. Y ¿usted?

5- How would you answer if somebody asked you «¿Cómo estás?»:

   a. Muy bien, gracias.   b. ¡Hola!   c. Hasta pronto.

Exercise 7: Translate from Spanish to English and vice versa.

Spanish	English
1- _____	Hello!/Hi! (informal)
2- _____	How are you? (formal)
3- Todo va bien.	_____
4- _____	Bye! (informal)
5- Buenas noches.	_____
6- Buenas tardes.	_____

Exercise 8: Translate this conversation from Spanish to English.

Tú: Buenos días, señor, ¿cómo está?   _____

Tú jefe: Bien, gracias, y ¿usted?   _____

Tú: Todo va bien, gracias. Hasta luego. _____

Tú jefe: Buenas tardes. _____

Exercise 9: Translate from Spanish to English and vice versa.

Spanish	English
1- Más o menos	_____
2- _____	Bye
3- Como siempre	_____
4- _____	Here we are
5- Estoy de maravilla	_____
6- _____	I'm good, thank you

Exercise 10: Translate this conversation from English to Spanish.

You: How's it going? _____

Your friend: I'm good, thank you, and you? _____

You: Well, here we are. _____

Your friend: As always. _____

You: As always! have a nice day, bye. _____

ANSWERS:

Exercise 1

1/ ¿Cómo estás? 2/ Buenos días 3/ Buenas noches 4/ Hasta luego 5/ *¿Cómo está usted?*

Exercise 2

1/ Good morning! / Hello! 2/ *¿Cómo estás?* 3/ Bien, gracias. 4/ Not very well. 5/ ¿Y usted? 5/ See you.

Exercise 3

(Possible) Answer:

Tú (you): Buenos días. ¿Cómo está usted?

Tú jefe (your boss): Bien, gracias, y ¿usted?

Tú (you): Bien. Buenas tardes.

Tú jefe (your boss): Hasta pronto.

Exercise 4

1/ Buenas tardes 2/ ¿Cómo estás? 3/ Very well. 4/ No muy bien. 5/ Y ¿usted? 6/ See you soon!

Exercise 5

Tú: Buenos días, ¿cómo estás?

Tú: Todo va bien. ¡Hasta pronto!

Tu amigo: Bien. Y ¿tú?

Tu amigo: ¡Adiós!

Exercise 6

1/ No muy bien. 2/ Buenos días. 3/ ¡Hasta pronto! 4/ Yo estoy bien, gracias. Y ¿usted? 5/ Muy bien, gracias.

Exercise 7

1/ Hola! 2/ ¿Cómo está? - ¿Cómo está usted? 3/ Everything is going well. 4/ **¡Adios! - ¡Bye!** 5/ Good night. 6/ Good afternoon.

Exercise 8

You: Good morning, Sir. How are you?   **Your boss:** Well, thank you. And you?

You: Everything is going well, thank you. Goodbye.   **Your boss:** Have a nice day.

Exercise 9

1/ More or less/ Not so good. 2/ Chao. 3/ As always. 4/ Aquí estamos. 5/ I'm great. 6/ Bien, gracias.

Exercise 10

Tu: ¿Qué tal?

Tu amigo: Bien, gracias, y ¿tú?

Tu: Bien, aquí estamos.

Tu amigo: Como siempre.

Tu: ¡Como siempre! Que tengas un buen día, chao.

Lesson 2. Introductions

One of the first things you need to know in order to speak Spanish is how to start. If you can't start a conversation, how are you ever going to practice? And, what better way to start a conversation than by introducing yourself?

That's where this lesson comes in. Here, you'll find some quick tips, phrases, and different ways of introducing yourself in Spanish and learning how to get the conversational ball rolling.

Getting Started

Listen to Track 4

Let's look at the very basics of how you'll go about letting the Spanish speaking world know just who you are.

In the previous lesson we talked about how to greet someone in Spanish. Using the greetings you've learned, you can already begin the conversation. Then you move on to….

Yo me llamo…

The logical next step, after saying "hello" to someone would be to tell them your name! You can't very well carry on a conversation with someone if you don't know who they are or don't let them know who you are. Once again, you have some options.

(Yo) me llamo…- The most commonly used, and literally translated means "I call myself".

Soy*…- If you're a fan of brevity, this introduction is for you! It's like saying "I'm…"

Mi nombre es… - The very practical "My name is…"

*This verb (which comes from *ser***, one of the two ways in Spanish to say "to be") will come in handy when introducing yourself, so make sure you keep it in the back of your mind, as we'll be seeing it again.

**This verb is used with permanent qualities. I am short; I am American; I am awesome. These things won't change! Temporary qualities take the verb *estar. Estoy enfadado*-I am angry. *Estoy triste*-I am sad, etc.

Getting Deeper

While it is important to know someone's name in order to strike up a conversation with them, if that's all you say, the chat will be very short-lived. So, what else can you say about yourself?

Soy de… Vivo en…

The verb *soy* was mentioned before and means "I am…". If you add the (very useful to remember) preposition "de" after it, you're saying "I am from…"

Soy de Chicago. I am from Chicago.

Just because you're from somewhere, doesn't necessarily mean that you live there. So, that's probably a good little piece of information to give someone about yourself. You say *vivo en* (I live in…)

Soy de Chicago, pero vivo en Chile. I'm from Chicago, but I live in Chile.

Tengo *X* años.

Saying your age is a little different. Surprisingly, you don't use *ser* or *estar* for this one. Pay attention here, because this is something that really gets a lot of English speakers in trouble. In Spanish you are not 20 years old... You have 20 years!! (I repeat "have *x* years")

Tengo 20 años-I have 20 years (Meaning - I am 20 years old).

Soy...

Hey! There's that verb again! I told you it'd be important.

Another important thing you should be able to mention about yourself is what you do–as in "what's your job"?

Soy estudiante/ profesor(a)/ abogado(a)/ dentista- I am a student/ teacher/ lawyer/ dentist (notice that the first and last one doesn't change gender).

Me gusta...

Another useful expression you may want to know when introducing/ talking about yourself is "me gusta...". This can be a tricky expression for English speakers, because its construction is a little different from how it's said in English. Literally translated it means "To me it is pleasing..."

So as not to get too complicated, let's just stick with using this construction with some verbs in the infinitive so we can say "To me it is pleasing to (insert verb here)."

Me gusta leer/ jugar basket/ cocinar/ ir al cine- I like to read/ play basketball/ cook/ go to the movies.

Examples

Let's take everything we've seen and put it all together. Below you will find two examples of people introducing themselves. They are both native English speakers who live/study in Mexico. They will use the aforementioned phrases, as well as adding in a few extra things about themselves.

Self-Introduction in Spanish: Example 1

Listen to Track 5

¡Buenos días! *Soy Ana. Tengo veintisiete años. Soy de Chicago, pero ahora vivo en una ciudad de México que se llama Guadalajara. Soy profesora de inglés en una preparatoria. Al volver a Estados Unidos, voy a continuar con mis estudios.*

Me gustaría hacer un doctorado en literatura mexicana. Pero, por ahora, estoy contenta de vivir en México e ir mejorando mi español poco a poco y de ir aprendiendo más de este país tan maravilloso. En mi tiempo libre me gusta leer, ver la tele y pasar tiempo con mis amigos, mi marido y mi perro.

Estudio español porque la historia del país me fascina. Y no solo eso, la cultura también me encanta y la gente es muy amable.

Translation: Good morning! I'm Ana. I'm 27 years old. I'm from Chicago, but now I live in a Mexican city called Guadalajara. I'm an English teacher in a high school. Upon returning to the United States, I'm going to continue my studies.

I would like to get a doctorate in Mexican literature. But for now I'm happy living in Mexico and improving my Spanish and learning more about this wonderful country. In my free time I like to read, watch TV, and spend time with my friends, my husband, and my dog.

I study Spanish because the history of the country fascinates me. It's not only that, but I also love the culture and the people are lovely.

Self-Introduction in Spanish: Example 2

Listen to Track 6

> *Hola, me llamo Nick y soy de Estados Unidos. Vivo en México y soy profesor de inglés. Tengo veintiséis años. Estoy casado con una mujer que se llama Ana y tengo un pequeño perro cuyo nombre es Joey. Llevo 8 años estudiando español y tengo una maestría en la lingüística del español. Me gusta estudiar español porque siempre me han gustado los idiomas y porque poder hablar con otro grupo de personas es algo que puede ser muy gratificante y beneficioso.*

Translation: Hello, my name is Nick and I'm from the United States. I live in Mexico and am an English teacher. I'm 26 years old. I have a wife named Ana and a little dog whose name is Joey. I have been studying Spanish for 8 years, and I have a Masters in Spanish Linguistics. I like studying Spanish because I have always liked languages and being able to speak with another group of people as it can be something very rewarding and beneficial.

Let's dive deeper into occupations, nationalities, and countries in the next section. Ready?

Let's talk about Jobs and Professions in Spanish

When talking to new acquaintances or friends, jobs often come up. To ask about what someone does for a living, you can say either of the following:

Listen to Track 7

- *¿Cuál es tu trabajo/profesión?* What is your job/profession?
- *¿En qué trabajas?* What do you work in?
- *¿Qué haces?/ ¿A qué te dedicas?* What do you do?

To respond, you say:

Soy ____. I'm a ____.

Listen to Track 8

abogado/a	lawyer
actor/actriz	actor/actress
agente de aduana	customs officer
agricultor/a	farmer
albañil	builder
arquitecto/a	architect
asistente	servant
asistente de ventas	shop assistant

astronauta	astronaut
bibliotecario/a	librarian
biólogo/a	biologist
bombero/a	fireman
camionero/a	lorry driver
cantante	singer
carnicero/a	butcher
carpintero/a	carpenter
cartero/a	postman
científico/a	scientist
cirujano/a	surgeon
cocinero/a	cook
conductor/a	driver
consultor/a	consultant
contador/a	accountant
dentista	dentist
despachador de farmacia	pharmacist
electricista	electrician
empleado de oficina	office worker
empleado/a	employee
empleado/a de banco	bank clerk
encargado/a	foreman
enfermero/a	nurse
escritor/a	writer
estudiante	student
fontanero/a	plumber
fotógrafo/a	photographer
geólogo/a	geologist
ginecólogo/a	gynecologist
granjero/a	farmer
guardia	guard
ingeniero/a	engineer
instructor/a	instructor
jardinero/a	gardener
joyero/a	jeweller
juez/a	judge
marinero/a	sailor
mecánico/a	mechanic
médico - doctor/a	doctor
mesero/a	waiter/waitress

minero/a	miner
modelo	model
monja	nun
monje	monk
músico	musician
niñera/o	nanny
obrero/a	labourer
panadero/a	baker
pastor/a	shepherd
peluquero/a	Hairdresser
periodista	journalist
pescador/a	fisherman
piloto	pilot
pintor/a	painter
policía	policeman
político	politician
portero/a	caretaker
profesor/a	teacher
psicólogo/a	psychologist
psiquiatra	psychiatrist
químico/a	chemist
recepcionista	receptionist
recolector de basura	garbage collector
relojero/a	watchmaker
reportero/a	reporter
sacerdote	priest
sastre	tailor
secretario/a	secretary
sobrecargo	flight attendant
soldado	soldier
taxista	taxi driver
técnico/a	technician
terapeuta	therapist
torero/a	bullfighter
traductor/a	translator
vendedor/a de libros	bookseller
vendedor/a	salesman
veterinario	vet
zapatero/a	shoemaker

Some important reminders about professions in Spanish:

- As a general rule, Spanish nouns pertaining to professions change according to the gender of the person they are referring to.

- Most profession nouns have masculine forms that end in o. To change it to feminine, simply replace the o with a. For example, *un maestro* becomes *una maestra*.

- Some profession nouns are exempted from this rule. This includes *un/una atleta* (athlete), *un/una piloto* (pilot), *un/una policía* (police,) and *un/una modelo* (model) which remain the same whether masculine or feminine.

- For profession nouns that end in a consonant, just add an *a* to make it feminine. Example: *una profesora, una bailarina*.

- There are profession nouns that change a lot in spelling when converted to their feminine form. For example, *un alcalde* (mayor) becomes *una alcaldesa*.

Countries and Nationalities in Spanish

When introducing yourself or getting to know someone, your country of origin and your nationality is bound to come up as a topic. In this section, let's talk about what the different countries and nationalities are called in Spanish.

Here's a sample conversation:

Listen to Track 9

Juan: *¿De dónde eres?* (Where are you from?)

Patti: *Soy de Estados Unidos. Soy americana/estadounidense. Y tú, ¿de dónde eres?* (I'm from the United States. I'm American. And you, where are you from?)

Juan: *Yo soy de México, pero vivo en Alemania.* (I'm from Mexico, but I live in Germany.)

Countries and Nationalities in Spanish:

Listen to Track 10

África – africano(a)

Alemania – alemán, alemana

Argentina – argentino(a)

Australia – australiano(a)

Austria – austriaco(a)

Bélgica – belga

Bolivia – boliviano(a)

Brasil – brasileño(a)

Bulgaria – búlgaro(a)

Canadá – canadiense

Chile – chileno(a)

China – chino(a)

Colombia – colombiano(a)

Corea del Norte – norcoreano(a)

Corea del Sur – surcoreano(a)

Cuba – cubano(a)

Dinamarca – danés, danesa

Egipto – egipcio(a)

Ecuador – ecuatoriano(a)

Escocia – escocés, escocesa

España – español(a)

Estados Unidos – americano(a)/estadounidense

Filipinas – filipino(a)

Finlandia – finlandés, finlandesa

Francia – francés, francesa

Grecia – griego(a)

Groenlandia – groenlandés, groenlandesa

Guatemala – guatemalteco(a)

Haití – haitiano(a)

Holanda – holandés, holandesa

Honduras – hondureño(a)

Hungría – húngaro(a)

India – indio(a)

Indonesia – indonesio(a)

Inglaterra – inglés, inglesa

Irán – iraní

Irak – iraquí

Irlanda – irlandés, irlandesa

Israel – israelí

Italia – italiano(a)

Jamaica – jamaicano(a)

Japón – japonés, japonesa

México – mexicano(a)

Nicaragua – nicaragüense

Noruega – noruego(a)

Nueva Zelanda – neozelandés, neozelandesa

Panamá – panameño(a)

Paraguay – paraguayo(a)

Perú – peruano(a)

Puerto Rico – puertorriqueño(a)/boricua

Portugal – portugués, portuguesa

Reino Unido – británico (a)

Rusia – ruso(a)

Suecia – sueco(a)

Suiza – suizo(a)

Turquía – turco(a)

Uruguay – uruguayo(a)

Venezuela – venezolano(a)

Some reminders:

- When talking about nationalities in Spanish, nationality adjectives are used. This means, they can take four forms: masculine singular, feminine singular, masculine plural, and feminine plural. For Example: francés (masculine singular), francesa (feminine singular), franceses (masculine plural), and francesas (feminine plural).

- Nationalities that end in e or an accented vowel have the same masculine or feminine singular form. For example, *iraquí, israelí,* and *iraní.*

Workbook Lesson 2: Presentarse, profesiones, países y nacionalidades - Introductions, professions, countries, and nationalities

Exercise 1: Fill in the blanks with the correct word/phrases to complete the following sentences.

1- ___ Antonio. (My name is Antonio.)

2- ___abogado. (I am a lawyer.)

3- ___ de Chicago. (I am from Chicago.)

4- ___ 20 años. (I am 20 years old.)

5- Ella___ arquitecta. (She is an architect.)

Exercise 2: Complete the table with nationalities in male, female and plural.

Singular / Plural

MASCULINO	FEMENINO	MASCULINO	FEMENINO
Brasileño	1 - _____	2 - _____	3 -_____
Iraní	4 - _____	Iraníes	5- _____
Costarricense	6 - _____	7 - _____	Costarricenses
Venezolano	8 - _____	9 - _____	10 - _____
Alemán	11 - _____	12 - _____	13 - _____

Exercise 3: Complete the following sentences with nationalities in masculine, feminine or plural form.

1- El rublo es la moneda _____ . (The ruble is the Russian coin.)

2- Gabriel García Márquez es un escritor _____ . (Gabriel García Márquez is a Colombian writer)

3- Berlín es una ciudad _____ . (Berlin is a German city.)

4- Camila es una chica_____. (Camila is an Argentine girl.)

5- Julia Roberts es una actriz_____ . (Julia Roberts is an American actress.)

Exercise 4: Translate the following sentences from English to Spanish.

1- Arturo is a fireman.

2- I am a foreman.

3- He is a farmer.

4- We are guards.

5- Pedro is a jeweller.

Exercise 5: Tick the right answer.

1- Yo___ llamo Pedro. (My name is Pedro.)

   a. me   b. te   c. se

2- Él es _____ . (He is mexican.)

   a. mexicano   b. mexicana   c.mexican

3- Yo ____ 21 años. (I am 21 years old.)

   a. tengo   b. llamo   c. soy

4- ____ de Nueva Zelanda. (I am from New Zealand.)

   a. Soy   b. Somos   c. Es

5- Me ____ el té. (I like tea.)

   a. gustan   b. gusta   c. llamo

Exercise 6: Translate the following text from Spanish to English.

Hola, me llamo Sara y soy de Marruecos. Vivo en Francia y soy profesora de árabe. Tengo treinta años. Tengo un novio que se llama Pierre y un pequeño gato cuyo nombre es Pete.

Exercise 7: Complete the following phrases with professions.

1- William es ____ . (William is a teacher.)

2- El señor García es ____ . (Mr García is a garbage collector.)

3- Él es ____ . (He is a carpenter.)

4- Antonio es ____ . (Antonio is a butcher.)

5- Pedro es____ . (Pedro is a scientist.)

Exercise 8: Translate the following text from English to Spanish.

1- Luis es ecuatoriano, vive en Quito.

2- Las pirámides son egipcias.

3- Los cubanos son amables.

4- Me gusta el chocolate holandés.

5- Susana vive en Madrid, pero es portuguesa.

Exercise 9: Correct grammatical errors in the following text.

¡Buenos días! Somos Antonia. Tenía veintisiete años. Soy a Chicago, pero ahora vive en una ciudad de México que se llama Tijuana. Soy asistente de ventas y trabajo en una tienda de ropa. (Good morning! I am Antonia. I'm 27. I'm from Chicago, but now I live in a Mexican city called Tijuana. I'm a shop assistant and I work in a clothing store.)

Exercise 10: Translate the following sentences from English to Spanish.

1- Vladimir Putin is President.

2- She is a writer.

3- They are students.

4- We are geologists.

5- Pablo is a judge.

ANSWERS:

Exercise 1

1/ mi nombre es 2/ soy 3/ soy 4/ Tengo 5/ es

Exercise 2

1/ Brasileña 2/ Brasileños 3/ Brasileñas 4/ Iraní 5/ Iraníes 6/ Costarricense 7/ Costarricenses 8/ Venezolana 9/ Venezolanos 10/ Venezolanas 11/ Alemana 12/ Alemanes 13/ Alemanas

Exercise 3

1/ Rusa 2/ Colombiano 3/ Alemana 4/ Argentina 5/ Estadounidense

Exercise 4

1/ Arturo es bombero. 2/ Yo soy encargado. 3/ Él es granjero. 4/ Nosotros somos guardias. 5/ Pedro es joyero.

Exercise 5

1/ me 2/ mexicano 3/ tengo 4/ Soy 5/ gusta

Exercise 6

Hi, my name is Sara and I'm from Morocco. I live in France and I'm an Arabic teacher. I'm 30. I have a boyfriend named Pierre and a little cat whose name is Pete.

Exercise 7

1/ profesor 2/ recolector de basura 3/ carpintero 4/ carnicero 5/ científico

Exercise 8

1/ Luis is Ecuadorian, he lives in Quito. 2/ The pyramids are Egyptian. 3/ Cubans are kind. 4/ I like Dutch chocolate. 5/ Susana lives in Madrid, but she's Portuguese.

Exercise 9

¡Buenos días! Soy Antonia. Tengo veintisiete años. Soy de Chicago, pero ahora vivo en una ciudad de México que se llama Tijuana. Soy asistente de ventas y trabajo en una tienda de ropa.

Exercise 10

1/ Vladimir Putin es presidente. 2/ Ella es escritora. 3/ Ellos son estudiantes. 4/ Nosotros somos geólogos. 5/ Pablo es juez.

Lesson 3. Pronunciation Guide

Spanish is a fairly easy language, considering that most Spanish words are pronounced exactly the way that they are spelt. It's not like English where they have some of the most absurd pronunciations. I mean, who decided that pony and bologna should rhyme?!

That being said, there are some tips and tricks to have you sounding like a local in no time. So sit back, grab a *cerveza* (pronounced ser-beh-sah) and let this book be your guide. We'll be like Gandalf and Spanish pronunciation. Will be your Middle Earth.

Let's start off with an important Spanish pronunciation tip...

Something about the Spanish language that is much more important than I realized when I started learning, is *which syllable you stress.*

I remember getting into a cab in Mexico and getting nervous when the cabbie didn't have a clue which street I was telling him to go to.

When I showed him the street name on my phone, I watched the light bulb go on above his head. He was quick to correct me and say that I had stressed the wrong syllable— and that small mistake had prevented him from understanding me at all.

But... Don't stress about the Stress!

(I'm sorry, I had to. It was just so easy.) There are some simple rules that you can memorize so that you always know which syllable you need to stress.

Some general rules to follow on stressing syllables

Listen to Track 11

If a word ends in a vowel, 'n', or 's', you need to stress the syllable that is next to the last one.

Por ejemplo (for example):

> *Cuenta* (the bill at a restaurant) is pronounced <u>Kwen</u>-tah.
> *Examen* (test/exam) is pronounced Ex-<u>ah</u>-men
> *Pestaña (eyelash) is pronounced Pez-<u>tah</u>-nya*

Words that end in a consonant (other than 'n' or 's' of course) are stressed on the last syllable.

Por ejemplo: Comer (to eat) is pronounced Koh-<u>mehr</u>

When there is an accent above a letter you must stress that syllable. Imagine that the accent is like that one attention-seeking friend we all have, and it's saying "Hey, stress me! I'm IMPORTANT!".

> *Por ejemplo: Próximo* (next) is pronounced <u>Prohk</u>-see-moh.

See, that was easy. Feeling a little less stressed now? Yes, as calm as a hippy in a commune. Now before you start growing your hair and exclusively wearing hemp clothing, let's move on to vowels!

Spanish Pronunciation Guide: How to Pronounce Spanish Vowels

Once you know what sounds the vowels make when speaking Spanish, you're pretty well in the clear because they very seldom change. That's great for you learners out there because it means that you need only memorize this Spanish pronunciation guide for vowels below.

Then, if you're sounding out a word and you use these vowel pronunciations, there is about a 99.5%* chance you've got it right! And those are odds we'd take to Vegas, baby!

*Rough estimate. Very rough estimate. But you get the point.

Listen to Track 12

Vowel	Pronunciation Guide	Example	What the Example Means
A	is pronounced 'ah' like apple	*Abajo*	Down/downstairs
E	is pronounced 'eh' like rent	*Antes*	Before
I	is pronounced 'ee' like free	*Amigo*	Friend
O	is pronounced 'oh' like fl**o**w	*Beso*	Kiss
U	is pronounced 'oo' like loose	*Nube (Noob-eh)*	Cloud
AI/AY	is pronounced 'y' like fly	*Bailar /Hay (Eye)*	Dance/There is
AU	is pronounced 'ow' like how	*Aunque*	Although
EI	is pronounced 'ay' like day	*Aceite*	Oil
IE	is pronounced 'yeh' like yes	*Bien*	Fine
UE	is pronounced 'weh' like well	*Cuello*	Neck/Collar

The (Usually) Constant Spanish Consonants and How to Say Them

Most of the consonants in Spanish are pronounced the same as in English. However, there are some that are different, and they can seem a little intimidating at first.

No worries though, we've gone ahead and listed all of the ones that vary from English below. That way, instead of having to spend time looking them up elsewhere, you can focus on more important things—like baking a birthday cake for your cat.

Listen to Track 13

Consonant	Pronunciation Guide	Example	What the Example Means
C (before 'e', 'i')	is pronounced 'th' like thanks	*Gracias/Cena*	Thank you/Dinner
C (before 'a','o','u')	is pronounced 'k' like corner	*Casa/Con/Cuando*	House/With/When
CC	is pronounced 'k' then 's'	*Dirección*	Address
D (between vowels)	Is pronounced 'th' like the	*Cada*	Each
G (before 'a','o','u')	is pronounced hard 'g' like grape	*Gris*	Grey
G (before 'e','i')	is pronounced a breathy 'h' like hi	*Gente (Hehn-teh)*	People
H	is not pronounced. Always silent.	*Hay (Eye)*	There is

J	is pronounced a breathy 'h' like hot	*Jamón*	Ham
L	is pronounced like 'l' in love	*Libre*	Free
LL	is pronounced a hard 'j' like Jacob	*Llamar*	To call
Ñ	is pronounced 'ny' like canyon	*Mañana*	Tomorrow
QU	is pronounced 'k' like keep	*Queso (Keh-soh)*	Cheese
R	is rolled only once	*Pero (pehr-oh)*	But
RR	Is rolled twice	*Perro (pehr-roh)*	Dog
V	is pronounced 'b' like beer	*Vale (Ball-eh)*	Okay
X	is pronounced 'cs' like exit	*Extranjero*	Foreign
Y	is pronounced like English 'y' in yard, except when by itself—it is pronounced 'ee'	*Ya(Yah)/Y(Ee)*	Already/And
Z	is pronounced 'th' like that	*Zapato*	Shoe

Important things to note about Spanish pronunciation for consonants

The letter 'B' is pronounced the same way as 'V' in Spanish—like 'B' in bad. This makes it difficult for my little Spanish host kids when trying to sound out words in their writing.

To further explain the tricky CC listed above, the example given—*dirección*, is pronounced like dee-rek-see-on. So, the first c behaves just like we have come to know and love, and the second is pronounced like 'th'.

When you pronounce the letter 'J' you should almost sound like someone who has smoked a pack of cigarettes a day for the past 25 years, and you're trying to clear your throat. Like you know that scene in Titanic where Jack is showing Rose how to "spit like a man", and he's hacking up something awful? Yeah, you should sound like that. If it doesn't almost hurt your throat, you're not doing it right.

The first 'N' example in the chart, the one where the 'N' is parading itself around like an 'M', isn't always in the word that the 'N' is in. For example, when saying *"con permiso"* (excuse me, when trying to get by someone) is pronounced like "compermiso". So, since those two words get all cozied up together like – and sound like one word - the 'N' to 'M' maneuver takes place.

I actually didn't notice this before I started learning Spanish, but in English the letter 'L' has two different sounds. The first is the obvious—'L' like in 'love'. The second is as sneaky as I am when ransacking the kitchen at 3am while I'm supposed to be on a diet. If you say the word 'ball', there you have the second 'L' pronunciation. It's a bit softer than the first. That 'L' sounds doesn't appear in Spanish. Always go with the first!

Bonus Topic: ¿What's With the Upside Down Question Marks?

You know how when you're reading something in English you generally ("generally" because English is weird and there are always exceptions. *Eye roll.*) know that it's a question before you get to the question mark at the end because of the word at the beginning? *Por ejemplo*: "Do you want something?"

I'm assuming that when reading that question, you put an upward inflection on it. That's because the word "do" tipped you off that it was a question and not a statement. Well, in Spanish they don't do that. Let me show you what I mean.

«Tú quieres algo.» / «¿ Tú quieres algo?»

The first is a statement. "You want something." The second is a question. "Do you want something?".

But the only way to tell the difference is by the punctuation. So, if you were reading the question, and there was no question mark doing a handstand at the beginning of it, you wouldn't know that it was a question until you got to the end.

The same goes for when you're speaking. It's super important to make sure that when asking a question, the inflection of your voice goes up.

It has to be clearly different from the inflection you use when making a statement. If not, you could end up saying something different from what you intended, and it could be a little embarrassing.

Yes, I did have an embarrassing experience with this. No, I'm not going to tell you about it.

Hopefully this Spanish pronunciation guide has helped you navigate through all the pronunciation confusion. If not, take another big swig of that *cerveza* we opened at the beginning and have another look. I always find my Spanish is better after a few drinks.

The Spanish Alphabet

The Spanish language officially has 27 letters in its alphabet or *abecedario*; just one letter more than the English alphabet. The extra letter is *la letra ñ (eñe)* which doesn't exist in the English alphabet.

However, this updated Spanish alphabet was only implemented by the *Real Academia Española* in 2010. Before that, the old Spanish dictionaries had sections for the now-defunct letters *ch* and *ll*. Other old resources would also previously include *rr* as another separate letter. Some would exclude the letters *k* and *w* because they only appear in words borrowed from other languages.

So it's a good thing that the Spanish alphabet has been sorted out and we're now officially using 27 letters only, don't you think? Fewer things to think about this way!

Here in this lesson, let's get to know the 27 different (official) letters of the Spanish alphabet.

Listen to Track 14

Letter	What it's called in Spanish	How to Pronounce its Spanish Name
Aa	*A*	AH
Bb	*Be*	BEH
Cc	*Ce*	SEH
Dd	*De*	DEH
Ee	*E*	EH
Ff	*Efe*	EH-feh
Gg	*Ge*	JEH
Hh	*Hache*	AH-cheh
Ii	*I*	EE
Jj	*Jota*	JOH-tah

Kk	Ka	KAH
Ll	Ele	EH-leh
Mm	Eme	EH-meh
Nn	Ene	EH-neh
Ññ	Eñe	EH-nyeh
Oo	O	OH
Pp	Pe	PEH
Qq	Cu	COO
Rr	Erre	EH-rreh
Ss	Ese	EH-seh
Tt	Te	TEH
Uu	U	OOH
Vv	Uve	OOH-beh
Ww	doble uve (also known previously as "uve doble," "doble ve," and "doble u")	DOH-bleh OOH
Xx	Equis	EH-kees
Yy	ye (often referred to as i griega)	YEH
Zz	Zeta	SEH-tah

Workbook Lesson 3: Pronunciación y alfabeto - Pronunciation and the alphabet

Exercise 1: Write down the following words, written as each letter sounds. You should find out what word it is.

1) Uve, a, ce, a _____

2) Ce, a, erre, ele, o, ese _____

3) Ene, i, eñe, o _____

4) Jota, a, erre, de, i, ene _____

5) Te, e, ele, e, uve, i, ese, i, o, ene_____

Exercise 2: What's the next letter? Choose the letter that follows in the alphabet.

1) A,B, _____

2) F,G, _____

3) L,M, _____

4) Q,R _____

5) T,U, _____

Exercise 3: Write down the following words, written as each letter sounds. You should also find out what each word means.

1- Jota, u, a, ene, e, ese____

2- Hache, a, be, ele, a, erre____

3- Hache, e, ele, a, de, o____

4- Ce, o, eme, pe, u, te, a, de, o, erre, a____

5- A, erre, eme, a, erre, i, o_____

Exercise 4: Write country names, starting with the following letters.

1- Ch:

2- V:

3- A:

4- C:

5- P:

Exercise 5: Write the sound of the following words.

1- Cuenta

2- Examen

3- Zapato

4- Comer

5- Próximo

Exercise 6: Spell the following surnames in Spanish.

1 — ¿Cómo se llama? —Rigoberta Menchú (What's her name?-Rigoberta Menchu)

. — ¿Puedes deletrearme el apellido? (Can you spell her surname?)

— _____

2. — ¿Cómo se llama? —Carolina. (What's her name?- Carolina)

— ¿Y de apellido? —Herrera. (And her surname?)

—¿Cómo se escribe? (How's it written?)

— _____

3. —¿Cómo se llama? (What's his name?)

—Antonio.

— ¿Cómo se escribe? (How's it written?)

— _____

Exercise 7: Write the letter next to the sound.

1- Hache ____

2- Ge ____

3- Eñe ____

4- Erre ____

5- Equis ____

Exercise 8: Write down the following words, written as each letter sounds. You should also find out what each word means.

1- A, erre, ge, e, ene, te, i, ene, a____

2- Efe, a, be, u, ele, o, ese, o____

3- Ge, u, a, te, e, eme, a, ele, a____

4- O, a, equis, a, ce, a____

5- Cu, u, i, te, o_____

Exercise 9: Write out the following professions, written as each letter sounds. You should also find out what each word means.

1- Ce, a, ene, t, a, ene, te, e____

2- Te, e, ce, ene, i, ce, o____

3- Uve, e, te, e, erre, i, ene, a, erre, i, o____

4- Zeta, a, pe, a, te, e, erre, o____

5- Ese, a, ese, te, erre, e_____

Exercise 10: Write country names, with the following letters:

1- F

2- H

3- G

4- A

5- L

ANSWERS:

Exercise 1

1/ Vaca 2/ Carlos 3/ Niño 4/ Jardín 5/ Televisión

Exercise 2

1/ C 2/ H 3/ N 4/ S 5/ V

Exercise 3

1/ Juanes 2/ Hablar 3/ Helado 4/ Computadora 5/ Armario

Exercise 4

1/ Chile, China 2/ Venezuela 3/ Albania, Argelia 4/ Colombia, Costa Rica 5/ Perú, Puerto Rico

Exercise 5

1/ <u>kwen</u>-tah 2/ ex-<u>ah</u>-men 3/ zah-<u>pah</u>-toh 4/ koh-<u>mehr</u> 5/ <u>prohk</u>-see-moh

Exercise 6

1/ eme, e, ene, che, u – eme, e, ene, ce, hache, u 2/ hache, e, erre, erre, e, erre, a 3/ a, ene, te, o, ene, i, o

Exercise 7

1/ h 2/ g 3/ ñ 4/ r 5/ x

Exercise 8

1/ Argentina 2/ Fabuloso 3/ Guatemala 4/ Oaxaca 5/ Quito

Exercise 9

1/ Cantante 2/ Técnico 3/ Veterinario 4/ Zapatero 5/ Sastre

Exercise 10

1/ Francia, Finlandia 2/ Honduras, Holanda 3/ Guyana, Guinea 4/ Australia, Alemania 5/ Líbano, Lituania

Lesson 4. Nouns

Ready to start the lesson? Let's begin!

What are Spanish nouns?

Spanish nouns, like their counterparts in all other languages, can either be a person, place, thing, or an idea.

Quick exercise

Listen to Track 15

Can you identify which among the words in the following Spanish conversation are nouns?

María: *Bienvenido a mi casa.* (Welcome to my house.)

Juan: *Gracias.* (Thank you.)

María: *Vamos al salón. Ahí tengo unas sillas y la televisión. Podemos ver algo. La comida está en la cocina. Todavía está en el horno.* (Let's go to the living room. There, I have chairs and the television. We can watch something. The food is in the kitchen. It's still in the oven.)

Juan: *¿Dónde está el baño?* (Where is the bathroom?)

María: *Hay dos baños en mi casa. Uno está aquí y el otro está cerca de la sala.* (There are two bathrooms in my house. One is here, and the other is near the living room.)

Here are the answers:

María, casa, Juan, sala, silla, televisión, comida, cocina, horno, baño.

María: *Bienvenido a mi **casa**.*

Juan: *Gracias.*

María: *Vamos al **salón**. Ahí tengo unas **sillas** y la **televisión**. Podemos ver algo. La **comida** está en la **cocina**. Todavía está en el **horno**.*

Juan: *¿Dónde está el **baño**?*

María: *Hay dos baños en mi casa. Uno está aquí, y el otro está cerca de la sala.*

Were you able to get the answers right?

Great! Now let's move on.

Spanish noun genders

Did you notice in the short exercise above that each Spanish noun comes with a different article before it?

Why is it *la televisión* and *la cocina* while it's *el horno* and *el baño*?

Say hello to Spanish noun genders!

Listen to Track 16

Here are more Examples:

Mesa – Table (feminine)
Perro – Dog (masculine)
Libro – Book (masculine)
Casa – House (feminine)

Now it may be confusing for new learners, but after a bit of exposure to this lesson, you'll understand that there is in fact, a system to it.

Here are some basic rules to remember on Spanish noun genders

Generally speaking, words that end in -o are masculine (perro/libro), and, generally, words that end in -a are feminine (mesa/ casa)

Seems simple enough! But be careful, because there are Spanish nouns that don't end in -o or -a. What about those?

In several cases, you'll be able to identify masculine or feminine nouns based on the gender associated with the word. Such as:

Mujer – Woman (feminine)
Hombre – Man (masculine)

But some of the word genders just do not seem easy to figure out.

Additional rules

Masculine

Ends in -o
Ends in an accented vowel (á, é, í, ó, ú)
Ends in -ma (be careful with this one!)
Ends in a consonant that isn't -d or -z
Ends in –e

Feminine

Ends in -a
Ends in -sión or -ción
Ends in -dad or -tad or -tud
Ends in -umbre
Ends in -d or -z

Note: As you will discover as we go along, there are ALWAYS exceptions in Spanish.

For example, *día* ("day") ends in an -a but is, in fact, masculine. And *lápiz* ("pencil") ends in "-z" but is masculine as well!

Is it a boy… no it's a girl! Oh, it's both!

Wait–it's not all cut-and-dried yet. Here are some more things you should know.

Words that end in -ista are used for both masculine and feminine. For example, *el artista/ la artista*, and *el pianista/ la pianista*.

Your giveaway would be the article that accompanies the noun.

In Spanish dictionaries, watch out for the (m) or (f) annotations after each word. This will give you a clue on the gender of the particular Spanish word.

Your best bet would be to learn the Spanish word together with the gender. This way, your ears will be more attuned to the sound of the Spanish word and its correct gender.

Spanish noun genders can be overwhelming for new learners. But don't let it get to you! Take it slowly and mind all the rules we shared above. With more and more exposure to the Spanish language, determining the gender will get easier in time.

Workbook Lesson 4: Sustantivos – Nouns

Exercise 1: Identify which words in the following Spanish conversation are nouns.

Marta: *Bienvenido a mi oficina.* (Welcome to my office.)

Julio: *Gracias.* (Thank you.)

Marta: *Vamos a la sala de conferencias. Ahí tengo un proyector y una televisión. Podemos ver el documental. La secretaria preparó café. Todavía está caliente.* (Let's go to the conference room. I have a projector and television there. We can watch the documentary. The secretary made coffee. It's still warm.)

Julio: *¿Dónde está el baño?* (Where is the bathroom?)

Marta: *Uno está aquí y el otro está en el primer piso.* (One is here, the other is on the first floor)

Exercise 2: Say whether the following nouns are male or female.

1- La periodista: M - F (The journalist)

2- El estudiante: M - F (The student)

3- La piloto: M - F (The pilot)

4- El doctor: M - F (The doctor)

5- La amiga: M - F (The friend)

6- El pintor: M - F (The painter)

7- La juventud: M - F (The youth)

Exercise 3: Classify the following nouns in the table.

<< Atención, lápiz, mano, vaso, problema, foto, casa, cama, día, cuaderno, cumpleaños, foto, hotel, habitación, libro, página, leche, teatro, noche, lámpara, museo, viernes >>

El		La	
___	___	___	___
___	___	___	___
___	___	___	___
___	___	___	___
___	___	___	___

Exercise 4: Tick the correct answer.

1- ___ casa de Juan (Juan's house)

    a. la   b. el   c. los

2- Ellos compran ___ pastel. (They buy the cake.)

    a. los   b. el   c. la

3- Nosotros no entendemos ___ problema. (We don't understand the problem.)

    a. la   b. el   c. los

4- Abre ___ ventana. (Open the window.)

    a. la   b. los   c. el

5- ¿Dónde está ___ hospital? (Where is the hospital?)

    a. el   b. la   c. los

Exercise 5: Translate the following from English to Spanish.

1- The kid

2- The room

3- The problem

4- Saturday

5- The language

Exercise 6: Create sentences with the correct noun, as in the example below.

Example: la / hija / de María / el. ➔ La hija de María (María's daughter)

1- la / planeta / Marte / el (The planet Mars)

2- el / la / chocolate/ suizo (Swiss chocolat)

3- universidad / el / la / alemana (German university)

4- león / la / el / africano (The African lion)

5- gata / el / la / blanca (The white cat)

Exercise 7: Translate the following phrases from Spanish to English.

1- La casa

2- El gallo

3- La foto

4- El lápiz

5- El cuaderno

Exercise 8: Locate the nouns in the following sentences.

1- Hoy iremos todos contigo al hospital. (Today we will all go with you to the hospital.)

2- Hubo personas heridas en el accidente. (There were people injured in the accident.)

3- Esta pelota es de aquellas personas. (This ball belongs to those people.)

4- Tu hermano tenía una moto. (Your brother had a motorcycle.)

5- Estos zapatos están muy rotos. (These shoes are very broken.)

Exercise 9: Translate the following phrases from English to Spanish.

1- The bicycle

2- The bottle

3- The table

4- The chair

5- The glass

Exercise 10: Change the masculine nouns to feminine:

1- Príncipe (The prince)

2- Padre (The father)

3- Tío (The uncle)

4- Caballo (The horse)

5- Primo (The cousin)

ANSWERS:

Exercise 1:

1/ Oficina 2/ Sala de conferencias 3/ Proyector 4/ Televisión 5/ Documental 6/ Café 7/ Baño

Exercise 2

1/ La Periodista – Fem. 2/ El estudiante – Mas. 3/ La piloto – Fem. 4/ El doctor - Mas. 5/ La amiga - Fem. 6/ El pintor - Mas. 7/ La juventud - Fem.

Exercise 3

EL/ el lápiz, el vaso, el problema, el día, el cuaderno, el cumpleaños, el hotel, el libro, el teatro, el museo, el viernes.

LA/ la atención, la mano, la foto, la casa, la cama, la foto, la habitación, la página, la leche, la noche, la lámpara.

Exercise 4

1/ la 2/ el 3/ el 4/ la 5/ el

Exercise 5

1/ El niño 2/ La habitación 3/ El problema 4/ El sábado 5/ El idioma

Exercise 6

1/ El planeta Marte 2/ El chocolate suizo 3/ La universidad alemana 4/ El león africano 5/ La gata blanca

Exercise 7

1/ The house 2/ The cock 3/ The picture 4/ The pen 5/ The notebook

Exercise 8

1/ Hospital 2/ Accidente 3/ Pelota 4/ Moto 5/ Zapatos

Exercise 9

1/ La bicicleta 2/ La botella 3/ La mesa 4/ La silla 5/ El vaso

Exercise 10

1/ Princesa 2/ Madre 3/ Tía 4/ Yegua 5/ Prima

Lesson 5. Numbers

This lesson is all about numbers! Clearly, they're an important part of any language, and are used every day, including for talking about dates, times, ages, prices... the list goes on!

Let's get the formalities out of the way first: Spanish numbers are either cardinal numbers or ordinal numbers. Don't worry, it's simpler than it sounds! Cardinal numbers are just, well, numbers. For example 'one,' 'five,' '200.' Ordinal numbers are similar but used for saying the position of something, e.g. 'first,' 'fifth,' '200th.'

Pronunciation

We've added a pronunciation guide, but hearing the numbers spoken by a native is also super important, to make sure you're doing it more or less right!

We've put an apostrophe at the beginning of a syllable to show that you put the emphasis on that syllable.

Number	Pronunciation
0 = cero	'seh-roh

CARDINAL NUMBERS

So, to learn how to count, we need the cardinal numbers.

Clearly we're not going to list every single number from 0 to 1,000 or 1,000,000 or beyond! Luckily, we have patterns that mean you only have to learn the small numbers (and the big multiples like 'hundred' and 'thousand') in order to be able to figure out how to say any number.

Let's start with 0-20:

Listen to Track 17

0	cero ('seh-roh)
1	uno* ('oo-noh)
2	dos (dohs)
3	tres (trehs)
4	cuatro ('kwah-troh)
5	cinco ('seehn-koh)
6	seis ('seh-ees)
7	siete (see-'eh-teh)
8	ocho ('oh- choh)
9	nueve (noo-'eh-beh)
10	diez (dee-'ehs)
11	once ('ohn-seh)
12	doce ('doh-seh)

13	*trece* ('treh-seh)
14	*catorce* (kah-'tohr-seh)
15**	*quince* ('keen-seh)
16***	*dieciséis* (dee-ehs-ee-'seh-ees)
17***	*diecisiete* (dee-ehs-ee-see-'eh-teh)
18***	*dieciocho* (dee-ehs-ee-'oh-choh)
19***	*diecinueve* (dee-ehs-ee-noo-'eh-beh)
20	*veinte* ('beh-een-teh)

* The number one is *uno*. However, if you want to say that you have one of something, you use *un* for a masculine noun, and *una* for a feminine noun! For example, '*Tengo un hermano y una hermana.*' ('I have one brother and one sister.')

** You may have heard of a celebration called the *quinceañera* that's celebrated in parts of Latin America and parts of the US. It marks a girl's 15th birthday and, as you can see, comes from the word *quince* ('15') and the word *año* ('year')!

*** The words for 16, 17, 18, and 19 are pretty smart. They come from mashing together words. For example, 17 comes from blending together the words *diez y siete* ('ten and seven').

Okay, let's move on to 21-30:

Listen to Track 18

21*	*veintiuno* (beh-een-tee-'oo-noh)
22	*veintidós* (beh-een-tee-'dohs)
23	*veintitrés* (beh-een-tee-'trehs)
24	*veinticuatro* (beh-een-tee-'kwah-troh)
25	*veinticinco* (beh-een-tee-'seehn-koh)
26	*veintiséis* (beh-een-tee-'seh-ees)
27	*veintisiete* (beh-een-tee-see-'eh-teh)
28	*veintiocho* (beh-een-tee-'oh-choh)
29	*veintinueve* (beh-een-tee-noo-'eh-beh)
30	*treinta* ('treh-een-tah)

With the twenties, we carry on blending words together, e.g. *veintidós* ('22') comes from *veinte y dos* (twenty and two).

* We mentioned earlier that *uno* becomes *un* or *una* before a noun. It's similar with 21, 31, and so on:

Tú tienes veintiún plátanos. Yo tengo veintiún manzanas. ('You have 21 bananas. I have 21 apples.')

Now, let's look at the 30s:

Listen to Track 19

31	*treinta y uno* (treh-een-tah ee 'oo-noh)
32	*treinta y dos* (treh-een-tah ee 'dohs)
33	*treinta y tres* (treh-een-tah ee 'trehs)

34	*treinta y cuatro* (treh-een-tah ee 'kwah-troh)
35	*treinta y cinco* (treh-een-tah ee 'seehn-koh)
36	*treinta y seis* (treh-een-tah ee 'seh-ees)
37	*treinta y siete* (treh-een-tah ee see-'eh-teh)
38	*treinta y ocho* (treh-een-tah ee 'oh-choh)
39	*treinta y nueve* (treh-een-tah ee noo-'eh-beh)
40	*cuarenta* (kwah-'rehn-tah)

In the thirties, we still do a little bit of math, but we don't need to worry about mashing words together now! For example, 35 is simply *treinta y cinco* (thirty and five').

The same rule applies for the 40s, 50s, all the way up to and including the 90s!

Now you know that, you just need to get to 100 in multiples of 10, so let's look at 10-100, to recap the earlier ones and advance up to higher numbers:

Listen to Track 20

10	*diez* (dee-'ehs)
20	*veinte* ('beh-een-teh)
30	*treinta* ('treh-een-tah)
40	*cuarenta* (kwah-'rehn-tah)
50	*cincuenta* (seen-'kwehn-tah)
60	*sesenta* (seh-'sehn-tah)
70	*setenta* (seh-'tehn-tah)
80	*ochenta* (oh-'chehn-tah)
90	*noventa* (noh-'behn-tah)
100	*ciento** OR *cien** (see-'ehn-toh) OR (see-'ehn)

When you're counting to 100, you can use either *ciento* or *cien*. When we're using it to count a noun, it has to be *cien*.

For example,

| I have a hundred puppies. | *Tengo cien perritos.* |

When we're using numbers from 101-199, we have to use *ciento:*

102	*ciento dos* (see-'ehn-toh dohs)
132	*ciento treinta y dos* (see-'ehn-toh 'treh-een-tah ee dohs)
160	*ciento sesenta* (see-'ehn-toh se-'sehn-tah)

Next, we'll look at the hundreds, from 100-900.

Listen to Track 21

| 100 | *ciento* OR *cien* (see-'ehn-toh) OR (see-'ehn) |
| 200 | *doscientos* (dohs-see-'ehn-tohs) |

300	*trescientos* (trehs-see-'ehn-tohs)
400	*cuatrocientos* (kwah-troh-see-'ehn-tohs)
500	*quinientos* (keen-ee-'ehn-tohs)
600	*seiscientos* (seh-ees-see-'ehn-tohs)
700	*setecientos* (seh-teh-see-'ehn-tohs)
800	*ochocientos* (oh-choh-see-'ehn-tohs)
900	*novecientos* (noh-beh-see-'ehn-tohs)

Some of them are just counting hundreds, e.g. *cuatrocientos* is a joined-up version of *cuatro cientos*. How many hundreds? Four hundreds. Others (500, 700, and 900) are a tiny bit different because what would Spanish be without exceptions to the rules?!

Now for the big 'uns! Let's look at 1,000-1,000,000,000!

Listen to Track 22

1.000*	*mil* (meel)
10.000	*diez mil* (dee-ehs 'meel)
100.000	*cien mil* (see-ehn 'meel)
1.000.000 (a million)	*un millón* (oon mee-'yohn)
1.000.000.000 (a billion)	*un billón* (oon bee-'yohn)

*In Spanish numbers, commas and decimal points are used the same as in Englis. To separate numbers higher than four digits, a comma is acceptable, nevertheless an space is also commonly used. (2,000 or 2 000)

How to say your age

In English, we use the verb 'to be' when it comes to age. In Spanish, we use 'to have.'

The word for 'year(s)' is *año(s)*. That little squiggle on the *ñ* is super important. If you skip it, you're talking about how many anuses you have. You have been warned.

Listen to Track 23

| I am 21 years old. | *Tengo veintiún años* OR *Tengo veintiuno.* |
| María is 69 years old. | *María tiene sesenta y nueve años.* |

ORDINAL NUMBERS

As we mentioned at the start, ordinal numbers are used for stating the position of something.

First of all (see what I did there?!) let's look at 1st-20th:

Listen to Track 24

First	*primero* OR *primer** (pree-'meh-roh) OR (pree-'mehr)
Second	*segundo* (seh-'goon-doh)
Third	*tercero* OR *tercer** (tehr-'seh-roh) OR (tehr-'sehr)

Fourth	*cuarto* ('kwahr-toh)
Fifth	*quinto* ('keen-toh)
Sixth	*sexto* ('sehks-toh)
Seventh	*séptimo* ('sehp-tee-moh)
Eighth	*octavo* (oc-'tah-boh)
Ninth	*noveno* (noh-'beh-noh)
Tenth	*décimo* ('deh-see-moh)
Eleventh	*undécimo* (oon-'deh-see-moh)
Twelfth	*duodécimo* (doo-oh-'deh-see-moh)
Thirteenth	*decimotercio* OR *decimotercero* (deh-see-moh-'tehr-see-oh) OR (deh-see-moh-tehr-'seh-roh)
Fourteenth	*decimocuarto* (deh-see-moh-'kwahr-toh)
Fifteenth	*decimoquinto* (deh-see-moh-'keen-toh)
Sixteenth	*decimosexto* (deh-see-moh-'sehks-toh)
Seventeenth	*decimoséptimo* (deh-see-moh-'sehp-tee-moh)
Eighteenth	*decimoctavo* (deh-see-moc-'tah-boh)
Nineteenth	*decimonoveno* (deh-see-moh-noh-'beh-noh)
Twentieth	*vigésimo* (bee-'heh-see-moh)

* *primero* becomes *primer* before a masculine singular noun, and the same happens with *tercero–>tercer.*

Note that the Spanish ordinals all end in -*o*, which is simpler than English (we have '-st' and '-nd' and '-rd' and '-th' to choose from!).

Instead of writing out whole words, in English we often use those last letters with the figure. We do the same in Spanish. The last letter is always *o* (or *a*, to agree with a feminine noun).

1st	1º
2nd	2º
3rd time	3ª *vez*
106th cookie	106ª galleta

Now things get a bit simpler (you're welcome). We'll look at 21st-100th:

Listen to Track 25

twenty-first	*vigésimo primero*
twenty-second, etc.	*vigésimo segundo, etc.*

From this point you just put the two words together, e.g. 20th (*vigésimo*) and 7th (*séptimo*) –> 27th (*vigésimo séptimo*)

Let's go up in multiples of ten from 10th-100th:

Tenth	*décimo* ('deh-see-moh)
twentieth	*vigésimo* (bee-'heh-see-moh)
thirtieth	*trigésimo** (tree-'heh-see-moh)
fortieth	*cuadragésimo* (kwah-drah-'heh-see-moh)

Fiftieth	*quincuagésimo* (keen-kwah-'heh-see-moh)
Sixtieth	*sexagésimo* (sehk-sah-'heh-see-moh)
seventieth	*septuagésimo* (sept-oo-ah-'heh-see-moh)
eightieth	*octogésimo* (oc-toh-'heh-see-moh)
ninetieth	*nonagésimo* (noh-nah-'heh-see-moh)
hundredth	*centésimo* (sehn-'teh-see-moh)

* 31st, 41st, etc. all have the same two options as 21st.

Now onto the really big ones (1,000th-1,000,000,000th):

thousandth	*milésimo* (mee-'leh-see-moh)
millionth	*millonésimo* (mee-yohn-'eh-see-moh)
billionth	*milmillonésimo* (meel-mee-yohn-'eh-see-moh)

Workbook Lesson 5: Los números – Numbers

Exercise 1: Complete the exercise following the example.

Example: Ochenta y cinco - (85)

1- Veintitrés

2- Ciento noventa

3- Cero

4- Cuarenta

5- Treinta y siete

Exercise 2: Complete the exercise by following the example.

Example: 90 - Noventa

1- 35

2- 78

3- 121

4- 345

5- 896

Exercise 3: Complete the exercise by adding the numbers.

1- Duermo ____ horas al día. (I sleep eight hours a day)

2- Él va al gimnasio ____ días a la semana. (He goes to the gym two days a week.)

3- Ellos van al cine ____ veces al mes. (They go to the movies three times a month.)

4- Camila estudia español ____ horas a la semana. (Camila studies Spanish seven hours a week.)

5- Pablo recibe dinero los días ____ de cada mes. (Paul receives money on the fifteenth of every month.)

Exercise 4: Translate the following sentences from Spanish to English.

1- La leche cuesta cuatro pesos el litro.

2- Mi cumpleaños es el doce de febrero.

3- Son las ocho y media de la noche.

4- Esta carne cuesta 100 pesos el kilo.

5- Trabajo por seis horas en la mañana.

Exercise 5: Complete the following dialogue.

Javier: Hola chicas, ¿cómo están? (Hey, girls, how are you?)

Lina: Hola Javier, muy bien, y ¿tú? (Hello Javier, very well, and you?)

Javier: Muy bien gracias, hace mucho no las veía. ¿Cuántos años tienen ahora? (All right, thank you. I haven't seen you in a long time. How old are you now?)

Lina: ¡Es cierto! pues yo tengo _____ años. (It's true! Well, I'm twenty-six.)

Carla: Yo tengo _____ años. Y tú, Carlos, ¿cuántos años tienes ahora? (I am twenty-one years old. And you, Carlos, how old are you now?)

Javier: Yo tengo_____ años (I'm thirty years old). Chicas, ¿qué hora es? Tengo trabajo a las ___. (Girls, what time is it? I have work at three.)

Lina: Es la __ y media (It's half past one.)

Exercise 6: Write the following numbers in words.

1- 15 de diciembre.

2- 45 kilómetros.

3- 11 alumnos.

4- 51 kilos.

5- 61 semanas.

Exercise 7: Write the phone numbers, as shown in the example.

Example: Pilar 977389583- nueve siete siete tres ocho nueve cinco ocho tres

1- Julián 9758328457

2- Pedro 9874338384

3- Sergio 31287384861

4- Camila 9872743338

5- Andrés 9384559285

Exercise 8: Complete the sentences with the numbers in the brackets.

1- La Habana tiene_____ de habitantes. (Havana has 2,000,000 million inhabitants.)

2- Carlos gana_____ pesos al mes. (Carlos gets 10,000 pesos a month.)

3- Alberto pesa_____ kilos. (Alberto weighs 108 kilos.)

4- Esta televisión cuesta___ bolívares. (This television costs 180 bolivars.)

5- La mujer más vieja del mundo tiene _____ años. (The oldest woman in the world is 109 years old.)

Exercise 9: Complete the sentences with the cardinal numbers in the brackets.

1- Antonio vive en el _____ piso. (Antonio lives on the fifth floor.)

2- Las oficinas de IKEA están en el _____ piso. (IKEA's offices are on the third floor.)

3- La sastrería está en la _____ planta. (The tailor's shop is on the eighth floor.)

4- La academia Cervantes está en la_____ planta. (The Cervantes Academy is on the second floor.)

5- Hay un despacho de abogados en el ___piso. (There is a law firm on the eleventh floor.)

Exercise 10: Write down the numbers that appear in brackets.

1- Valencia es el (1°) _____ en la liga. (Valencia is the first in the league.)

2- La Ñ es la letra (15°) _____ del alfabeto. (Ñ is the fifteenth letter of the alphabet.)

3- Teresa y Jésica acabaron (5°)__ en el campeonato de tenis. (Teresa and Jesica finished fifth in the Tennis Championship.)

4- Javi es el (3°) ____ de sus hermanos. (Javi is the third of his brothers.)

5- Febrero es el (2°) ____ mes del año. (February is the second month of the year.)

ANSWERS:

Exercise 1

1/ 23 2/ 190 3/ 0 4/ 40 5/ 37

Exercise 2

1/ Treinta y cinco 2/ Setenta y ocho 3/ Ciento veintiuno 4/ Trescientos cuarenta y cinco 5/ Ochocientos noventa y seis

Exercise 3

1/ Duermo ocho horas al día. 2/ Él va al gimnasio dos días a la semana. 3/ Ellos van al cine tres veces al mes. 4/ Camila estudia español siete horas a la semana. 5/ Pablo recibe dinero los días quince de cada mes.

Exercise 4

1/ Milk costs four pesos a litre. 2/ My birthday is on February 12th. 3/ It's 8:30 at night. 4/ This meat costs a hundred pesos per kilo. 5/ I work for six hours in the morning.

Exercise 5

1/ Lina: ¡Es cierto! pues yo tengo veintiséis años. 2/ Carla: Yo tengo veintiún años. 3/ Javier: Yo tengo treinta años. 4/ Javier: Chicas, ¿qué hora es? Tengo trabajo a las tres. 5/ Lina: Es la una y media.

Exercise 6

1/ Quince de diciembre. 2/ Cuarenta y cinco kilómetros. 3/ Once alumnos. 4/ Cincuenta y un kilos. 5/ Sesenta y un semanas.

Exercise 7

1/ Nueve siete cinco ocho tres dos ocho cuatro cinco siete. 2/ Nueve ocho siete cuatro tres tres ocho tres ocho cuatro. 3/ Tres uno dos ocho siete tres ocho cuatro ocho seis uno. 4/ Nueve ocho siete dos siete cuatro tres tres tres ocho. 5/ Nueve tres ocho cuatro cinco cinco nueve dos ocho cinco

Exercise 8

1/ La Habana tiene dos millones de habitantes. 2/ Carlos gana diez mil pesos al mes. 3/ Alberto pesa ciento ocho kilos. 4/ Esta televisión cuesta ciento ochenta bolívares. 5/ La mujer más vieja del mundo tiene ciento nueve años.

Exercise 9

1/quinto 2/ tercer 3/ octavo 4/ segunda 5/ undécimo

Exercise 10

1/ primero 2/ decimoquinta 3/ quintas 4/ tercero 5/ segundo

Lesson 6. Hay ('There Is'/'There Are')

In this lesson, we'll look at how to say 'there is' and 'there are' in Spanish. It's simpler than you might think!

Two forms of *haber*:

The verb we're going to need is the verb *haber,* which roughly translates as 'to have/to be.'

There are two ways to use it! The first one is by conjugating it like this:

Listen to Track 26

Yo he	Nosotros hemos
Tú has	Ustedes han
Él/ella/usted ha	Ellos/ellas han

The second way is when we want to use *haber* to denote that something exists, i.e. to say 'there is' or 'there are.' To do this, we only ever need the third person singular, but instead of using *ha*, we use *hay* (don't ask why we add the 'y'!). For Example:

Hay pan en la cocina.	There is bread in the kitchen.

Hay is so useful in Spanish, so it's worth knowing how it's pronounced. It's not like hay, the stuff that horses eat. It's more like 'ay ay ay!'

Singular and plural

Hay is amazing because it's the same whether you're saying 'there is one thing' (singular) or 'there are multiple things' (plural)!

And as it's only ever the third person *hay* that's used, there's essentially no conjugation for gender or number!

The only changes we need to make are for different tenses. And in each tense, there's no need to conjugate for gender or number!

How *hay* can be used

Hay can be used in pretty much every tense you can think of.

Let's check out some examples.

Present

Listen to Track 27

As we've seen, the word to use is *hay.*

¿Hay algún lugar aquí que venda fruta?	Is there any place here that sells fruit?
Hay lugares hermosos en Bolivia.	There are beautiful places in Bolivia.

Preterite

Listen to Track 28

To use it in the preterite, which is a past tense, we need to say *hubo*.

Hubo una reunión esta mañana.	There was a meeting this morning.
Hubo muchos problemas durante la reunión.	There were lots of problems during the meeting.

Imperfect

Listen to Track 29

[handwritten: Imperf. había = they were ...]

The imperfect (another past tense) version is *había*.

Pasé una hora buscando pero no había nadie en el edificio.	I spent an hour searching but there was nobody in the building.
Vi que había dos computadoras libres en la biblioteca.	I saw that there were two free computers in the library.

Future

Listen to Track 30

[handwritten: habrá = there will be]

For the future tense, the verb is *habrá*.

Habrá mucha gente en la fiesta.	There will be lots of people at the party.
Alicia, habrá dos chicos en el departamento cuando regreses del trabajo. No te asustes, son amigos míos.	Alicia, there'll be two guys in the apartment when you get home from work. Don't be scared, they're friends of mine.

Future (*ir a ...*)

[handwritten: va a haber = going to be]

The other way of forming future phrases (especially for the near future) uses *ir a* + infinitive, so here we use *ir a* + *haber*. *Ir* will be in the present tense third person singular (*va*), and *haber* stays in the infinitive.

Va a haber otro restaurante en la avenida principal.	There's going to be another restaurant on *the main avenue.*
Va a haber 500 vasos y botellas de agua para los participantes de la carrera.	There are going to be 500 cups and bottles of water for the participants of the race.

Conditional

Listen to Track 31

To use *haber* to say that 'there would be' something, use *habría*. *[handwritten: would be: habría]*

This is useful for 'if ... then ...' phrases.

Si un genio me concediera un deseo, ya no había guerra en el mundo.	If a genie granted me one wish, there would be no more war in the world.
Si enfrentaras a tu ex, había más discusiones insignificantes. No valdría la pena.	If you confronted your ex, there would be more petty arguments. It wouldn't be worth it.

Hay can be used in compound tenses, like the perfect, pluperfect, future perfect, and conditional perfect.

These tenses all consist of the verb *haber* conjugated in the third person singular in the appropriate tense, and then a past participle (in this case *habido*).

Perfect

Listen to Track 32

Don't get confused here, just follow the formula that we taught you in <u>this lesson</u>: *haber* (conjugated as we did in the table at the top) + *habido*.

The formula is always *ha + habido*. It's similar to *ha + existido* but just happens to be a double whammy of '*haber*'s!

—¿Qué ha pasado aquí?	What's happened here?
—Ha habido una pelea.	There's been a fight.
Ha habido varias denuncias contra el jefe.	There have been several complaints made against the manager.

*Although the Perfect tense is correct (in Spanish *Pretérito Perfecto*), in the day-to-day communication **in Mexico** is not commonly used. Instead, Simple Past is utilized. (¿Que **pasó** aquí? – **Hubo** una pelea). Nevertheless, it is very important to know about it and its estructure, because you'll never know when you will have to use it.

Pluperfect

Listen to Track 33

This is similar to the perfect, but 'further back' in time. (More info at the end of <u>this lesson</u>.)

You need to use *había + habido*.

Alguien llamó la policía porque había habido una pelea.	Someone called the police because there had been a fight.
Despidieron al jefe porque había habido varias denuncias contra él.	The manager was sacked because there had been several complaints about him.

*The same thing applies as with the Perfect tense. The Pluperfect (in Spanish *Pluscuamperfecto*) is almost only used in literature. It is replaced, once again, by Simple Past (*Alguien llamó a la policía porque **hubo** una pelea – Despidieron al jefe porque **hubo** varias denuncias contra él*)

Future Perfect

Listen to Track 34

We use this tense to talk about what will have existed.

Again, it's similar to the other compound tenses. Instead of saying something like *habrá existido*, we can use *habrá + habido*. #haberdoublewhammy

Habrá habido una investigación sobre la pelea para el viernes.	There will have been an investigation into the fight by Friday.
Cuando llegue el nuevo jefe, habrá habido cuatro jefes diferentes en un solo año.	When the new manager arrives, there will have been four different managers in only a year.

*One more thing! As in the past two tenses, this one is rarely utilized in Mexican Spanish. The Simple Future comes in, leaving the Future Perfect out the picture. (**Habrá** (there will be) *una investigación sobre la pelea para el viernes*) or it will, as well, be replaced by another word (*Cuando llegue el Nuevo jefe, **serán** cuatro jefes diferentes en un año*).

Conditional Perfect

Listen to Track 35

habría habado
would have been a lot

This one is about what would have existed, had a certain condition been met.

We use the phrase *habría* + *habido* to mean something along the lines of *habría existido*.

Si la policía no hubiera llegado tan pronto, habría habido mucha más violencia.	If the police hadn't turned up so soon, there would have been much more violence.
Habría habido menos problemas con el jefe si hubieran hecho una revisión de antecedentes.	There would have been fewer problems with the manager if they'd done a background check.

The word *hay* is so versatile, we can even put it in the subjunctive (which is technically a ~mood~ rather than a tense).

Present Subjunctive

Listen to Track 36

The subjunctive form that you'll need is *haya*.

Voy a la fiesta siempre que haya buena música.	I'll go to the party as long as there's good music.
Avísame cuando haya más noticias.	Let me know when there's more news.

The Imperfect Subjunctive

Listen to Track 37

The way to use it in this mood is with *hubiera* (more common in Latin America) or *hubiese* (more common in Spain). (The imperfect subjunctive has two forms.)

This is useful in certain types of 'if … then …' phrases! (*Si hubiera …* , forma verbal condicional.)

Si hubiera/hubiese más dinero en mi cuenta bancaria, no tendría que trabajar.	If there were more money in my bank account, I wouldn't have to work.
Si hubiera/hubiese millones de dólares en tu cuenta bancaria, ¿me comprarías un coche?	If there were millions of dollars in your bank account, would you buy me a car?

Useful phrases

Listen to Track 38

So far, we've used *hay* + noun(s) to mean 'there is/are' + noun(s).

It's pretty cool to know that there are some other ways to use the word *hay*. Here we're giving you a few set phrases to get you started.

Hay que …

This is used for something that you have to do, and can be translated as 'one must …' (or, more colloquially 'you have to …').

Al llegar, hay que marcar el ingreso.	Upon arrival, you must sign in.
Hay que ser amable, siempre.	One must be kind, always.

Listen to Track 39

Hay de todo

This means 'there's a bit of everything.'

—¿Qué tipo de comida hay en tu restaurante?	What type of food is there at your restaurant?
—Es un bufé internacional. Hay de todo.	It's an international buffet. There's a bit of everything.
En este tianguis hay de todo.	At this flea market, there's all sorts.

Listen to Track 40

Es lo que hay

This phrase looks at life from a realist's point of view. It could mean 'such is life,' 'it is what it is,' 'that's the way the cookie crumbles,' '*c'est la vie,*' 'it be like that sometimes,' and so on.

—Odio tener tantas tareas. No me interesan todas las materias. —Bueno, somos estudiantes. ¡Es lo que hay!	I hate having so much homework. Not all the subjects interest me. Well, we're students. That's life!
—¡Hace demasiado calor! —En este país, es lo que hay.	It's too hot! In this country, that's how it is!

Workbook Lesson 6: Hay – There is / There are

Exercise 1: Create sentences similar to the example below.

Example: Flores/Jardín. ➔ En el jardín, hay flores (In the garden, there are flowers.)

1- Nubes/Cielo. (Clouds/sky)

2- Estudiantes/escuela. (Pupils/school)

3- Juguetes /cuarto del niño. (Toys/kid's room)

4- Mesas/Salón. (Tables/classroom)

5- Ropa/lavadora. (Clothes/washing machine)

Exercise 2: Transform these affirmative sentences into negative ones.

Example: Hay un perro. (There is a dog) ➔ No hay un perro. (There's no dog)

1- Hay un espejo en la sala. (There's a mirror in the living room.)

2- Hay leche en el refrigerador. (There's milk in the fridge.)

3- Hay aves en el cielo. (There are birds in the sky.)

4- Hay coches en el estacionamiento. (There are cars in the parking lot.)

5- Hay lápices en mi estuche. (There is a pencil in my pencil case.)

Exercise 3: Create questions using « Hay » (see the example below).

Example: Un perro/ jardín ➔ ¿Hay un perro en el jardín? (Is there a dog in the garden?)

1- Una habitación libre/ hotel. (A free room/hotel)

2- Azúcar /café. (Sugar/coffee)

3- Las clases de baile/ gimnasio. (Dance classes/gym)

4- Un león/ zoológico (A lion/zoo)

5- Baños/ aquí. (Toilets/here)

Exercise 4: Create questions using « Hay » (see the example below).

Example: Hay un perro. ➔ ¿Hay un perro? (Is there a dog?)

1- Hay un concierto. (There is a concert.)

2- Hay aire acondicionado en la habitación. (There is an air conditioner in the room.)

3- Hay un balcón en el departamento. (There is a balcony in this apartment.)

4- Hay un banco cerca de aquí. (There is a bank near here.)

5- Hay taxis aquí. (There are taxis here.)

Exercise 5: What is in your room? Imagine you are in your room and create sentences like the example, either affirmative or negative.

Example: No hay espejo (There's no mirror) – un espejo ➔ Hay un espejo.

1- una mesa (a table)

2- una lámpara (a lamp)

3- una televisión (a television)

4- un reloj (a clock)

5- un sofá (a sofa)

Exercise 6: What is in your fridge? Write phrases using « hay », in affirmative or negative forms.

1- leche: _____ (milk)

2- agua: _____ (water)

3- mantequilla: _____ (butter)

4- huevos: _____ (eggs)

5- yogures: _____ (yoghurt)

Exercise 7: Transform these negative sentences to affirmative ones.

1- En mi colonia no hay metro. (There is no metro in my neighborhood.)

2- ¿No hay una cafetería por aquí? (Isn't there a coffee shop around here?)

3- En Guadalajara no hay muchos museos. (There aren't many museums in Guadalajara.)

4- No hay diez alumnos en mi clase. (There aren't ten students in my class.)

5- En mi casa no hay dos albercas. (There aren't two pools in my house.)

Exercise 8: Re-order these words to create sentences that make sense.

1- para ti / un paquete/ hay

2- para comer / hay / algo

3- ratón / en / un/ mi / habitación/ hay

4- en mi calle / un hotel / hay

5- algo / hay /en mi sopa

Exercise 9: Translate these sentences from English to Spanish.

1- There is no more beer.

2- There is a hospital nearby.

3- Excuse me, where is the pharmacy?

4- There´s a gentleman who wants to talk with you.

5- There´s a key at the reception.

Exercise 10: Form sentences with the correct words. Follow the example.

Example: Hay / luna / llena/hoy/ media ➜ Hay luna llena hoy.

1- súper / pueblo/ en el / hay / de/ un

2- pan / en la / refri / hay / sillas

3- cafeteria / hay / una/ la entrada/ en / caja

4- camas / dos oficinas / en este/ edificio / hay

5- hay / ¿dónde/ una / papelería/ usted / por aquí?

ANSWERS:

Exercise 1

1/ Hay nubes en el cielo. 2/ Hay estudiantes en la escuela. 3/ Hay juguetes en el cuarto del niño. 4/ Hay mesas en el salón. 5/ Hay ropa en la lavadora.

Exercise 2

1/ No hay espejo en la sala. 2/ No hay leche en el refrigerador. 3/ No hay aves en el cielo. 4/ No hay coches en el estacionamiento. 5/ No hay lápices en mi estuche.

Exercise 3

1/ ¿Hay una habitación libre en el hotel? 2/ ¿Hay azúcar para el café? 3/ ¿Hay clases de baile en el gimnasio? 4/ ¿Hay un león en el zoológico? 5/ ¿Hay baños aquí?

Exercise 4

1/ ¿Hay un concierto? 2/ ¿Hay aire acondicionado en la habitación? 3/ ¿Hay un balcón en el departamento? 4/ ¿Hay un banco cerca de aquí? 5/ ¿Hay taxis aquí?

Exercise 5

1/ No hay una mesa. 2/ Hay una lámpara. 3/ Hay una televisión. 4/ No hay un reloj. 5/ Hay un sofá.

Exercise 6

1/ hay leche 2/ hay agua 3/ no hay mantequilla 4/ hay huevos 5/ hay yogures

Exercise 7

1/ En mi colonia hay metro. 2/ Hay una cafetería por aquí. 3/ En Guadalajara hay muchos museos. 4/ Hay diez alumnos en mi clase. 5/ En mi casa hay dos albercas.

Exercise 8

1/ Hay un paquete para ti. 2/ Hay algo para comer. 3/ Hay un ratón en mi habitación. 4/ En mi calle hay un hotel. 5/ Hay algo en mi sopa.

Exercise 9

1/ No hay más cerveza. 2/ Hay un hospital cerca. 3/ Disculpe, ¿dónde hay una farmacia? 4/ Hay un señor que quiere hablar con usted. 5/ Hay una llave en la recepción.

Exercise 10

1/ Hay un súper en el pueblo. 2/ Hay pan en el refri. 3/ Hay una cafetería en la entrada. 4/ Hay dos oficinas en este edificio. 5/ ¿Dónde hay una papelería por aquí?

Lesson 7. El presente simple – Present tense

Okay, so you know a bit of Spanish vocabulary, and now you want to know how to use it in sentences. The best place to start? Right here, right now, with the present tense!

Three types of verb

To form sentences in the present tense, we need to know how to conjugate verbs with the correct present tense endings.

In Spanish, verbs can be split into three main types:

-ar

-er

-ir

Each group has its own conjugation pattern. To conjugate a verb, you need to remove the infinitive ending (*-ar, -er,* or *-ir*) and add on the appropriate present tense ending.

-ar verbs

Let's take the common *-ar* verb *hablar* (to talk) as an example.

First, you remove the *-ar.*

Hablar → *habl-*

Then you add one of the following endings:

Yo (I)	-o	Nosotros (We)	-amos
Tú (You)	-as	Ustedes (You plural) (In Spanish is the second person in plural)	-an
Él/ella/usted (He/she/it/you formal)	-a	Ellos/ellas (They)	-an

For example, 'I talk' would be: *habl- + -o* → *hablo*

*If you want to know more about "*Ustedes*" go to page 279 "Usted and Ustedes command".

So, what we end up with is a conjugation table like this:

Listen to Track 41

Yo	hablo	Nosotros	hablamos
Tú	hablas	Ustedes	hablan
Él/ella/usted	habla	Ellos/ellas	hablan

-er verbs

This table shows you the present tense endings for -er verbs:

Yo (I)	-o	Nosotros (We)	-emos
Tú (You)	-es	Ustedes (You plural)	-en
Él/ella/usted (He/she/it/you formal)	-e	Ellos/ellas (They)	-en

*Remember that in most of Latin America, *Usted* is used in familiar contexts when addressing, for example, grandparents or even parents!

One of the most common -er verbs is *vender* (to sell). The conjugation table looks like this:

Listen to Track 42

Yo	vendo	Nosotros	vendemos
Tú	vendes	Ustedes	venden
Él/ella/usted	vende	Ellos/ellas	venden

-ir verbs

Yo (I)	-o	Nosotros (We)	-imos
Tú (You)	-es	Ustedes (You plural)	-en
Él/ella/usted (He/she/it/you formal)	-e	Ellos/ellas (They)	-en

The common verb *vivir* (to live) is conjugated like this:

Listen to Track 43

Yo	vivo	Nosotros	vivimos
Tú	vives	Ustedes	viven
Él/ella/usted	vive	Ellos/ellas	viven

The good news...

That may feel like a lot of tables, but don't be overwhelmed! If we simplify things a little, you'll see that there aren't actually that many differences. Check out this table which shows them side by side.

-ar	-er	*ir*
-o	-o	-o
-as	-es	-es
-a	-e	-e
-amos	-emos	-imos
-an	-en	-en
-an	-en	-en

Not so bad, right?

Null-subject language

Spanish is what we call a 'null-subject language.'

This means that, due to the variety of endings, we can leave out the subject of the verb and still make sense. Take the verb *vender* as an example. In English, most of the verb endings are the same:

I	sell	We	sell
You	sell	You (plural)	sell
He/she/it	sells	They	sell

So if you were to say 'sell houses' you'd have no idea who is doing the selling. For that reason, in English we have to include the subject, to differentiate between 'I sell houses,' 'you sell houses,' 'we sell houses,' and 'they sell houses.'

But in Spanish, each person pretty much has its own verb ending. So if I say '*vendo* casas,' it's perfectly clear that it's me selling the houses, because of the '*o*' at the end. There's no need to say '*yo vendo casas.*'

Examples

Take a look at these examples, and try to spot how the verb endings often allow us to drop the subject:

-ar verbs

Listen to Track 44

Yo hablo.	I speak.
¿Por qué tú me miras?	Why are you looking at me?
Carolina baila bien.*	Carolina dances well.
Nosotros nadamos en el mar.	We swim in the sea.
¿Ustedes trabajan por aquí?	Do you (You plural) work around here?
Ellas toman riesgos.	They take risks.

*Examples like this are a little more complicated. The verb ending -*a* could refer to he or she or it or you (formal), so it may be necessary to include the subject to clarify who exactly we are talking about. But don't forget the power of context.

If we were reading a book all about Carolina the ballerina then we wouldn't need to say *'Carolina es bailarina de ballet. Carolina baila bien. Carolina tiene 30 años.'* It would be clear that we were talking about Carolina, so we could drop her name and just say: *'Carolina es bailarina de ballet. Baila bien. Tiene 30 años.'*

-er verbs

Listen to Track 45

Yo tomo té.	I drink tea.
Tú aprendes rápido.	You learn fast.
Él no teme a nada.	He fears nothing.
Nosotras comemos por la noche.	We eat in the evening.
Ustedes venden muchas cosas.	You (You plural) sell lots of things.
Ustedes leen libros.	You (You plural) read books.

-ir verbs

~~Yo~~ vivo en Inglaterra.	I live in England.
¿~~Tú~~ recib**es** mensajes de él?	Do you receive messages from him?
¿Qué ocurr**e**?	What is happening?
~~Nosotros~~ permit**imos** animales.	We permit animals.
~~Ustedes~~ asist**en** al colegio.	You attend school.
Los destapacorchos abr**en** botellas.	Bottle openers open bottles.

Irregular verbs

There are quite a few irregular verbs in Spanish, but it's important to learn the most common ones, as they're some of the most useful verbs in the language.

ir (to go)

Listen to Track 46

voy	vamos
vas	van
va	van

Examples:

Voy al mercado.	I'm going to the market.
Juan va al gimnasio.	Juan goes to the gym.
Vamos a la playa.	We are going to the beach.

Listen to Track 47

hacer (to do/to make)

hago	hacemos
haces	hacen
hace	hacen

Examples:

Los martes, hago el súper.	On Tuesdays, I do the grocery shopping.
¿Qué haces?	What are you doing?
Hacen mucho ruido.	They're making a lot of noise.

ser (to be)*

Listen to Track 48

soy	somos
eres	son
es	son

Examples:

Eres hermosa.	You are beautiful.
Son idiotas.	You are idiots.
Son hombres.	They are men.

estar (to be)*

Listen to Track 49

estoy	estamos
estás	están
está	están

Examples:

¿Dónde está la biblioteca?	Where is the library?
Están en mi casa.	You (plural) are in my house.
¿Señores, cómo están?	Gentlemen, how are you?

*The differences between these two versions of 'to be' can be quite subtle and take a while to learn. Just remember that there are two verbs that mean 'to be.'

haber (to have)*

Listen to Track 50

he	hemos
has	han
ha/hay	han

This verb is usually used in compound tenses.

Another use of *haber* is that the third person singular form *hay* is used to mean 'there is'/'there are.'

He terminado.	I have finished.
Juan ha escrito algo.	Juan has written something.
Hay un ratón en la casa.	There is a mouse in the house.

tener (to have)

Listen to Track 51

tengo	tenemos
tienes	tienen
tiene	tienen

Examples:

Julia tiene fiebre.	Julia has a fever.
Tenemos muchos problemas.	We have a lot of problems.
Los perros tienen muchos juguetes.	The dogs have lots of toys.

poner (to put)

Listen to Track 52

pongo	Ponemos
pones	Ponen
pone	Ponen

Examples:

¿Te pongo más ensalada?	Shall I give you more salad?
¿Por qué pones tus cosas en mi habitación?	Why are you putting your things in my room?
La radio pone mis canciones favoritas.	The radio puts on my favorite songs.

decir (to say)

Listen to Track 53

Digo	Decimos
Dices	Dicen
Dice	Dicen

Examples:

Digo la verdad.	I'm telling the truth.
A veces mi padre dice groserías.	Sometimes my dad says swear words.
Dicen que todo pasa por alguna razón.	They say that everything happens for a reason.

ver (to see)

Listen to Track 54

veo	vemos
ves	ven
ve	ven

Examples:

Ya me has hecho daño, ¿ves?	Now you've hurt me, see?
Ven demasiadas películas.	You watch too many films.
Tus profesores lo ven todo.	Your teachers see everything.

saber (to know something/to taste)

Listen to Track 55

sé	sabemos
sabes	saben
sabe	saben

Examples:

No lo sé.	I don't know.
La nieve sabe a vainilla.	The ice cream tastes of vanilla.
Sabemos cantar.	We know how to sing.

venir (to come)

Listen to Track 56

vengo	venimos
vienes	vienen
viene	vienen

Examples:

Ya vengo.	I'm coming.
¿Señora, viene a la reunión?	Madame, are you coming to the meeting?
Vienen a la fiesta.	They are coming to the party.

conocer (to know someone)

Listen to Track 57

Conozco	conocemos
Conoces	conocen
Conoce	conocen

Examples:

Conozco a Joan.	I know Joan.
¿Ustedes se conocen?	Do you know each other?
Conocen a Shakira.	They know Shakira.

dar (to give)

Listen to Track 58

doy	damos
das	dan
da	dan

Examples:

Doy mis consejos.	I give my advice.
¿Me das tu número de teléfono?	Will you give me your number?
Estamos dando pasos para mejorar la situación.	We are taking steps to improve the situation.

salir (to go out)

Listen to Track 59

salgo	salimos
sales	salen
sale	salen

Examples:

Salgo cada viernes.	I go out every Friday.
Sale más barato así.	It works out cheaper this way.
Normalmente salen por esa puerta.	Normally they go out through that door.

Stem-changing verbs

Also known as radical-changing verbs, these don't follow the regular conjugations, but they aren't fully irregular, either!

In some verbs, the $o \rightarrow ue$

In some verbs, the $e \rightarrow ie$

In some verbs, the $e \rightarrow i$

The changes occur in the *yo*, *tú*, *él/ella/usted*, and *ustedes/ellos/ellas* forms. No changes occur in the *nosotros* form.

poder (to be able to)

Listen to Track 60

$o \rightarrow ue$

p**ue**do	podemos
p**ue**des	p**ue**den
p**ue**de	p**ue**den

Examples:

No puedo ir.	I can't go.
¿Pueden venir?	Can you (plural) come?
Puede entrar.	You (formal) may enter.

volver (to return)

Listen to Track 61

o → ue

v*ue*lvo	volvemos
v*ue*lves	v*ue*lven
v*ue*lve	v*ue*lven

Examples:

Los lunes vuelvo a casa a medianoche.	On Mondays I return home at midnight.
Sandra siempre vuelve con su ex.	Sandra always goes back to her ex.
¿Chicas, a qué hora vuelven?	Girls, what time are you coming back?

querer (to want)

Listen to Track 62

e → ie

qu*ie*ro	queremos
qu*ie*res	qu*ie*ren
qu*ie*re	qu*ie*ren

Examples:

Te quiero.	I love you.
¿Quieres un sandwich?	Do you want a sandwich?
Queremos ir a Japón.	We want to go to Japan.

empezar (to start)

Listen to Track 63

e → ie

emp*ie*zo	empezamos
emp*ie*zas	emp*ie*zan
emp*ie*za	emp*ie*zan

Examples:

La película empieza pronto.	The movie starts soon.
Cuando estamos arregladas, nos dan ganas de salir.	When we're dressed up, we feel like going out.
Las canciones empiezan bien.	The songs start well.

pensar (to think)

Listen to Track 64

e → ie

pienso	pensamos
piensas	piensan
piensa	piensan

Examples:

¿Piensas en mí?	Do you think about me?
Tu madre y yo pensamos que eres muy inteligente.	Your mother and I think that you're very intelligent.
Ana y María están pensando en rentar el departamento.	Ana and María are thinking about renting the apartment.

preferir (to prefer)

Listen to Track 65

e → ie

prefiero	preferimos
prefieres	prefieren
prefiere	prefieren

Examples:

Prefiero vivir en Alemania.	I prefer living in Germany.
¿Cuál prefiere usted?	Which one do you (formal) prefer?
¿Prefieren pastel o helado?	Do you (plural) prefer cake or ice cream?

repetir (to repeat)

Listen to Track 66

e → i

repito	repetimos
repites	repiten
repite	repiten

Examples:

Repito: no vas a la fiesta.	I say again: you are not going to the party.
A veces cenamos y luego repetimos.	Sometimes we have dinner then have second helpings.
Repiten los mismos errores.	They make the same mistakes.

pedir (to ask for)

Listen to Track 67

e → i

p*i*do	pedimos
p*i*des	p*i*den
p*i*de	p*i*den

Examples:

No pido nada de él.	I'm not asking anything from him.
El gato pide leche.	The cat pleads for milk.
Piden voluntarios.	They are looking for volunteers.

Good job!

That's a lot of example sentences to get through, so well done! It's okay if you don't memorize all this at once. Start by trying to learn the regular verb endings, practicing a little every day, then think about moving onto the irregular ones!

Workbook Lesson 7: El presente simple – Present tense

Exercise 1: Conjugate the verbs between brackets in the simple present tense.

1- Yo (amar) ___ mucho esta película. (I really like this movie.)

2- Ellos (trabajar) ___ día y noche. (They work day and night.)

3- Ella (habla) ___ muy bien español. (She speaks Spanish very well.)

4- Nosotros (comer) ___ fuera esta noche. (We eat out tonight.)

5- ¿Usted (pagar) ___ en efectivo o con tarjeta de crédito? (Are you going to pay in cash or by credit card?)

Exercise 2: Change the verbs in the following sentences into plural.

1- Él come un pastel. (He eats a cake.)

2- Yo adoro la música. (I adore music.)

3- Tú bailas muy bien. (You dance very well.)

4- Ella juega a las cartas. (She plays cards.)

5- Yo busco los baños. (I'm looking for the toilets.)

Exercise 3: Conjugate the verbs between brackets in the simple present tense.

1- Ella (terminar) ___ sus tareas antes de jugar. (She finishes her homework before playing.)

2- Nosotros (pensar) ___en una solución. (We are thinking about a solution.)

3- En mi casa (cenar) ___ muy temprano. (We have dinner very early in my house.)

4- ¿Usted (elegir) ___ cuál opción? (You choose which option?)

5- Ellos (aplauden) ___ cuando el espectáculo se termina. (They applaud when the show is over.)

Exercise 4: Rewrite the following sentences in the singular.

1- Nosotros elegimos ir de vacaciones. (We choose to go on vacation.)

2- Ellos terminan el examen a tiempo. (They finish the exam in time.)

3- Ellos crecen muy rápido. (They grow up so fast.)

4- Ustedes piensan mucho. (You think a lot.)

5- Ellos no obedecen órdenes. (They don't obey orders.)

Exercise 5: Conjugate the verbs between brackets in the simple present tense.

1- Nostros (esperar) ___ el resultado desde la mañana. (We've been waiting for the results since this morning.)

2- ¿Qué ruta (tomar) ___ para ir al súper? (Which road do I take to go to the supermarket?)

3- Ellos (vender) ___ ropa bonita. (They sell beautiful clothes.)

4- Ella (responder) ___ al teléfono rápidamente. (She answers the phone quickly.)

5- ¿Usted (bajar) ___ aquí? (Are you coming down here?)

Exercise 6: Change the following sentences from singular into plural, or from plural into singular.

1- Yo espero desde hace mucho tiempo. (I've been waiting for a long time.)

2- Nosotros visitamos a nuestra abuela. (We visit our grandmother.)

3- Él escucha un ruido raro que viene de afuera. (He hears a weird sound coming from outside.)

4- Responde a nuestras preguntas. (Answer the questions.)

5- Yo siempre pierdo las llaves. (I always lose my keys.)

Exercise 7: Conjugate the verbs between brackets in the simple present tense.

1- Él (hablar) ___ bien inglés. (He speaks English well.)

2- Ellas (responder) ___ a todas las preguntas. (They answer all the questions.)

3- Nosotros (elegir) ___ dormir en el hotel esta noche. (We choose to sleep at the hotel tonight.)

4- Yo (esperar) ___ el metro. (I'm waiting for the metro.)

5- Usted (caminar) ___ muy rápido. (You walk very fast.)

Exercise 8: Choose the right translation for these sentences.

1- Yo no bebo vino.
   a. I don't drink wine.   b. I never drink wine.   c. I drink wine.

2- Ella ya no trabaja más.
   a. She's always working.   b. She doesn't work.   c. She doesn't work anymore.

3- Ellos comen muchos chocolates.
   a. They eat a lot of chocolates.   b. He eats a lot of chocolates.   c. They are eating a lot of chocolates.

4- Arturo trabaja en una fábrica.
   a. Arturo works in a factory.   b. Arturo is working in a factory.   c. Arturo has been working in a factory.

5- Pedro estudia historia.
   a. Pedro studied history.   b. Pedro studies history.   c. Pedro is studying history.

Exercise 9: Tick the correct answer.

1- Yo __ Italiano. (I speak Italian.)
   a. hablo   b. hablan   c. hablas

2- Ellos ___ a Europa. (They travel to Europe.)
   a. viajar   b. viajan   c. viaja

3- Nosotros __ en Monterrey (We live in Monterrey.)
   a. vivimos   b. viven   c. vivo

4- Ustedes __ la televisión. (You watch TV.)
   a. miras   b. miran   c. miro

5- Tú __ mucho. (You walk a lot.)
   a. caminas   b. caminan   c. camina

Exercise 10: Conjugate the verbs between brackets in the simple present tense.

1- Las ballenas (vivir) ____ en aguas frías. (Whales live in cold waters.)

2- Los argentinos (hablar) ____ español. (Argentines speak Spanish.)

3- Lola y yo nunca (viajar) ____ en avión. (Lola and I never travel by plane.)

4- Nosotros no (abrir) ____ esta noche. (We don't open tonight.)

5- ¿Dónde (pasar) ____ los veranos usted? (Where do you spend your summers?)

ANSWERS:

Exercise 1

1/ Yo amo mucho esta película. 2/ Ellos trabajan día y noche. 3/ Ella habla muy bien español. 4/ Nosotros comemos fuera esta noche. 5/ ¿Usted paga en efectivo o con tarjeta de crédito?

Exercise 2

1/ Ellos comen un pastel. 2/ Nosotros adoramos la música. 3/ Ustedes bailan muy bien. 4/ Ellas juegan a las cartas. 5/ Nosotros buscamos los baños.

Exercise 3

1/ Ella termina sus tareas antes de jugar. 2/ Nosotros pensamos en una solución. 3/ En mi casa cenamos muy temprano. 4/ ¿Usted elige cuál opción? 5/ Ellos aplauden cuando el espectáculo se termina.

Exercise 4

1/ Yo elijo ir de vacaciones. 2/ Ella termina el exámen a tiempo. 3/ Él crece muy rápido. 4/ Tú piensas mucho. 5/ Él no obedece órdenes.

Exercise 5

1/ Nosotros esperamos el resultado desde la mañana. 2/ ¿Qué ruta tomo para ir al súper? 3/ Ellos venden ropa bonita. 4/ Ella responde al teléfono rápidamente. 5/ ¿Usted baja aquí?

Exercise 6

1/ Nosotros esperamos desde hace mucho tiempo. 2/ Yo visito a mi abuela. 3/ Ellos escuchan un ruido raro que viene de afuera. 4/ Responden a nuestras preguntas. 5/ Nosotros siempre perdemos las llaves.

Exercise 7

1/ Él habla bien inglés. 2/ Ellas responden a todas las preguntas. 3/ Nosotros elegimos dormir en el hotel esta noche. 4/ Yo espero el metro. 5/ Usted camina muy rápido.

Exercise 8

1/ I don't drink wine. 2/ She doesn't work anymore. 3/ They eat a lot of chocolates. 4/ Arturo works in a factory. 5/ Pedro studies history.

Exercise 9

1/ Yo hablo italiano. 2/ Ellos viajan a Europa. 3/ Nosotros vivimos en Monterrey. 4/ Ustedes miran la televisión. 5/ Tú caminas mucho.

Exercise 10

1/ Las ballenas viven en aguas frías. 2/ Los argentinos hablan español. 3/ Lola y yo nunca viajamos en avión. 4/ Nosotros no abrimos esta noche. 5/ ¿Dónde pasa usted los veranos usted?

Lesson 8. How to ask questions

If any conversation is going to go very far, you have to know how to ask questions. It would be very boring if two people just went back and forth, telling each other random statements about themselves.

Asking questions isn't just good for that, however. If you travel through a Spanish speaking country, you may want to know things, such as "where are the bathrooms?" and "how much does this cost?"

This lesson will give you a quick guide to the different rules, structures, and important vocabulary you should know when asking questions in Spanish.

The Basics

Let's start at the very beginning. Like in English, we have two options for asking questions in Spanish. The first is with a "question word." The other is by changing a statement into a question with just a little shifting around of the words and/or changing the intonation of your voice.

Something unique about questions in Spanish is the way they are written. You've seen the "¿" before. Well, this is your chance to use it! In Spanish, there will be the inverted question mark at the beginning of the statement, and the normal one at the end. *¿Qué quieres hacer?* – What do you want to do?

Questions with Question Words

So, let's start with the first possible way to ask questions in Spanish–with "Question Words" or "Interrogatives." These are words that make our statement a question. For example, in English we can say "Where is the train station?" In the example, "where" is our question word, letting the listener know we are asking for information.

In Spanish, our question words are:

Listen to Track 68

Qué- What

Dónde- Where

Cuánto/a- How much

Cuántos/as- How many

Por qué- Why

Cuál- Which

Quién- Who

Cómo- What

Cuándo- When

You'll notice that ALL of these words have accents! If they are used in a statement, they do not have the accent, but the pronunciation will stay the same.

Listen to Track 69

Example: *¿Dónde está Juan? ¡No sé donde está!* – Where is Juan? I don't know where he is!

Generally speaking, the verb will go right after our question word.

¿Por qué tengo que ir? – Why do I have to go?

¿Dónde está la biblioteca? – Where is the library?

¿Cómo está? – How is he/she/it? OR How are you (singular/formal)?

You'll notice that with some questions, it's pretty clear what we're talking about. With others, however (the last in the list above, for example), unless we can infer it from the conversation, we need to specify a little. If this is the case, the subject will come after the verb.

¿Cómo está ella? – How is she?

¿Cómo está usted? – How are you (singular/ formal)?

Word Order and Intonation

Sometimes you may have a question that doesn't use a question word. This is very common, in both Spanish and English. So, let's look at how those would be formed.

In Spanish, like in English, we can also create questions by moving around the words. However, there is a little more freedom in Spanish as to where those words should go.

For example, the question "Is she going to the store?" could be said:

Listen to Track 70

¿Va a la tienda? – no subject because due to the conversation we're all aware we're talking about the subject "she."

The following are ways of putting in the subject for specification purposes (in case you weren't paying close enough attention during the conversation, or you just want to double check). This is because the verb conjugation can go with any number of subjects (he, she, it, you).

¿Va ella a la tienda?

*¿Ella va a la tienda?***

You'll notice that in English, we use an auxiliary or "helping" verb ("is") whereas in Spanish we do not. To form the question in Spanish, the helping verb isn't required.

Or, the question "Do you want to go to the movies?" could be said:

¿Quieres ir al cine? – There's no subject because the conjugation tells us who we are talking about.

The following are examples with the subject. Note: when we have a verb conjugated to a subject that can only be one thing (i.e. "tú" "yo" "nosotros" "ustedes") we add in the subject, more often than not, because we want to emphasize it. The following are like saying "*You* want to go to the movies? (as in, you never want to go to the movies, and I'm surprised!).

¿Quieres ir tú al cine?

*¿Tú quieres ir al cine?***

You'll notice here that the word "do" in English is another type of "question word." Other than turning the statement "you want to go to the movies" into the question "do you want to go to the movies?", it has no other purpose. In Spanish, we don't have this type of construction. We simply change the order of the words, and make sure our intonation goes up, up, up at the end of our question.

** These questions have word orders that are identical to their statement forms. In these cases it is VERY important to use the correct intonation, or the listener will be confused.

One last thing…

Listen to Track 71

You can also take a statement and turn it into a question by adding a sort of "question tag" to the end. For Example: "You're coming tonight, right?".

Vienes esta noche, ¿verdad?

Notice how the question marks only go around the part of the statement that is the question.

Tienes que estudiar, ¿no? – You have to study, no?

Voy a la fiesta, ¿y tú? – I'm going to the party, are you?

Asking questions in Spanish isn't unlike asking questions in English. The important thing to remember? Your intonation. This is the key!

Word order is a little more relaxed, and (other than the "question words" we looked at before) you don't have to worry about throwing in any "helping" words along the way. The best way to become more familiar and comfortable with asking questions is simple…by doing it! So, get out there and practice, practice, practice!

Workbook Lesson 8: Hacer preguntas – Asking questions

Exercise 1: Choose the correct answer.

1- You want to ask somebody his/her name. You should say:

    a. ¿Cómo te llamas? (informal)/ ¿Cómo se llama usted? (formal)

    b. ¿Quién eres? (informal)/ ¿Quién es usted? (formal)

    c. ¿Tú te llamas cómo? (informal)/ ¿Usted se llama cómo? (formal)

2- You want to ask somebody his/her age. You should say:

    a. ¿Cuál es tu edad?

    b. ¿Qué edad tienes tú? / ¿Qué edad tiene usted?

    c. ¿Cuántos años tienes? / ¿Cuántos años tiene usted?

3- You want to know where the toilets are. You should say:

    a. ¿Hay baños aquí?

    b. ¿Dónde están los baños?

    c. ¿Cuántos baños hay aquí?

4- You want to know when the train arrives. You should say:

    a. ¿Dónde está el tren?

    b. ¿Cuál es el tren a París?

    c. ¿Cuándo llega el tren?

5- You want to know how much this cost. You should say:

    a. ¿Cuáles cuesta esto?

    b. ¿Cuánto cuesta esto?

    c. ¿Por qué cuesta tanto?

Exercise 2: Change these statements into questions.

1- Usted ama Argentina. (You like Argentina.)

2- Es su perro. (It's your dog.)

3- Usted habla español. (You speak Spanish.)

4- Él es un buen amigo. (He's a good friend.)

5- Ella ha llegado. (She arrived.)

Exercise 3: Choose the correct translation.

1- What are you doing this weekend?

    a. ¿Qué has hecho este fin de semana?

    b. ¿Qué haces este fin de semana?

    c. ¿Cuándo es el fin de semana?

2- When are you coming?

    a. ¿De dónde vienes?

    b. ¿Cuándo vienes?

    c. ¿Cómo vienes?

3- Where do you live?

    a. ¿Dónde vives?

    b. ¿Quién vive contigo?

    c. ¿Por qué vives tú aquí?

4- Do you have brothers or sisters?

    a. ¿Cuántos hermanos y hermanas tienes?

    b. ¿Tienes hermanos o hermanas?

    c. ¿Dónde están tus hermanos o hermanas?

5- Which one of them is your dog?

    a. ¿Dónde está tu perro?

    b. ¿Cómo está tu perro?

    c. ¿Cuál de éstos es tu perro?

Exercise 4: Complete these questions with the right question words.

1- ¿___ cuesta este teléfono? (___ does this phone cost?)

2- ¿___ hermanos y hermanas tienes? (___ brothers and sisters do you have?)

3- ¿___ están mis zapatos nuevos? (___ are my new shoes?)

4- ¿___ le hago para ir a la estación de tren? (___ to do to go to the train station?)

5- ¿___ te gustan los perros? (__ do you like dogs?)

Exercise 5: Change these statements into questions using inversion.

1- Tú amas el chocolate. (You like chocolate.)

2- Tú sabes cocinar. (You know how to cook.)

3- Usted tiene frío. (You are cold.)

4- Tú has visitado París. (You visited Paris.)

5- Usted me comprende. (You undestand me.)

Exercise 6: Change these statements into questions using « ¿No es así? » or « ¿No? ».

1- Él hace deporte. (He plays sports.)

2- Ella está en la casa (She's at home.)

3- Tú has lavado los platos. (You washed the dishes.)

4- Tú amas el vino. (You like wine.)

5- Ellos están juntos. (They are together.)

Exercise 7: Choose the correct translation.

1- Do you like cats?

    a. ¿Qué gato te gusta?

    b. ¿Por qué te gustan los gatos?

    c. ¿Te gustan los gatos?

2- Where is he?

    a. ¿Dónde está él?

    b. ¿Cuándo va a llegar él?

    c. ¿Quién es él?

3- Did you eat lunch today?

    a. ¿Has comido hoy?

    b. ¿Quisieras comer hoy?

    c. ¿Cuándo es que has comido hoy?

4- Who sings this song?

    a. ¿Quién canta esta canción?

    b. ¿Quién cantó esa canción?

    c. ¿Dónde se canta esta canción?

5- Which one of you is María?

    a. ¿Quién de ustedes es María?

    b. ¿Cuál de ustedes es María?

    c. ¿Quién es María?

Exercise 8: Complete these questions with the right question words.

1- ¿___ empiezan las clases? (___ do classes begin?)

2- ¿___ de ustedes es médico?(___of you is a doctor?)

3- ¿___ es el presidente de Francia? (___ is the president of Francia?)

4- ¿___ es tu película favorita? (___ is your favourite movie?)

5- ¿___ significa « hola » en español ? (__ does « hola » mean in Spanish?)

Exercise 9: Tick the right answer.

1- ¿___ ha llamado por teléfono? (Who called on the phone?)

    a. Cuál   b. Quién   c. Cómo

2- ¿___ vende esa señora? (What is that lady selling?)

    a. Qué   b. Quién   c. Cuáles

3- ¿___ son los ganadores? (Who are the winners?)

    a. Quiénes   b. Quién   c. Cuándo

4- ¿___ tienes en la mano? (What do you have in your hand?)

  a. Quién   b. Qué   c. Cuál

5- ¿___ viven Alberto y Diana? (Where do Alberto and Diana live?)

  a. Cuándo   b. Dónde   c. Quién

Exercise 10: Translate these sentences from English to Spanish.

1- What are the Amazon countries?

2- Who is Camilo's father?

3- How old is Ernesto?

4- Why is he always late?

5- Where do you come from?

ANSWERS:

Exercise 1

1/ ¿Cómo te llamas? (informal)/ ¿Cómo se llama usted? (formal) 2/ The three options are correct /¿ Qué edad tiene usted? 3/ ¿Dónde están los baños? 4/ ¿Cuándo llega el tren? 5/ ¿Cuánto cuesta esto?

Exercise 2

1/ ¿Ama usted Argentina? 2/ ¿Es su perro? 3/ ¿Habla usted español? 4/ ¿Es él un buen amigo? 5/ ¿Ha llegado ella?

Exercise 3

1/ ¿Qué haces este fin de semana? 2/ ¿Cuándo vienes? 3/ ¿Dónde vives? 4/ ¿Tienes hermanos o hermanas? 5/ ¿Cuál de éstos es tu perro?

Exercise 4

1/ ¿Cuánto cuesta este teléfono? 2/ ¿Cuántos hermanos y hermanas tienes? 3/¿Dónde están mis zapatos nuevos? 4/ ¿Cómo hago para ir a la estación de tren? 5/ ¿Por qué te gustan los perros?

Exercise 5

1/ ¿Amas el chocolate? 2/ ¿Sabes cocinar? 3/ ¿Tiene usted frío? 4/ ¿Has visitado París? 5/ ¿Usted me comprende?

Exercise 6

1/ Él hace deporte, ¿no es así?/¿no? 2/ Ella está en la casa, ¿no es así?/¿no? 3/ Tú has lavado los platos, ¿no es así?/¿no? 4/ Tú amas el vino, ¿no es así?/¿no? 5/ Ellos están juntos, ¿no es así?/¿no?

Exercise 7

1/ ¿Te gustan los gatos? 2/ ¿Dónde está él? 3/ ¿Has comido hoy? 4/ ¿Quién canta esta canción? 5/ ¿Quién de ustedes es María?

Exercise 8

1/ ¿Cuándo empiezan las clases? 2/ ¿Quién de ustedes es médico? 3/ ¿Quién es el presidente de Francia? 4/ ¿Cuál es tu película favorita? 5/ ¿Qué significa «hola» en español?

Exercise 9

1/ Quién 2/ Qué 3/ Quiénes 4/ Qué 5/ Dónde

Exercise 10

1/ ¿Cuáles son los países amazónicos? 2/ ¿Quién es el padre de Camilo? 3/ ¿Cuántos años tiene Ernesto? 4/ ¿Por qué él siempre llega tarde? 5/ ¿De dónde vienen ustedes?

Lesson 9. Ser and Estar

¡Hola! Undoubtedly one of the most important words in English is the verb 'to be.' Well, 'to be' in Spanish is also super important, but there's a catch: there are two Spanish verbs that both mean 'to be': *ser* and *estar*.

Although they both mean 'to be', they aren't the same in Spanish, and can't just be used interchangeably. That's where this lesson comes in!

A super-simplified rule for the difference between *ser* and *estar* is that *ser* is for permanent things, and *estar* is for temporary things. However, the rules go so much deeper than that, and we want you to be able to use the right verb at the right time!

SER

Conjugation

Listen to Track 72

First of all, let's learn how to conjugate *ser* in the present tense. It's very irregular.

yo	soy
tú	eres
él/ella/usted	es
nosotros	somos
ustedes	son
ellos/ ellas	son

When to use *ser*

A common device for learning the uses of *ser* is to remember the acronym '**DOCTOR.**' Each letter stands for a situation where you'd use *ser*.

D = *Descriptions*

Listen to Track 73

This refers to the permanent or essential qualities of a person or object. Let's look at some examples.

Soy Juan.	I'm Juan.
Eres un hombre guapo.	You are a handsome man.
Ana es una chica.	Ana is a girl.
Somos altos.	We are tall.
¿Son ingleses?	Are you guys English?
Los coches son negros.	The cars are black.

O = *Occupations*

Listen to Track 74

When you're saying what someone does, use *ser*. It could be a job or just something that they do as a hobby.

Soy médico*.	I'm a doctor.
Eres pianista.	You're a pianist.
Jaime es mesero en un gran restaurante.	Jaime is a waiter in a big restaurant.
Tenemos muchos exámenes porque somos estudiantes.	We have lots of exams because we are students.
Señores, ¿son bomberos?	Gentlemen, are you firefighters?
Pablo y Paula son enfermeros.	Pablo and Paula are nurses.

*Note that in Spanish, you don't have to use 'a' or 'an' before an occupation. You say *'soy médico'* rather than *'soy un médico.'*

C = *Characteristics*

As we said earlier, *ser* is used for descriptions, and this includes the characteristics of someone's personality.

Listen to Track 75

Yo soy flojo.	I am lazy.
Eres una persona feliz.	You are a happy person (in general).
Ignacio es aventurero.	Ignacio is adventurous.
Somos amables.	We are nice.
Son muy graciosos	You (plural) are very funny.
Las chicas de mi clase son inteligentes.	The girls in my class are intelligent.

T = *Times*

When you're talking about times, use *ser*. This doesn't just mean times of the day—it also includes days, months, etc.

Listen to Track 76

Ya son las tres.	It's already three o'clock.
Hoy es viernes.	Today is Friday.
¡Es mi cumpleaños!	It's my birthday!
Es marzo.	It's March.

O = *Origins*

Listen to Track 77

We use *ser* to talk about the origin of something or someone. This includes what something is made of.

Soy de Dinamarca.	I'm from Denmark.
Eres de Uruguay, ¿verdad?	You're from Uruguay, right?
La puerta es de madera.	The door is made from wood.
La guitarra es de Michoacán.	The guitar is from Michoacán.

R = *Relations*

Listen to Track 78

When you're describing how people are related to each other, use *ser*.

Soy la tía de Pepe.	I'm Pepe's aunt.
Eres mi novio.	You are my boyfriend.
Nuria es mi abuela.	Nuria is my grandmother.
Miki es el hermano de Ricky.	Miki is Ricky's brother.

ESTAR

Conjugation

Listen to Track 79

Here's how to conjugate *estar* in the present tense:

yo	estoy
tú	estás
él/ella/usted	está
nosotros	estamos
ustedes	están
ellos/ellas	están

When to use *estar*

A useful way to remember when to use *estar* is the acronym 'PLACE.'

P = *Position*

We use *estar* to say where something is, or how it's positioned.

Listen to Track 80

Estoy a tu lado.	I'm by your side.
¿Estás enfrente del hotel?	Are you in front of the hotel?
La biblioteca está al lado del mercado.	The library is next to the market.
Estamos acostados en el parque.	We are lying in the park.
Están sentados.	You're sitting/seated.
Mis padres están cerca.	My parents are nearby.

L = *Location*

Listen to Track 81

As 'PLACE' can help you remember, *estar* is used to talk about the place that someone or something is in. In other words, that person or thing's location, whether it's temporary or permanent!

Estoy en el baño.	I'm in the bathroom.
¿Estás?	Are you there?
La estación está a tu derecha.	The station is on your right.
Estamos en Nueva York.	We're in New York.
Están en mi casa.	You (plural) are in my house.
Los perritos están en el jardín.	The puppies are in the yard.

There is an exception to this one. When you're saying where an event is being held, you use *ser*.

So, it would be *'la fiesta es en mi casa'* rather than *'la fiesta está en mi casa.'*

A = *Action*

Estar is used in the gerund, which can be used in past, present, future, etc. This is when you want to say what someone is do**ing**, e.g. he is swimm**ing**, she was sing**ing**, he'll be laugh**ing**, etc. For more on the gerund, click here.

Listen to Track 82

Estoy pensando en él.	I'm thinking about him.
Estás bailando.	You are dancing.
Dani está cambiando el mundo.	Dani is changing the world.
María y yo estamos buscando departamento.	María and I are looking for an apartment.
Chicos, ¿están caminando o corriendo?	Boys, are you walking or running?
Señoras, ¿están esperando?	Ladies, are you waiting?

C = *Condition*

When talking about a physical or emotional condition that is changeable (as opposed to personality traits, which are pretty much set), use *estar*.

For Example:

Listen to

Estoy mareado.	I'm feeling dizzy.
Mamá, ¿estás lista? ¡Vámonos!	Mom, are you ready? Let's go!
Carla está enamorada de Lucía.	Carla is in love with Lucía.
Estamos muy cansados.	We are very tired.
Puedo ver que están enfermos hoy. No tienen que hacer sus tareas.	I can see that you're unwell today. You don't have to do your homework.
Ayer mis abuelos estaban confundidos.	Yesterday my grandparents were confused.

E = *Emotion*

Okay, so this one is pretty self-explanatory. Use *estar* for emotional states.

Listen to Track 84

Estoy aburrida en esta clase.	I am bored in this class.
¿Estás contento?	Are you happy?
Victoria está feliz porque está con su hermana.	Victoria is happy because she's with her sister.
Ambos estamos muy emocionados (o: Los dos estamos muy emocionados).	We are both very excited.
Se ve que están tristes por sus calificaciones.	It's clear that you (plural) are feeling sad about the grades.
Tus amigos están preocupados por ti.	Your friends are worried about you.

Words that change meaning

Interestingly, some adjectives can be used with either *ser* or *estar*, and they have different meanings with each!

Sometimes the difference is subtle and linked to the permanence of the adjective, and sometimes it's quite a big difference in meaning.

It's tricky, but helpful to learn them. Some of the common ones are in the table below.

Listen to Track 85

ser aburrido (to be boring)	estar aburrido (to be bored)
ser consciente (to be aware)	estar consciente (to be conscious)
ser un enfermo (to be chronically ill)	estar enfermo (to be unwell)
ser feliz (to be happy - personality trait)	estar feliz (to be happy - a temporary state)
ser frío (to be cold - personality trait)	estar frío (to be cold - current temperature)
ser guapo (to be good-looking)	estar guapo (to be looking good now)
ser listo (to be smart/clever)	estar listo (to be ready)
ser malo (to be bad)	estar malo (to be ill)
ser orgulloso (to be proud - as a person; could have negative connotation)	estar orgulloso (to be proud of someone or something)
ser rico (to be rich)	estar rico (to be tasty)
ser seguro (to be safe)	estar seguro (to be sure)
ser verde (to be green)	estar verde (to be unripe)
ser viejo (to be old)	estar viejo (to be looking old)
ser vivo (to be quick/sharp)	estar vivo (to be alive)

Be careful with these... the last thing you want is to try and say you're rich but accidentally claim to be tasty!

Well done!

If you've followed this lesson, then you've done well, as the differences between *ser* and *estar* can be subtle. It takes practice before they start to come naturally, so do a little bit of Spanish every day and watch the improvement!

Workbook Lesson 9: Ser y estar - The verb « to be »

Exercise 1: Tick the correct answer.

1- Yo ___ mexicano. (I am Mexican.)

   a. es   b. soy   c. son

2- Ellos ___ casados. (They are married.)

   a. están   b. eres   c. es

3- Nosotros ___ felices. (We are happy.)

   a. son   b. somos   c. eres

4- Ustedes ___ mis mejores amigos. (You are my best friends.)

   a. son   b. somos   c. eres

5- Tú ___ muy amable. (You are very nice.)

   a. es   b. soy   c. eres

Exercise 2: Re-order these words to make sentences that make sense.

1- estoy/yo/en Puerto Vallarta (am/I/in Puerto Vallarta)

2- aburrida/estas/tú (bored/are/you)

3- ella/loca/está (she/crazy/is)

4- estamos/nosotros/cansados (we/are/tired)

5- está/sucia/la casa (is/dirty/the house)

Exercise 3: Conjugate the verb « ser » in the present tense.

1- Él ___ un chico bueno. (He is a nice kid.)

2- Nosotros ___ italianos. (We are Italian.)

3- Ustedes ___ muy bien parecidos (You are very good looking.)

4- Ellas ___ hermanas. (They are sisters.)

5- Él ___ buena persona (He is a good person.)

Exercise 4: Complete this dialogue with the right form of the verb «Estar» or «Ser».

Pablo: Buenos días, ¿___ aquí Maria? (Hello, is Maria there?)

La mama de María: No, ella no ___. ___ en el doctor con su papá. Ellos ___ enfermos. ¿Quieres dejarle un mensaje? Tú ___? (No, she's not here. She went to the doctor with her dad. They are both sick. Do you want to leave a message for her? You are…?

Pablo: Pablo. ___ Pablo. Sí, muchas gracias. (Pablo. I am Pablo. Yes, thank you very much.)

Exercise 5: Translate these sentences from English to Spanish.

1- I am Mexican.

2- He is tall.

3- They are doctors. (m.)

4- We are smart.

5- You are nice. (pl.)

Exercise 6: Conjugate the verb « Estar » in the present tense.

1- Este café____ muy caliente. (This coffe is so hot.)

2- Este árbol___ muerto. (This tree is dead.)

3- Hoy no ___ feliz. (I am not happy today.)

4- Este libro___ roto. (This book is broken.)

5- Mi ropa ___ sucia. (My clothes are dirty.)

Exercise 7: Complete these sentences using the verb « Ser ».

1- Ellos ___ franceses. (They are French.)

2- Ella ___ alta. (She is tall.)

3- Yo ___ africana. (I am African.)

4- Tú ___ tonto. (You're stupid.)

5- Ellos ___ amables. (They're kind)

Exercise 8: Find the mistake in each sentence and re-write it correctly.

1- Ellos están Bolivia. (They are in Bolivia.)

2- Nosotros estás enfermos. (We are sick.)

3- Ella estamos embarazada. (She is pregnant.)

4- Ustedes estamos hablando mucho. (You are talking a lot.)

5- Tu es retrasado. (You're late.)

Exercise 9: Conjugate the verb « Ser » in the present tense.

1- ¿De dónde ___ tú? (Where are you from?)

2- ¿De dónde ___ tus padres? (Where are your parents from?)

3- ¿Cuántos ___ en tu familia? (How many are in your family?)

4- Diana ___ muy inteligente. (Diana is very smart.)

5- El coche de Eduardo ____ rojo. (Eduardo´s car is red.)

Exercise 10: Tick the correct answer.

1- Omar____ muy delgado. (Omar is very thin.)

   a. estamos   b. está   c. estoy

2- Yo __ en Perú. (I'm in Peru.)

   a. está   b. estoy   c. están

3- Carla y Luis ___ de luna de miel. (Carla and Luis are on honeymoon.)

   a. estamos   b. están   c. estoy

4- Estos cristales___ muy sucios. (These crystals are very dirty.)

   a. están   b. estamos   c. estás

5- Este plato ___ delicioso. (This dish is delicious.)

   a. estoy   b. está   c. están

ANSWERS:

Exercise 1

1/ soy 2/ están 3/ somos 4/ son 5/ eres

Exercise 2

1/ Yo estoy en Puerto Vallarta. 2/ Tú estás aburrida. 3/ Ella está loca. 4/ Nosotros estamos cansados. 5/ La casa está sucia.

Exercise 3

1/ Él es un chico bueno. 2/ Nosotros somos italianos. 3/ Ustedes son muy bien parecidos. 4/ Ellas son hermanas. 5/ Él es buena persona.

Exercise 4

Pablo: Buenos días, ¿está aquí María? (Hello, is Maria there?)

La mama de María: No, ella no está. Está en el doctor con su papá. Ellos están enfermos. ¿Quieres dejarle un mensaje? ¿Tú eres…? (No, she's not here. She went to the doctor with her dad. They are both sick. Do you want to leave a message for her? You are…?

Pablo: Pablo. Soy Pablo. Sí, muchas gracias. (Pablo. I am Pablo. Yes, thank you very much.)

Exercise 5

1/ Yo soy mexicano. 2/ Él es alto. 3/ Ellos son médicos/doctores. 4/ Nosotros somos inteligentes. 5/ Ustedes son amables.

Exercise 6

1/ Este café está muy caliente. 2/ Este árbol está muerto. 3/ Hoy no estoy feliz. 4/ Este libro está roto. 5/ Mi ropa está sucia.

Exercise 7

1/ Ellos son franceses. 2/ Ella es alta. 3/ Yo soy africana. 4/ Tú eres tonto. 5/ Ellos son amables.

Exercise 8

1/ Ellos están en Bolivia. 2/ Nosotros estamos enfermos. 3/ Ella está embarazada. 4/ Ustedes están hablando mucho. 5/ Tu estás retrasado.

Exercise 9

1/ ¿De dónde eres tú? 2/ ¿De dónde son tus padres? 3/ ¿Cuántos son en tu familia? 4/ Diana es muy inteligente. 5/ El coche de Eduardo es rojo.

Exercise 10

1/ está 2/ estoy 3/ están 4/ están 5/ está

Lesson 10. Singular and Plural Nouns

¡Buenos días! Today we're looking at how to make singular nouns plural! The only background knowledge you need is that when we say a noun is 'singular,' it means there's only one of them. When we refer to it as 'plural,' there's more than one.

We've made a list of rules to help you form all sorts of plurals, but generally it's pretty simple.

- **Rule #1: Change the article**

The first rule is that when you make a singular noun plural, you must remember to change the article that goes with it (the article is the tiny word in front), for example *la chica* becomes *las chicas*.

Here's how to change the common articles, with Examples:

Listen to Track 86

El	los
el chico (the boy)	*los chicos* (the boys)
La	las
la chica (the girl)	*las chicas* (the girls)
Un	unos
un chico (a boy)	*unos chicos* (some boys)

- **Rule #2: Add an -s when it ends in a vowel**

When a Spanish noun ends in an unstressed vowel, it's a simple case of adding an -s to the end of it.

Listen to Track 87

un lobo (one wolf)	*dos lobos* (two wolves)
una manzana (one apple)	*dos manzanas* (two apples)

- **Rule #3: Add an -s when it ends in -é or -ó**

We've seen what to do with unstressed vowels, but what if the vowel at the end of the noun has an accent? Words ending in -é or -ó also take their plurals by adding -s, just like in Rule #2. Nice and simple.

Listen to Track 88

un café (a coffee)	*dos cafés* (two coffees)
el buró (the coffee table)	*los burós* (the coffee tables)

- **Rule #4: Add an -es if it ends in -á, -í, or -ú (exceptions apply)**

If a noun ends in -á or -í or -ú, we usually add -es.

Listen to Track 89

el panamá (Panama hat)	*los panamáes* (Panama hats)
el bisturí (the scalpel)	*los bisturíes* (the scalpels)
el tabú (the taboo)	*los tabúes* (the taboos)

There are exceptions to this rule. Some of these nouns (a lot of the common ones, actually) form their plurals irregularly, such as *mamá*, or *menú*, for which we just stick an *-s* on the end.

la mamá y el papá (the mommy and the daddy)	*las mamás y los papás* (the mommies and the daddies)
el menú (the menu)	*los menús* (the menus)

- **Rule #5: Add an *-es* when it ends in a consonant other than *s***

The general rule for words ending in consonants is that we add *-es*.

Listen to Track 90

el color (the color)	*los colores* (the colors)
la ciudad (the city)	*las ciudades* (the cities)
un rey (one king)	*cinco reyes* (five kings)

- **Rule #6: If the noun ends in *-s*, leave it as it is**

As long as there's no stress on the final syllable, the noun remains unchanged in the plural.

Listen to Track 91

el jueves (Thursday)	*los jueves* (Thursdays)
la tesis (the thesis)	*las tesis* (the theses, e.g. 'The students submitted their theses')
el cactus (cactus)	*los cactus* (cacti)

This rule often applies to Spanish compound nouns. We're talking about words where a verb and a noun are joined together to make a bigger word, e.g. *paraguas* = *parar* (to stop) + *agua* (water)!

mi paraguas (my umbrella)	*mis paraguas* (my umbrellas)
su cumpleaños (his birthday)	*sus cumpleaños* (his birthdays)
el limpiaparabrisas (the windshield wiper)	*los limpiaparabrisas* (the windshield wipers)

But if the final syllable is stressed ...

- **Rule #7: Add an *-es* when the noun ends in a stressed vowel + *-s***

If the noun ends in *-s* and the emphasis is on the last syllable when spoken (which will also be the case for words that only have one syllable!), then add *-es*.

Listen to Track 92

el mes (month)	*los meses* (months)
el autobús* (bus)	*los autobuses** (buses)

*see rule #8 to find out why we removed the accent.

- **Rule #8: If the noun ends in a consonant and the last syllable has an accent, you can usually remove it**

In Spanish, we have rules surrounding stress and emphasis within words. If our noun ends in a consonant, then we're most likely going to be adding -*es*, which adds an extra syllable onto the end of the word.

This means that we don't need the accent anymore. Don't worry, you won't mess up the stress—follow the rules and the syllables sort themselves out!

Listen to Track 93

un autobús (a bus)	*unos autobuses* (some buses)
el francés (Frenchman)	*los franceses* (Frenchmen)
un rehén (a hostage)	*ocho rehenes* (eight hostages)

- **Rule #9: If the noun ends in -*en*, do the opposite of #8!**

Sometimes making a noun plural means we actually have to add an accent, to maintain the stress when we add the new -*es* syllable. This usually applies to words ending in -*en*.

Listen to Track 94

el crimen (the crime)	*los crímenes* (the crimes)
una imagen (an image)	*unas imágenes* (some images)

- **Rule #10: If it's a foreign word, just add -*s***

One of the cool things about languages is that they're always borrowing and adapting words from each other! When a non-Spanish word (or an adapted version of it) is used in Spanish, we usually just add an -*s* to it!

Listen to Track 95

el chalet (chalet)	*los chalets* (chalets)
un hacker (one hacker)	*dos hackers* (two hackers)

- **Rule #11: Families**

When we use a surname to talk about members of a family, we don't add -*s* or -*es*. (Royalty is an exception.)

Listen to Track 96

Soy Ana Smithson. (I'm Ana Smithson.)	*Somos los Smithson.* (We're the Smithsons.)
Estoy enamorado de una Jones. (I'm in love with a Jones.)	*Estoy enamorado de una de las Jones.* (I'm in love with one of the Joneses.)

- **Rule #12: Some nouns are only ever plural anyway**

So you don't need to worry about changing these, e.g. *los celos* (jealousy), and *las tijeras* (scissors). You can't have just one scissor—you need a pair!

- **Rule #13: Some nouns are only ever singular anyway**

So you don't need to worry about making these plural, e.g. *el tenis* (tennis). You can have more than one **game of** tennis, but you can't have more than one tennis. These nouns are called mass nouns. They're uncountable.

- **Rule #14: Spelling changes!**

This one is just a quick note on spelling. If the noun in the singular form ends in *-z,* we'll need to change it to a *-c* before we add *-es.* Don't worry, change can be a good thing.

Listen to Track 97

un pez (a fish)	*unos pe**ces*** (some fish)
la voz (the voice)	*las vo**ces*** (the voices)

- **Rule #15: To pluralize a noun that is written in both its masculine and feminine way in the same sentence, it is necessary to use the masculine one.**

When, for example, you invite one female friend and one male friend to a party, in English (plural) it rests the same: "I invited two **friends**". In spanish you use the plural ***Amigos*** eventhough you invited ***un amigo*** (male) and ***una amiga*** (female). To sumarize, you must pluralized them as if you were only using the masculine one, without forgettins its correct article!

un ciudadano y una ciudadana (citizen)	*unos ciudadan**os*** (some citizens)
un amigo y una amiga (friend)	*unos amig**os*** (some friends)
un niño y una niña (kid)	*unos niñ**os*** (some children)
el cliente y la clienta (costumer)	*los client**es*** (the costumers)

Quiz

Try and figure out the plural form of each of the following nouns! The parts in parentheses give you the meaning of the singular noun in English, and then the plural that you want to get to. Don't forget to change the article!

Listen to Track 98

1. *un libro* (a book -> some books)
2. *el tentempié* (the snack -> the snacks)
3. *una mamá* (a mommy -> some mommies)
4. *el corazón* (the heart -> the hearts)
5. *el lápiz* (the pencil -> the pencils)
6. *el germen* (germ -> germs)
7. *una vez* (one time -> a few/several times)
8. *un guardaespaldas* (one bodyguard -> two bodyguards)
9. *una computadora (a computer -> three computers)*
10. *la crisis* (the crisis -> the crises)

So there are your rules! Now you know how to turn Spanish singular nouns into plurals ... which is a very useful skill to have, otherwise you'd only ever be able to talk about one of anything (#notideal)! ¡Hasta la próxima!

Workbook Lesson 10: Sustantivos singulares y plurales - Singular and plural nouns

Exercise 1: Write the plural of the following nouns.

1- Actriz.

2- Pantalones.

3- Camión.

4- Pez.

5- Jueves.

Exercise 2: Replace the underlined words, as in the example.

Example: Camila tiene un hijo y dos hijas ➔ Camila tiene tres hijos.

1- Una amiga y un amigo mío están en Buenos Aires. (Friends of mine are in Buenos Aires.)

2- El abuelo y la abuela de Claudia viven en Bogotá. (Claudia's grandfather and grandmother live in Bogota.)

3- En mi escuela hay un profesor y dos profesoras. (In my school there is a male teacher and two female teachers.)

4- El rey y la reina de Francia viven en París. (The king and queen of France live in Paris.)

5- En mi grupo hay tres chicos y dos chicas. (In my group there are three boys and two girls.)

Exercise 3: Choose the correct plural of the following words.

1- calcetín: a. calcetíns   b. calcetines

2- pez: a. peces   b. pezes

3- plátano: a. plátanes   b. plátanos

4- jueves: a. jueves   b. jueveses

5- lámpara: a. lámparas   b. lampares

Exercise 4: Write the plural of these words.

1- mesa (table)

2- mal (bad)

3- edad (age)

4- bici (bike)

5- pera (pear)

Exercise 5: Write the plural of the following sentences.

1- La flor del jardín de María Victoria. (Maria Victoria's flower garden.)

2- El frijol mexicano es delicioso. (The Mexican bean is delicious.)

3- Nuestro mejor cocinero es de Tailandia. (Our best chef is from Thailand.)

4- Una raíz muy grande. (A huge root.)

5- El pastel de maracuyá. (Passion fruit cake)

Exercise 6: Translate the following phrases from English to Spanish.

1- Nokia cellphones

2- green folders

3- skater boys

4- security officers

5- corn circles

Exercise 7: Choose the right plural for each phrases.

1- Una discoteca

    a. unes discotecas   b. unas discotecas   c. unas discotecs

2- Una alberca

    a. unas albercas   b. unes alberques   c. unas alberques

3- Un cuaderno

    a. los cuadernos   b. les cuadernos   c. unos cuadernos

4- Un diccionario

    a. unos diccionaries b. unes diccionarios   c. unos diccionarios

5- Un pizarrón

    a. unas pizarronas   b. unos pizarrones   c. unos pisarones

Exercise 8: Change these affirmative sentences into negative ones.

1- Los tabúes son malos. (Taboos are bad.)

2- Los champús son caros. (Shampoos are expensive.)

3- Las leyes son duras. (Laws are tough.)

4- Las crisis son buenas. (Crises are good.)

5- El cáliz de la flor es grande. (The flower's calyx is big.)

Exercise 9: Translate the following phrases from Spanish to English.

1- Las estrellas mágicas

2- Los libros de terror

3- Los mapas del mar

4- Los museos de arte

5- Los gorilas de África

ANSWERS:

Quiz

1/ unos libros 2/ los tentempiés 3/ unas mamás 4/ los corazones 5/ los lápices 6/ los gérmenes 7/ unas veces 8/ dos guardaespaldas 9/ unas computadoras 10/ las crisis

Exercise 1

1/ Actrices 2/ Pantalones 3/ Camiones 4/ Peces 5/ Jueves.

Exercise 2

1/ Dos amigos míos están en Buenos Aires. 2/ Los abuelos de Claudia viven en Bogotá. 3/ En mi escuela hay tres profesores. 4/ Los reyes de Francia viven en París. 5/ En mi grupo hay cinco chicos.

Exercise 3

1/ calcetines 2/ peces 3/ plátanos 4/ jueves 5/ lámparas

Exercise 4

1/ mesas 2/ males 3/ edades 4/ bicis/bicicletas 5/ peras

Exercise 5

1/ Las flores del jardín de María Victoria. 2/ Los frijoles mexicanos son deliciosos. 3/ Nuestros mejores cocineros son de Tailandia. 4/ Unas raíces muy grandes. 5/ Los pasteles de maracuyá.

Exercise 6

1/ celulares Nokia 2/ carpetas verdes 3/ chicos patinadores 4/ agentes de seguridad 5/ círculos del maíz

Exercise 7

1/ unas discotecas 2/ unas albercas 3/ unos cuadernos 4/ unos diccionarios 5/ unos pizarrones

Exercise 8

1/ Los tabúes no son malos. 2/ Los champús no son caros. 3/ Las leyes no son duras. 4/ Las crisis no son buenas. 5/ El cáliz de la flor no es grande.

Exercise 9

1/ magical stars 2/ terror books 3/ sea maps 4/ art museums 5/ African gorilas

Lesson 11. Adjectives

Adjectives take a dull, plain thought and make it more exciting.

They can make a boring sentence dynamic, a nice sentiment sweeter and a harsh word, well… even harsher.

If you want to be able to do anything in terms of describing something, you need to be able to use this handy, and necessary, part of speech!

In Spanish, adjectives are a little more complicated than they are in English. But don't fret! Below you will find a quick guide to how you can spice up your conversations.

The Basics

Let's start by first figuring out what is an adjective? It's simple, really. Adjectives are the words we add to a sentence to define our nouns. They *describe* a person, place, thing or idea.

For Example:

The house- The <u>red</u> house

The boy- The <u>handsome</u> boy

The building- The <u>tall</u> building

So, let's look at how these parts of speech work in Spanish.

Do you need a girl or a boy adjective?

All right, it's not really a "girl" or "boy" adjective, but one thing about Spanish that is very different from English is that words have a gender. They can be "feminine" or "masculine."

As you learnt in lesson 4, even just a little bit, you've realized that a lot of words end in *O* or *A*. Well, the "o" words are masculine, and the "a" words are feminine*. Like the nouns they modify, <u>the adjectives will need to be either masculine or feminine</u>.

For Example: "The red house"- here, the word "house" in Spanish is feminine (casa) so you will need the *feminine* form of the adjective "red" (roja).

*Remember- Not ALL nouns will end in either "o" or "a". But ALL nouns WILL have a gender! This means it's something you'll have to memorize. **Example:** *coche*– (car) masculine; *leche*– (milk) feminine

And how many "reds" will you need?

Just like agreeing in gender, <u>your adjectives need to agree in number</u>. If you have more than one house, you will have more than one "red."

For Example: "The red house"- here, we have only one, singular red house, so our adjective would be *roja* (singular). But if we were to say "the red houses", our adjective would become the plural version *rojas*. No matter if we have 2 or 23 red houses, if there is more than one, they will be *rojas*.

I know this seems a little weird, but it's really not all that difficult. Just remember that your adjectives have to AGREE, AGREE!! (Two agrees, for two criteria- <u>gender, number</u>.)

Almost time to put it all together

Just one last little detail to throw your way before we can dive in a little deeper to the really juicy technical stuff.

<u>In Spanish, the adjectives come after the noun.</u>

Let's go back to our **Example:** "The red house"- In Spanish this little phrase would be *"La casa roja."* So, literally you're saying "The house red."

Examples:

Listen to Track 99

The handsome boy- *El chico* (the boy) *guapo* (handsome/ attractive)

The tall building- *El edificio* (the building) *alto* (tall)

The handsome boys- *Los chicos guapos*

The tall buildings- *Los edificios altos*

The Technicalities

Some adjectives will be able to take ALL the possible forms we looked at briefly above (masculine, feminine, singular, plural) while some, actually, will only take a few of them.

You will find, generally speaking, three different types of adjectives.

Adjectives that end in "o"

Adjectives that end in "e"

Adjectives that end in a consonant

To make this a little easier, why don't we look at these in a chart.

Listen to Track 100

Adjective	Meaning	Masculine	Feminine	Singular	Plural
Bonito	Pretty	*Bonito*	*Bonita*	*Bonito(a)*	*Bonitos/as*
Tímido	Shy	*Tímido*	*Tímida*	*Tímido(a)*	*Tímidos/as*
Grande	Big	--------------	--------------	*Grande*	*Grandes*
Inteligente	Intelligent	--------------	--------------	*Inteligente*	*Inteligentes*
Leal	Loyal	--------------	--------------	*Leal*	*Leales*
Joven	Young	--------------	--------------	*Joven*	*Jóvenes*

As you can see in the chart above, there are a few small differences between the three different types of adjectives you'll find.

Adjectives that end in "o"

Can be <u>masculine</u> or <u>feminine</u>

Can be <u>singular</u> or <u>plural</u>

Listen to Track 101

The shy boy	*El chico tímido*	Singular/ Masculine
The shy girl	*La chica tímida*	Singular/ Feminine
The shy children	*Los chicos tímidos*	Plural/ Masculine**

Adjectives that end in "e"

Will only change between the <u>singular</u> and <u>plural</u> forms

To make the plural form, simply add an "s"

Listen to Track 102

The intelligent boy	*El chico inteligente*	Singular
The intelligent girl	*La chica inteligente*	Singular (doesn't change gender)
The intelligent children	*Los chicos inteligentes*	Plural (no gender)

Adjectives that end in a consonant

Will only change between the <u>singular</u> and <u>plural</u> forms

To make the plural form, add "es"

Listen to Track 103

The loyal boy	*El chico leal*	Singular
The loyal girl	*La chica leal*	Singular (doesn't change gender)
The loyal children	*Los chicos leales*	Plural (no gender)

**Note: When describing a group of something, the adjective will become masculine even if only one of the things in the group is masculine. For example- a group of 7 shy girls and only 1 shy boy will still be described using the masculine adjective (los niños tímidos). But if you have a group of 7 shy girls without the boy, you will make it feminine (las niñas tímidas). The same as in the rule #15, but with Adjectives.

Of course, the exceptions…

Like with almost everything when learning a language, this part of speech comes with its own little list of exceptions to the rules.

Adjectives ending in -or, -án, -ín, -ón

This group, although they end in consonant, will in fact still <u>have a feminine form</u>.

Listen to Track 104

Example	Meaning	Masculine	Feminine	Singular	Plural
Hablador	Talkative	*Hablador*	*Habladora*	*Hablador(a)*	*Habladores/as*

Adjectives that go before the noun

There are some adjectives in Spanish that do, actually, go before the noun they are modifying.

The first group of adjectives that you will find in front of the noun are those relating to a quantity. They describe the amount of something.

For Example: There are a few people in the house. *Hay poca gente en la casa.*

You may be able to put a descriptive adjective before the noun if you are not trying to differentiate (or single out) the noun you are describing.

For Example: If I were to say "The intelligent students" (los estudiantes inteligentes) I'm talking about a specific group of students within an even large group of not as bright students.

However, if I said "los inteligentes estudiantes" I'm implying that ALL the students are intelligent.

Adjectives that change meaning when they change location

There is a handful of adjectives that can go before OR after the noun, but they will change their meaning depending on where you put them.

The most common are:

Listen to Track 105

Adjective	Meaning before	Meaning after
Antiguo	Former, Ex-	Old, Ancient
Pobre	Poor (as in unfortunate)	Poor (as in no money)
Gran/Grande	Great	Big, Large
Viejo	Old (as in long-standing)	Old (as in age)
Único	Only	Unique

This has just been a quick overview of the basics behind using adjectives in Spanish. At first glance, this very useful part of speech may seem strange and even intimidating to the native English speaker. But the truth is, it's really not all that complicated! It just takes lots of practice and adjusting your mindset a little bit.

Remember–your adjectives need to AGREE, AGREE!

Workbook Lesson 11: Adjetivos – Adjectives

Exercise 1: Complete the sentences with the correct form of the adjectives in brackets.

1- Lola tiene los ojos (verde)___, es (rubio)____ y tiene el pelo (corto)___ y (rizado)___ (Lola has green eyes, is blonde, and has short, curly hair.)

2- Él es muy (simpático) ____ , (alegre)____ y muy (charlatán)____(He is very likeable, cheerful, and very talkative.)

3- Las hijas de Andrés son muy (joven)____ (Andrew's daughters are very young.)

4- Me gustan las rosas (blanco)____ (I like white roses)

5- Esta gata está (enfermo)_____ (This cat is sick.)

Exercise 2: Translate the following sentences from English to Spanish.

1- I am very tired.

2- This saxophone is old.

3- The Spanish language is a difficult language.

4- They are talkers.

5- Charles is very poor.

Exercise 3: Complete the sentences with a noun and an adjective, as in the example.

Example: El chico inteligente

<<Rojo, vieja, China, ojo, azul, comida, flor, ropa, bueno, nuevo, preferido>>

1- Pablo tiene los _____ (Paul has blue eyes.)

2- La rosa es una _____ (The rose is a red flower.)

3- Esta computadora es muy _____ (This computer is very old.)

4- Necesito comprar_____ (I need to buy new clothes.)

5- Voy a comprar _____ (I am going to buy Chinese food.)

Exercise 4: Choose the correct adjective of the following sentences.

1- Elena y Camila son muy:	a. trabajador	b. trabajadoras
2- Me he comprado unos zapatos:	a. negres	b. negros
3- Marco y Andrés son:	a. altos y morenos	b. altes y morenos
4- Él es un hombre:	a. leale	b. leal
5- Ella es muy:	a. tímida	b. tímidas

Exercise 5: Translate the following phrases from English to Spanish.

1- The shy children

2- The kind lady

3- The intelligent children

4- The old cheerful man

5- The strong man

Exercise 6: Complete the sentences with the correct form of the adjectives in brackets.

1- Estoy muy (gordo)_____. (I'm very fat.)

2- Estamos muy (cansado)_____. (We are very tired.)

3- Somos los (campeón)_____. (We are the champions.)

4- Ella está (triste)_____. (She is sad.)

5- Marta es muy (alegre)_____. (Marta is very cheerful.)

Exercise 7: Change these affirmative sentences into negative ones.

1- Los belgas son muy amables. (Belgians are very kind.)

2- Las rusas son muy bonitas. (Russian women are very pretty.)

3- Iván es cubano. (Ivan is cuban.)

4- La bandera argentina es azul y blanca. (The Argentine flag is blue and white.)

5- Shakira es colombiana. (Shakira is Colombian.)

Exercise 8: Complete the following dialogue by changing the adjectives.

Camilo: Hola Liliana. Mira, esta es mi amiga Sofía es (Chile)____.

Liliana: Hola Sofía, mucho gusto, yo soy (Panamá)_____.

Sofía: ¡Mucho gusto! Uff, me gusta mucho vivir en Panamá, hace calor y el clima es muy agradable. La ciudad es muy (bonito)_____, el aire está muy (limpio) _____ y la plaza _____(antiguo) es muy (bello)____.

Exercise 9: Complete the sentences with a noun and an adjective from the example.

<<moneda, escritor, capital, China, ruso, ciudad, México, italiano, capital, escrito, británico>>

1- El rublo es la _____ _____.

2- Shanghái es una _____ _____.

3- La Ciudad de México es la _____ _____.

4- J. K. Rowling es una _____ _____.

5- Roma es la _____ _____.

Exercise 10: Translate the following phrases from Spanish to English.

1- El perro amigable

2- El profesor japonés

3- Unos sellos alemanes

4- Un coche italiano

5- La blusa amarilla

ANSWERS:

Exercise 1

1/ Lola tiene los ojos verdes, es rubia, y tiene el pelo corto y rizado. 2/ Él es muy simpático, alegre y muy charlatán. 3/ Las hijas de Andrés son muy jóvenes. 4/ Me gustan las rosas blancas. 5/ Esta gata está enferma.

Exercise 2

1/ Estoy muy cansado. 2/ Este saxofón es antiguo. 3/ El español es un idioma difícil. 4/ Ellos son comunicativos. 5/ Charles es muy pobre.

Exercise 3

1/ Pablo tiene los ojos azules. 2/ La rosa es una flor roja. 3/ Esta computadora es muy vieja. 4/ Necesito comprar ropa nueva. 5/Voy a comprar comida china.

Exercise 4

1/ Trabajadoras 2/ Negros 3/ Altos y morenos 4/ Leal 5/ Tímida

Exercise 5

1/ Los niños tímidos 2/ La señora amable 3/ Los niños inteligentes 4/ El viejo alegre 5/ El hombre fuerte

Exercise 6

1/ Estoy muy gordo. 2/ Estamos muy cansados. 3/ Somos los campeones. 4/ Ella está triste. 5/ Marta es muy alegre.

Exercise 7

1/ Los belgas no son muy amables. 2/ Las rusas no son bonitas. 3/ Iván no es cubano. 4/ La bandera argentina no es azul y blanca. 5/ Shakira no es colombiana.

Exercise 8

Camilo: Hola Liliana. Mira, ésta es mi amiga Sofía, es chilena. (Hi Liliana, look this is my friend Sofia, she is Chilean.)

Liliana: Hola Sofía, mucho gusto, yo soy panameña. (Hi Sofia, glad to meet you, I am Panamanian.)

Sofía: ¡Mucho gusto! Uff me gusta mucho vivir en Panamá, hace calor y el clima es muy agradable. La ciudad es muy bonita, el aire está muy limpio y la plaza antigua es muy bella. (Nice to meet you! I really like living in Panama, it's hot and the weather is very nice. And the city is very pretty. The air is very clean and the Old Square is very beautiful.)

Exercise 9

1/ El rublo es la moneda rusa. 2/ Shanghái es una ciudad china. 3/ La Ciudad de México es la capital mexicana. 4/ J.K. Rowling es una escritora británica. 5/ Roma es la capital italiana.

Exercise 10

1/ The friendly dog 2/ The Japanese teacher 3/ Some German stamps 4/ An Italian car 5/ The yellow blouse

¡Hola!

Telling the time is an important skill, so in this lesson we're learning about telling the time in Spanish, split into handy sections.

I. Numbers

Let's get started with the basics.

First up: numbers! You'll need to know the numbers 1 to 59 to tell the time, but once you've mastered a few, you'll be fine with them all. 0 to 15 are probably the most difficult to learn, because they're all quite different.

N.B. where we've given the pronunciation, the apostrophe at the beginning of a syllable denotes that the stress falls on that syllable, e.g. in 'oo-no, the first syllable is emphasized.

0	cero	'seh-roh*
1	uno/una	'oo-noh/'oo-nah
2	dos	dohs
3	tres	trehs
4	cuatro	'kwah-troh
5	cinco	'seehn-koh
6	seis	'seh-ees
7	siete	see-'eh-teh
8	ocho	'oh-choh
9	nueve	noo-'eh-beh
10	diez	dee-'ehs
11	once	'ohn-seh
12	doce	'doh-seh
13	trece	'treh-seh
14	catorce	kah-'tohr-seh
15	quince	'keen-seh

From number 16 onward, things start to look a bit more logical. All you need to remember is that "y" (pronounced *ee*) means "and."

Example: 17 => 10 + 7 => ten and seven => diez y siete => diecisiete

16	*dieciséis*	dee-ehs-ee-'seh-ees
17	*diecisiete*	dee-ehs-ee-see-'eh-teh
18	*dieciocho*	dee-ehs-ee-'oh-choh
19	*diecinueve*	dee-ehs-ee-noo-'eh-beh

Then we get to 20, or "veinte." Instead of pronouncing "veinte-**ee**-uno," we mush it all together, making the word flow better: "veintiuno."

Example: 27 => 20 + 7 => twenty and seven => veinte y siete => veintisiete

20	*Veinte*	'beh-een-teh
21	*veintiuno*	beh-een-tee-'oo-noh
22	*veintidós*	beh-een-tee-'dohs
23	*veintitrés*	beh-een-tee-'trehs
24	*veinticuatro*	beh-een-tee-'kwah-troh
25	*veinticinco*	beh-een-tee-'seehn-koh
26	*veintiséis*	beh-een-tee-'seh-ees
27	*veintisiete*	beh-een-tee-see-'eh-teh
28	*veintiocho*	beh-een-tee-'oh-choh
29	*veintinueve*	beh-een-tee-noo-'eh-beh

At this point, we stop mushing things together. It's simply 'tens' **y** 'units.' You've probably got to grips with the pattern by now, but here they are all laid out, just in case:

30	*treinta*	'treh-een-tah
31	*treinta y uno*	'treh-een-ta ee 'oo-noh
32	*treinta y dos*	'treh-een-ta ee dohs
33	*treinta y tres*	'treh-een-ta ee trehs
34	*treinta y cuatro*	'treh-een-ta ee 'kwah-troh
35	*treinta y cinco*	'treh-een-ta ee 'seehn-koh
36	*treinta y seis*	'treh-een-ta ee 'seh-ees
37	*treinta y siete*	'treh-een-ta ee see-'eh-teh
38	*treinta y ocho*	'treh-een-ta ee 'oh-choh
39	*treinta y nueve*	'treh-een-ta ee noo-'eh-beh
40	*Cuarenta*	kwah-'rehn-tah
41	*cuarenta y uno*	kwah-'rehn-tah ee 'oo-noh
42	*cuarenta y dos*	kwah-'rehn-tah ee dohs
43	*cuarenta y tres*	kwah-'rehn-tah ee trehs
44	*cuarenta y cuatro*	kwah-'rehn-tah ee 'kwah-troh
45	*cuarenta y cinco*	kwah-'rehn-tah ee 'seehn-koh
46	*cuarenta y seis*	kwah-'rehn-tah ee 'seh-ees
47	*cuarenta y siete*	kwah-'rehn-tah ee see-'eh-teh
48	*cuarenta y ocho*	kwah-'rehn-tah ee 'oh-choh
49	*cuarenta y nueve*	kwah-'rehn-tah ee noo-'eh-beh
50	*Cincuenta*	seehn -'kwehn-tah
51	*cincuenta y uno*	seehn -'kwehn-tah ee 'oo-noh
52	*cincuenta y dos*	seehn -'kwehn-tah ee dohs
53	*cincuenta y tres*	seehn -'kwehn-tah ee trehs

54	*cincuenta y cuatro*	seehn -'kwehn-tah ee 'kwah-troh
55	*cincuenta y cinco*	seehn -'kwehn-tah ee 'seehn-koh
56	*cincuenta y seis*	seehn -'kwehn-tah ee 'seh-ees
57	*cincuenta y siete*	seehn -'kwehn-tah ee see-'eh-teh
58	*cincuenta y ocho*	seehn -'kwehn-tah ee 'oh-choh
59	*cincuenta y nueve*	seehn -'kwehn-tah ee noo-'eh-beh
(...and for luck) 60	*Sesenta*	seh-'sehn-tah

Well done for getting through all that counting!

Asking for the Time

Next, we want to know enough vocabulary to ask for the time!

Listen to Track 106

The time/the hour	*La hora*	lah 'oh-rah
Minute	*El minuto*	ehl mee-'noo-toh
Have you got the time?	*¿Tiene(s) la hora?*	tee-'eh-neh(s) lah 'oh-rah
What time is it?	*¿Qué hora es?**	keh 'oh-rah ehs
What time do you make it?	*¿Qué hora tiene(s)?*	keh 'oh-rah tee-'eh-neh(s)
To tell the time	*Decir la hora*	deh-'seer lah 'oh-rah
To ask for the time	*Preguntar la hora*	preh-goon-'tahr lah 'oh-rah

*In Mexico and other parts of Latin America you might also hear "¿qué horas son?", which is also correct. *So feel free to use it, as well as all the other formats.*

To respond to this question, we use the verb "ser" ("to be"). Instead of x o'clock, Spanish speakers count hours.

Example: Son las 8 => it is 8 (hours) => it is 8 o'clock.

Usually, you'll need to use "son las..." (*sohn lahs*) to mean "it is" but occasionally you use "es la" (*ehs lah*). This is because "son las" is used for plural times, i.e. anything bigger than 1 o'clock. "Es la" is singular, so it's used for 1 o'clock (and x minutes past 1).

II. O'clock

So, let's have a look at the following times:

Listen to Track 107

It's 1 o'clock.	*Es la una.*
It's 3 o'clock.	*Son las tres.*
It's 6 o'clock.	*Son las seis.*
It's 11 o'clock.	*Son las once.*

BONUS:

Usually, when we say "it's 12 o'clock," we know whether it's the middle of the day or the middle of the night by, like, seeing if it's dark outside. But sometimes we prefer to make it extra clear:

Listen to Track 108

It's midday.	*Es mediodía.*	ehs meh-dee-oh-'dee-ah
It's midnight.	*Es medianoche.*	ehs meh-dee-ah-'noh-cheh

III. Half past

When it's half past the hour, we use "y media," (*ee 'meh-dee-ah*) which means "and half." See if these examples make sense:

Listen to Track 109

It's 1:30.	*Es la una y media.*
It's 5:30.	*Son las cinco y media.*
It's 7:30.	*Son las siete y media.*
It's 12:30.	*Son las doce y media.*

IV. Quarter past

To say that it's quarter past the hour, we add "y cuarto" (*ee 'kwahr-toh*), which means "and quarter."

Listen to Track 110

It's 1:15.	*Es la una y cuarto.*
It's 4:15.	*Son las cuatro y cuarto.*
It's 8:15.	*Son las ocho y cuarto.*
It's 10:15.	*Son las diez y cuarto.*

Makes sense, right?!

V. Quarter to

Like in English, we can still use the word for "quarter." If we say it as the literal translation *cuarto a la una* ('*kwahr-toh* ah lah '*oo-nah*) is perfect. But in Mexico there are also two other versions to mean the same things:

"*Falta un cuarto para las x.*" There's a missing quarter to x (where is it ?!)

"*Es cuarto para las x.*" Using the verb "to be" (*Ser*) to complement.

Listen to Track 111

It's 12:45 (quarter to one).	*Falta un cuarto para la una.*
It's 1:45 (quarter to two).	*Es cuarto para las dos.*
It's 8:45 (quarter to nine).	*Es cuarto para las nueve.*
It's 9:45 (quarter to ten).	*Falta un cuarto para las diez.*

VI. Minutes past

For highly specific numbers (i.e. not quarters or halves), we have a pretty simple rule! We just say the "o'clock" bit and then add the number of minutes past the hour!

Listen to Track 112

It's 1:23.	*Es la una veintitrés.*
It's 1:47.	*Es la una cuarenta siete.*
It's 4:05.	*Son las cuatro cinco.*
It's 4:59.	*Son las cuatro cincuenta y nueve.*
It's 6:11.	*Son las seis once.*

VII. Minutes to

And for minutes **to** the hour, we use *"para la/las..."* (*pahrah lah/lahs*) or *"a la/las..."* (*ah lah/lahs*). You just have to say how many minutes are left.

*For 1 use *"la"* and for all the other hours 2-12 use *"las"*. Also, have in mind you can use *"Son..."at the beginning or just go straight to it.*

Listen to Track 113

It's 12:55 (five minutes to one).	*(Son) cinco **para la** una.*
It's 8:52 (8 minutes to 9).	*(Son) ocho **a las** nueve. #arithmetic*
It's 2:45 (15 minutes to 3).	*(Son) quince **a las** tres .*
It's 11:40 (20 minutes to 12).	*(Son) veinte **para las** doce.*

In Mexico this format is used when there aren't many minutes left to the next hour (max. 25 minutes.)

VIII. A few extras:
Listen to Track 114

The morning	*La mañana*	*la mah-'nyah-nah*
It's 8 in the morning/8am.	*Son las ocho de la mañana.*	
The afternoon	*La tarde*	*lah 'tahr-deh*
It's 2 in the afternoon/2pm.	*Son las dos de la tarde.*	
The evening/night	*La noche*	*lah 'noh-cheh*
It's 11 at night/11pm.	*Son las once de la noche.*	
The early hours of the morning	*La madrugada*	*lah mah-droo-'gah-dah*
Go to sleep! It's 2am!	¡Duérmete! ¡Son las dos de la madrugada!	
... and a bit.	*... y pico**	*ee 'peeh-koh*
It's a few minutes past 7.	*Son las siete y pico.*	
Around	*Alrededor de más o menos*	*ahl-reh-deh-'dohr deh mahs oh 'meh-nohs*
It's around 5.	*Son alrededor de las cinco. Son las cinco más o menos.*	

On the dot.	En punto.	ehn 'poon-toh
It's 6 on the dot.	Son las seis en punto.	
At ...	A la/las ...	ah lah/lahs
We cook at 2.	Cocinamos a las dos.	
The party starts at 1.	La fiesta empieza a la una.	

* "Y pico," /"Y algo" is understood as a "a few minutes past", but it could also refer to anything up to around 50 minutes past the hour.

IX. 12-hour vs 24-hour clock

Depending on where you're from, you may be more used to the 12-hour clock than the 24-hour clock (military time). In Spanish-speaking destinations, you could encounter both. Like in English, spoken Spanish tends to use the 12-hour clock, even if the time is sometimes written in the 24-hour format. For example, if you were reading out theater times, the page in front of you might say "15:00," but you'd say to your friend on the phone, "it sarts at 3."

X. Mini-test

It's **time** (see what I did there?) for a mini-test!

Use the guide we've given you and see if you can figure out what the following phrases mean.

Listen to Track 115

1. *Es la una.*
2. *Es mediodía.*
3. *Son las tres y media.*
4. *Son las cuatro y cuarto.*
5. *Falta un cuarto para las siete.*
6. *Son las ocho diez.*
7. *Son cinco a las nueve.*
8. *Son las once en punto.*
9. *Son las once de la mañana.*

Keep practicing ...

Whether you've struggled with this or found it pretty easy, practicing Spanish daily will help you get to grips with telling the time. Numbers are used often in everyday life, so the more you speak, the more opportunity you'll get to practice them! If you know any native Spanish-speakers, try and practice what you've learnt with them.

Spanish Calendar Vocabulary: Days and Months in Spanish

Another year is here! A whole new set of twelve months to look forward to. You know what's a good way to mark this occasion? Learn Spanish words about the calendar!

Here in this lesson, we'll talk about Spanish words for the different days of the week, the Spanish names of the months, as well as how to talk about dates in Spanish.

The Basics

Before we proceed to the different names of days and months, let us tackle the basic words first.

Listen to Track 116

el calendario	calendar
el día	day
la semana	week
el mes	month
la fecha	date

The Days of the Week

Now let's move on to the days of the week (*días de la semana*).

Listen to Track 117

Lunes	Monday
Martes	Tuesday
Miércoles	Wednesday
Jueves	Thursday
Viernes	Friday
Sábado	Saturday
Domingo	Sunday

Take note that, unlike in English, the names of the days of the week are not capitalized in Spanish.

Let's see some examples below.

Listen to Track 118

Necesito ir al médico el jueves. I need to go to the doctor on Thursday.

Mi cumpleaños es el martes. My birthday is on Tuesday.

El nuevo capítulo sale cada miércoles. The new chapter comes out every Wednesday.

Voy a la iglesia el domingo. I go to church on Sunday.

Months in Spanish

Now let's move on to the different months of the year.

Listen to Track 119

Enero	January
Febrero	February
Marzo	March
Abril	April

Mayo	May
Junio	June
Julio	July
Agosto	August
Septiembre	September
Octubre	October
Noviembre	November
Diciembre	December

Just like the days of the week, the names of the months are also not capitalized in Spanish!

Let's take a look at some example sentences below.

Listen to Track 120

El cumpleaños de Luis es en febrero. Luis's birthday is in February.

Las vacaciones terminan en septiembre. Vacation ends in September.

Mi boda será en enero. My wedding will be in January.

Talking about Dates in Spanish

Dates will always come up during conversations, so make sure you know how to say the date in Spanish!

Here are a few reminders:

When talking about dates in Spanish, the month is said after the day. **For Example:** Hoy es el nueve de enero. Today is January 9.

The format for saying dates in Spanish is: el + day + de + month (+ del -from 2000- + year). **For Example:** *el dos de septiembre del 2015.* September 2, 2015

*You only use "*el*" when you are talking about a past event or something that hasn't happened yet. If someone ask you: When was the party? You answer "*el 10 de diciembre.*" But, if some demands to know what day is today, you tell them just "15 de mayo del 2020".

Cardinal numbers (*uno, dos, tres*) are used when talking about dates in Spanish, except for the first day of the month, where an ordinal number is needed.

Example: *Hoy es primero de enero.* Today is January 1st.

But for all other dates, cardinal numbers are still used.

Here are some more **Examples:**

Listen to Track 121

*Hoy es 5 de Diciembre **del** 2018.* Today is December 5, 2018.

*Ella nació **el** 12 de febrero **de** 1990.* She was born on February 12, 1990.

*Nuestra primera cita fue **el** 10 de julio **del** 2018.* Our first date was on July 10, 2018.

Workbook Lesson 12: Cómo decir la hora – How to tell time

Exercise 1: Write the right time in Spanish from the following phrases.

1- It's 1:20 _____

2- It's 6:30 _____

3- It's 7 o'clock_____

4- It's 11:15 ____

5- It's 5:45 (quarter to six) ____

Exercise 2: Translate the following sentences from English to Spanish.

1- I work in the morning and study in the afternoon.

2- The party is on Sunday at nine.

3- The match is at four.

4- I leave work at seven.

5- They go to the cinema at one o'clock.

Exercise 3: Translate the following phrases from Spanish to English.

1- Alrededor de

2- A la/las …

3- Once

4- Faltan cinco a la una

5- La madrugada

Exercise 4: Complete the next exercise with the days of the week.

1- Antes del martes está el ____

2- Antes del sábado está el ____

3- Antes del jueves está el ____

4- Antes del miercoles está el ____

5- ___, sábado, domingo

Exercise 5: Translate the following phrases from Spanish to English:

1- La semana

2- El calendario

3- El día

4- El mes

5- La fecha

Exercise 6: Reorder the letters in each word to discover the hidden month.

1- LUJIO:_____

2- TOGOSA:_____

3- ROEEN:_____

4- SBREEPTMIE:_____

5- YMAO:_____

Exercise 7: Complete the next exercise with the correct month.

1- La navidad siempre es en _____.

2- El verano empieza en _____.

3- _____ es el primer mes del año.

4- Me gusta _____ por las flores hermosas.

5- San Valentín es en _____.

Exercise 8: Reorganize the following words into a sentence.

1- Cumpleaños/ el / de / pedro / es / en marzo

2- La final/ de / en julio/ la liga / es

3- Yo termino / en noviembre / mis /estudios

4- Ellos / en octubre / se casaron

5- El / febrero / es / carnaval de Río

Exercise 9: Change these affirmative sentences into negative ones.

1- En agosto hace mucho calor.

2- Ella nació el 5 de abril.

3- El día de los muertos en México es en noviembre.

4- El día de San Patricio es el 17 de marzo.

5- En octubre se celebra *Halloween*.

ANSWERS:

Mini-test

1/ It's 1:00. 2/ It's midday. 3/ It's 3:30. 4/ It's 4:15. 5/ It's 6:45. 6/ It's 8:10. 7/ It's 8:55. 8/ It's exactly 11/11 on the dot. 9/ It's 11am.

Exercise 1

1/ Es la una veinte 2/ Son las seis y media 3/ Son las siete en punto 4/ Son las once y cuarto 5/ Son quince a las seis

Exercise 2

1/ Trabajo por la mañana y estudio por la tarde. 2/ La fiesta es el domingo a las nueve. 3/ El partido es a las cuatro. 4/ Yo salgo del trabajo a las siete. 5/ Ellos van al cine a la una en punto.

Exercise 3

1/ Around 2/ At … 3/ Eleven 4/ Five minutes to one 5/ Early morning

Exercise 4

1/ Lunes 2/ Viernes 3/ Miércoles 4/ Martes 5/ Viernes, sábado, domingo

Exercise 5

1/ The week 2/ The calendar 3/ The day 4/ The month 5/ The date

Exercise 6

1/ Julio 2/ Agosto 3/ Enero 4/ Septiembre 5/ Mayo

Exercise 7

1/ La navidad siempre es en diciembre. 2/ El verano empieza en junio. 3/ Enero es el primer mes del año. 4/ Me gusta abril por las flores hermosas. 5/ San Valentín es en febrero.

Exercise 8

1/ El cumpleaños de Pedro es en marzo. 2/ La final de la liga es en julio. 3/ Yo termino mis estudios en noviembre. 4/ Ellos se casaron en octubre. 5/ El carnaval de Río es en febrero.

Exercise 9

1/ En agosto no hace mucho calor. 2/ Ella no nació el 5 de abril. 3/ El día de los muertos en México no es en noviembre. 4/ El día de San Patricio no es el 17 de marzo. 5/ En octubre no se celebra Halloween.

Lesson 13. Negatives

It's time to get negative! Using negatives in Spanish is important and can make your language seem a lot more sophisticated, so let's look at how to do it (but stay positive throughout the lesson)!

Double negatives in Spanish are okay!

When making negative statements in Spanish, you can either use *no* (which means 'no' or 'not'), or you can use a negative word with it! (Sometimes you can use the negative word without the *no*, but more on that later.)

Don't let the apparent double negatives confuse you. We're taught in English not to use double negatives, because a negative and a negative make a positive, so using it can get quite confusing (and grammatically incorrect), i.e.

I have**n't** got **nothing**. = I have actually got something.

But in Spanish, a negative and a negative remain negative!

No tengo nada. = I haven't got anything/ I've got nothing.

Word order

The basic rule is that we put the *no* before the main verb in the phrase. If there are pronouns, then stick it in front of those. The other negative word (if applicable) goes right after the verb.

Listen to Track 122

No voy a la biblioteca.	I don't go to the library.
No voy *nunca* a la biblioteca	I never go to the library.

When using a compound tense (the perfect, the pluperfect, etc.), you still put the *no* before the verbs. You then put the other negative word **after both** verbs.

No he dicho *nada*.	I haven't said anything.
No había venido *nadie*.	No one had arrived.

Okay, so earlier we said that negative words usually need to be used with *no* as well. However, sometimes it will be more natural to use the negative word alone, without *no*. In this case, you'd put the negative word before the verb(s).

No cantó nadie. → Nadie cantó.	Nobody sang.
No bailas nunca. → Nunca bailas.	You never dance.

Another simple way to use negatives is as one-word answers (so we don't have to worry about word order!).

Listen to Track 123

—¿Quieres tomar algo conmigo?	—Do you want to get a drink with me?
—No.	—No.
—¿Qué haces?	—What are you doing?
—Nada.	—Nothing.
—¿Has estado alguna vez en Brasil?	—Have you ever been to Brazil?
—¡Nunca!	—Never!

No

This one is versatile! It can simply mean 'no,' or it can mean 'not' when used to negate statements. Put it at the beginning of a phrase, before the verb, and before pronouns if there are any.

Listen to Track 124

—¿Vienes a la fiesta?	—Are you coming to the party?
—No.	—No.
Hay fruta en casa.	There's fruit at home.
No hay fruta en casa.	There isn't fruit at home.
Lo sé.	I know.
No lo sé.	I don't know.
Me lo dio.	He gave it to me.
No me lo dio.	He didn't give it to me.

Sometimes, *no* is used as a question tag. We can make a statement then stick a *no* on the end, to see if the person you're talking to agrees or not.

Listen to Track 125

Ana es muy inteligente, ¿no?	Ana is very intelligent, isn't she?
Has hecho la tarea, ¿no?	You've done the homework, haven't you?
La clase es mañana, ¿no?	The class is tomorrow, right?

Ni... ni...

This means 'neither... nor....' Its opposite is *o... o...* ('either... or...').

Listen to Track 126

Ni canto ni bailo.	I neither sing nor dance.
No canto ni bailo.	I don't sing or dance.

Ni (siquiera)

Ni and *ni siquiera* mean 'not even.'

Listen to Track 127

No sé ni (siquiera) tocar el piano, mucho menos el órgano.	I don't even know how to play the piano, let alone the organ.
Ni (siquiera) Juan viene.	Not even Juan is coming.
Ni (siquiera) tengo una hora libre.	I don't even have one hour free.

Nada

Nada means 'nothing.' It's the opposite of *algo* ('something').

Listen to Track 128

No dije nada.	I didn't say anything.
No hay nada en el refri.	There is nothing in the refrigerator.
Nada nos puede separar.	Nothing can separate us.

Nadie

This one means 'no one' or 'nobody.' Its opposite would be *alguien* ('someone'/'somebody').

Listen to Track 129

¿No viste a nadie?	You didn't see anyone?
No hay nadie en el equipo que me pueda ayudar.	There is no one on the team who can help me.
Aquí nadie se rinde.	Nobody quits here.

Ninguno/a/os/as

Ninguno means 'not any.' It's what we call an 'indefinite adjective,' and it modifies a noun.

When it's used before a masculine singular noun, *ninguno* becomes *ningún*.

Listen to Track 130

No hay ninguna mujer en el edificio.	There aren't any women/there are no women in the building.
No hay ningún hombre aquí.	There aren't any men/there are no men here.
Ningún hombre en esta oficina sabe qué hacer en esta situación.	No man (none of the men) in this office knows what to do in this situation.

Ninguno/a/os/as

Similar to the above, this one means 'neither one'/'none.' This is an 'indefinite pronoun,' and it's slightly different as it's used as a replacement for the noun.

There's no shortening to *ningún* in this case.

Listen to Track 131

—¿Cuál chico prefieres?	—Which guy do you prefer?
—Pues ninguno.	—Well, neither/none.
—¿Tienes ideas?	—Do you have any ideas?
—No, no tengo ninguna.	—No, I don't have any/I have none.

Nunca/Jamás

Usually, *nunca* and *jamás* mean 'never.' (They can also be used in the sense of 'ever,' but don't worry about that right now!) Naturally, their opposite is *siempre* (always).

Listen to Track 132

No voy nunca a su casa.	I never go to her house.
Nunca vienes a mi casa.	You never come to my house.

Tampoco

Last but not least, this one means '(n)either.' It's the opposite of *también* ('also').

Listen to Track 133

Ella no va tampoco/Ella tampoco va.	She's not going either.
—No quiero salir con David.	—I don't want to go out with David.
—Yo tampoco.	—Me neither.
Tampoco quiere salir con nosotras.	Nor does he want to go out with us/he doesn't want to go out with us either.

Workbook Lesson 13: La negación – Negation

Exercise 1: Choose the right translation for each sentence.

1- I don't like onions.

    a. No me gustan las cebollas.   b. Ya no gusta las cebollas.   c. No gusta las cebollas.

2- I have never been to Cuba.

    a. Yo nunca no fui a Cuba.   b. Yo nunca he ido a Cuba.   c. Yo iré a Cuba.

3- We have nothing to lose.

    a. No tenemos nada que perder.   b. Nunca tenemos que perder.   c. No tenemos nunca que perder.

4- I don't love you anymore.

    a. Ya no más te amo.   b. Ya no te amo más.   c. No más te amo.

5- I don't see anyone.

    a. Yo no veo a nadie.   b. Yo no veo a nada.   c. Yo no veo más nada.

Exercise 2: Change these affirmative sentences into negative ones.

1- Yo amo las manzanas. (I love apples.)

2- Él hace deporte. (He plays sports.)

3- Ellos están casados. (They are married.)

4- El vestido es rojo. (The dress is red.)

5- Ella trabaja aquí. (She works here.)

Exercise 3: Change these negative sentences into affirmative ones.

1- Esa falda no es verde. (This skirt is not green.)

2- Esta película no es mala. (This movie is not bad.)

3- Ellos no son malos. (They are not mean.)

4- Este trabajo no es difícil. (This work is not hard.)

5- Yo no estoy cansado. (I am not tired.)

Exercise 4: Choose the right translation for these sentences.

1- El nunca ha manejado.

    a. He always drove.

    b. He never drove.

    c. He doesn't drive.

2- Ella no trabaja más.

    a. She's always working.

    b. She doesn't work.

    c. She doesn't work anymore.

3- Yo no conozco a nadie aquí.

    a. I know everybody here.

    b. I don't know anybody here.

    c. I don't know anymore.

4- Yo no tengo suficiente dinero para comprar una casa.

    a. I don't have enough money to buy a house.

    b. I have enough money to buy a house.

    c. I don't have enough money to buy a house anymore.

5- Yo no tengo nada que darte.

    a. I have nothing to give you.

    b. I have nothing to give you anymore.

    c. I have something to give you.

Exercise 5: Change these affirmative sentences into negative ones.

1- Yo aún te amo. (I still love you.)

2- La casa es grande. (The house is big.)

3- La ventana está abierta. (The window is open.)

4- Yo entiendo todo. (I understand everything.)

5- Yo hablo español. (I speak Spanish.)

Exercise 6: Choose the right answer.

1- «No me gustan las aceitunas » « A mí tampoco ». What does « A mí tampoco » mean here?

    a. Me neither / Nor me.

    b. I don't.

    c. Me too.

2- Which one of these is said in an informal conversation?

    a. Yo no amo más las fresas.

    b. Yo amo no las fresas.

    c. Yo no amo las fresas.

3- «¿Quién rompió ese jarrón?!» «¡Yo no!». What does «Yo no!» mean here?

    a. Me!

    b. Not me!

    c. Him!

4- «Mamá, ¿puedo salir esta tarde?» «¡De ninguna manera!». What does «¡De ninguna manera!» mean here?

    a. No way!

    b. Don't!

    c. No question

Exercise 7: Transform these affirmative sentences into negative ones.

1- Yo te escucho. (I hear you.)

2- Él le ha regalado dinero. (He gave him/her money.)

3- Yo lo vi ayer. (I saw him yesterday.)

4- Ella le preguntó su número de teléfono. (She asked him for his phone number.)

5- Yo le hablo en francés. (I talk to him in French.)

Exercise 8: Complete these sentences with «No», «Nunca», «Nada»,

«Nadie».

1- Me encantaba esta película, pero ahora ya___ me gusta más. (I liked this movie before. Now, I don't like it anymore.)

2- Me gustaría viajar. Yo ___ lo he hecho. (I would like to travel. I've never done it.)

3- No he hecho ___ en todo el día. (I've done nothing all day long.)

4- ¿Dónde está la gente? No veo a ___ aquí. (Where are the people? I don't see anyone here.)

5- Ayer lavé los platos. Hoy ___ los he lavado. (Yesterday, I washed the dishes. Today, I didn't do it.)

Exercise 9: Transform these negative sentences into affirmative to ones.

1- No eres de Brasil. (You are not from Brazil.)

2- Pedro no come nieve. (Pedro doesn't eat ice-cream.)

3- Ellos no están disponibles. (They are not available.)

4- Él no conoce a Camila. (He doesn't know Camila.)

5- Ella no habla chino. (She doesnt speak Chinese.)

Exercise 10: Tick the correct answer.

1- Ellos ___ saben cocinar. (They don't know to cook.)

  a. Nadie   b. No   c. Nunca

2- Martin ___ está en casa (Martin is not at home.)

  a. Nunca   b. No   c. Nadie

3- ___ aquí entiende este tema. (Nobody here undestand this theme.)

  a. No   b. Nadie   c. Nunca

4- ___ puedes fumar aquí. (You cannot smoke here.)

  a. No   b. Nadie   c. Nunca

5- ___ debes hablar por teléfono aquí. (You mustn't talk on the phone here.)

  a. Nunca   b. Nadie   c. No

ANSWERS:

Exercise 1

1/ No me gustan las cebollas. 2/ Yo nunca he ido en Cuba. 3/ No tenemos nada que perder. 4/ Ya no te amo más. 5/ Yo no veo a nadie.

Exercise 2

1/ Yo no amo las manzanas. 2/ Él no hace deporte. 3/ Ellos no están casados. 4/ El vestido no es rojo. 5/ Ella no trabaja aquí.

Exercise 3

1/ Esa falda es verde. 2/ Esta película es mala. 3/ Ellos son malos. 4/ Este trabajo es difícil. 5/ Yo estoy cansado.

Exercise 4

1/ He never drove. 2/ She doesn't work anymore. 3/ I don't know anybody here. 4/ I don't have enough money to buy a house. 5/ I have nothing to give you.

Exercise 5

1/ Yo no te amo más. 2/ La casa no es grande. 3/ La ventana no está abierta. 4/ Yo no entiendo nada. 5/ Yo no hablo español.

Exercise 6

1/ Me neither. 2/ Yo no amo las fresas. 3/ Not me! 4/ No way!

Exercise 7

1/ Yo no te escucho. 2/ Él no le ha regalado dinero. 3/ Yo no lo vi ayer. 4/ Ella no le preguntó su número de teléfono. 5/ Yo no le hablo en francés.

Exercise 8

1/ No 2/ Nunca 3/ Nada 4/ Nadie 5/ No

Exercise 9

1/ Eres de Brasil. 2/ Pedro come nieve. 3/ Ellos están disponibles. 4/ Él conoce a Camila. 5/ Ella habla chino.

Exercise 10

1/ No 2/ No 3/ Nadie 4/ No 5/ No

Lesson 14. Prepositions

Prepositions are small words that pack a big punch. They define, identify, and explain, and are an essential part of everyday speech.

They help you identify the girl <u>with</u> the long hair, and you need them to explain that dinner is <u>on</u> the table. It's almost impossible to say a single sentence <u>without</u> (see what I mean?) one of these useful little words!

Learning to use prepositions in Spanish isn't overly difficult but does take some practice. Read on for a quick introduction to these very useful little words.

Let's start at the beginning...

Before we dive in too deep with what the Spanish prepositions are and how we use them, let's take a step back and review what prepositions are.

What are prepositions and why are they so important?

A preposition is a (usually) little word that can have a big impact on what you're saying. It is what forms the connections and relations between different elements in a sentence.

For example (prepositions in bold):

The girl **from** Cuba

The boy **across** the street

The store **in** the mall

They can be very important because there's a big difference between saying: "The dog is on the table" and "the dog is under the table", and it would make absolutely no sense to say "the dog is in the table".

Prepositional Phrases

A preposition is always followed by an object (a noun or pronoun). In the examples given previously, the <u>prepositional phrases</u> would be:

The girl <u>from Cuba</u>

The boy <u>across the street</u>

The store <u>in the mall</u>

These phrases function as either adjectives or adverbs. In the examples above, the prepositional phrases are all functioning as adjectives, describing the nouns (girl, boy, store) answering the question "Which girl/boy/store?"

An example of a prepositional phrase functioning as an adverb would be the set of examples relating to the dog.

The dog is <u>under the table</u>

Here, the prepositional phrase answers the question "Where (is the dog)?"

Prepositions in Spanish

Prepositions in Spanish function much as they do in English. They always take an object, and they serve as either an adverb or adjective.

While on the surface they appear pretty easy (since they're like English and all), sometimes they can cause a few problems. Mainly, this comes when deciding which preposition to use when.

For example, one of the prepositions that gets misused frequently in Spanish by English speakers is *en*.

Listen to Track 134

Spanish	English	Examples
En	In, On, At	*Estoy en la tienda.*
		Está en la mesa.
		Estoy en la casa de un amigo.

Two of its uses are pretty easy (in, on) since it sounds like its English equivalents.

Estoy en la tienda - I'm in the store.

Está en la mesa.- It's on the table.

This little word causes problems, however, with its third meaning "at". Often times, as English speakers, we want to use the Spanish preposition *a* in place of *en* because we associate the *a* with our own "at". This is wrong, though.

For Example:

Estoy en la casa de un amigo - I'm at a friend's house.

NOT: Estoy a la casa de un amigo.

Let's look at some of the most common prepositions in Spanish and their different meanings and uses.

Most Common Prepositions in Spanish

In addition to *en* which we've already seen, you will also commonly hear/see the following prepositions in Spanish:

Listen to Track 135

Spanish	English	Examples
A	to, at (for time)	*Voy a la tienda.* (I'm going to the store.)
		Estaré ahí a las tres. (I'll be there at 3:00.)
Antes de	before	*Debes estirar antes de hacer ejercicio.* (You should stretch before doing exercise.)
Cerca de	near	*Estamos cerca de tu casa.* (We are near your house.)
Con	with	*Ella está con sus padres.* (She is with her parents.)
De	of, from, indicating possession	*¿Qué piensas de la película nueva?* (What do you think of the new movie?)
		Soy de Estados Unidos. (I am from the USA.)
		Estamos en (la) casa de María. (We are at Maria's house.)

(A)dentro de	inside	Mi coche está (a)dentro del garaje. (My car is inside the garage.)
Desde	since, from	No he estado ahí desde hace un mes. (I haven't been there since last month).
		Tiró la pelota desde aquí. (He threw the ball from here.)
Después de	after	Después de clase, voy a estudiar. (After class, I'm going to study.)
Detrás de (Atrás de)	behind	El pan está detrás de los huevos. (The bread is behind the eggs.)
		La mochila está atrás del sillón (The backpack is behind the couch.)
Durante	during	Durante el vuelo, dormí. (During the flight, I slept.)
Encima de	on top of	La sal está encima de la mesa. (The salt is on top of the table.)
Enfrente de	opposite (across from)	Nos veremos enfrente de la biblioteca. (We'll meet across from the library).
		*Note: This is another one that usually trips up English speakers since it sounds like our version of "in front of".
		If you want to say "We'll meet in front of the library" it would be Nos veremos en (at) la biblioteca.
Entre	between, among	Entre nosotros (nos), no me gusta el profe de inglés. (Between us, I don't like the English teacher.)
		Hay un traidor entre nosotros. (There's a traitor among us.)
Fuera de (Afuera de)	outside	Los baños están (a)fuera de la estación. (The restrooms are outside the station.)
Hasta	until	No llegaré hasta las seis. (I won't arrive until 6:00).
Para	for, in order to	Compré el regalo para ti. (I bought the gift for you.)
		Para aprender español, tienes que estudiar mucho. (In order to learn Spanish, you have to study a lot.)
Por	for, by, through	Les damos las gracias por su paciencia. (We are thankful for your patience.)
		El Quijote fue escrito por Cervantes. (Quixote was written by Cervantes.)
		Tenemos que atravesar por el parque para llegar a la escuela. (We have to pass through the park in order to get to the school.)
Sin	without	No puedo vivir sin ti. (I can't live without you.)
Sobre	over, about	El avión vuela sobre el océano. (The plane flies over the ocean.)
		El libro es sobre la Guerra Civil. (The book is about the Civil War.)

Some tricky verb/ preposition combinations

So, now that we have a working list of the most common prepositions in Spanish, let's look at some of the verb/ preposition combinations that tend to be more difficult for English speakers.

A lot of verbs in Spanish take a specific preposition. For Example:

Listen to Track 136

Empezar a- to start

Acabar de- to finish

Dejar de- to quit

The best way to learn these is simply by familiarizing yourself with them as you come across them. Below, however, I want to list the ones that seem to be common pitfalls for English speakers because we would also use a preposition with the verb. However, the preposition we use is different from the one used in Spanish (i.e. they don't translate exactly).

Listen to Track 137

Pensar de- We saw this one on our list. It means to think of.

This is used to give an opinion (as in the example given above).

Pensar en- Meaning to think about. This is where the verb *pensar* with a preposition can get tricky. The translation isn't exact (as it would be "think in/on").

This is used to say "I've been thinking about him a lot" or "I'm thinking about going to England for the summer."

He estado pensando mucho en él. Or *Estoy pensando en ir a Inglaterra durante el verano.*

NOT an opinion.

Soñar con- Meaning to dream about/ of.

For Example: *Anoche soñé con ir a París.* (Last night I dreamed about/ of going to Paris.)

NEVER *soñar* de.

Enamorarse de- Meaning to fall in love with

For Example: *Me enamoré de Bolivia.* (I fell in love with Bolivia).

NEVER *enamorarse* con

Depender de- Meaning to depend on

For Example: *Esto depende de lo que hace él.* (This depends on what he does.)

NEVER *depender* en

Contar con- Meaning to count on

For Example: *Cuento mucho contigo.* (I count on you a lot.)

NEVER *contar* en

The dreaded "por" and "para"

These two little words can easily incite a sense of fear in English speaking Spanish students everywhere. Given that, more often than not, we translate both of them to our preposition "for", knowing when to use each one can be a little confusing.

While giving an in-depth explanation of when to use each one may be a little too much for this specific lesson (don't worry, there's a specific lesson for that in the next topic), let's just look at a quick chart that might help to clear up a few things.

Por	Para
Used to show something in process. There's no finality associated with it.	Used to show the "end" of something. There's a sense of finality with it.
Commonly means or is used for:	Commonly means or is used for:
"Through"	Indicating destination
"By"	Showing the purpose of an object
"On behalf of"	Indicating the recipient of something
Expressing gratitude or extending an apology	"In order to"
Exchanging (including sales)	Expressing a deadline
Expressing cause or reason	

Example:

Listen to Track 138

Compré un regalo para (recipient) *mi madre. Pagué 200 pesos por* (exchange-sale) *él. También tuve que comprar otro regalo para* (recipient) *mi hermano. Tuve que buscar por* ("indicating destination) *toda la ciudad, porque él es muy difícil de complacer.*

I bought a present for my mom. I paid 200 Pesos for it. I also had to buy another present for my brother. I had to search all over town because he's really hard to please.

Contractions in Spanish

There are only 2 contractions in Spanish, and they both happen to relate to prepositions. So, let's just go ahead and take a quick look at those, shall we?

Listen to Track 139

A+el=Al

In you ever find these two little words (*a* and *el*) right next to each other, you can go ahead and mush them into one!

Quiero ir a el cine= Quiero ir al cine. (I want to go to the movies.)

De+el=Del

You can do the same thing if you come across these two words (*de* and *el*).

Vengo de el dentista= Vengo del dentista. (I'm coming from the dentist.)

On the surface, Spanish prepositions appear to be just like the ones in English. However, there are a few little nuances that every English-speaking Spanish student should be familiar with. These little, but extremely useful, words can be confusing sometimes. But, don't worry! The more you practice them, the easier they become.

Workbook Lesson 14: Preposiciones – Prepositions

Exercise 1: Complete the sentences with the appropriate prepositions.

1- Despiértame _____ las ocho. (Wake up me at eight.)

2- Los domingos solo trabajo ___ la mañana. (I only work in the morning on Sundays.)

3- Mi cumpleaños es el 30___ noviembre. (My birthday is November 30.)

4- Ana no puede estudiar ___ la noche, se duerme. (Anna cannot study at night, she falls asleep.)

5- Podemos vernos ___ las siete. (We can meet at seven.)

Exercise 2: Complete the sentences with the corresponding prepositions using << a, hasta, desde, de, o dentro de >> to create the expressions in brackets.

1- Trabajé en una empresa mexicana _____ el año pasado. (I worked for a Mexican company until last year.)

2- Patricio vive en la Ciudad de México _____ 2003. (Patricio has lived in Mexico City since 2003.)

3- Los bancos abren _____ ocho _____ cuatro. (Banks open from eight to four.)

4- Quiero ir a México_____ dos meses. (I want to go to Mexico in two months.)

5- Katia lleva enferma_____ el martes. (Katia has been sick since Tuesday.)

Exercise 3: Complete the sentences with the corresponding prepositions using << a, hasta, desde, de, o dentro de >>.

1- Diego estuvo con nosotros (el principio, fin de otoño)___. (Diego was with us from the beginning to the end of autumn.)

2- Emilio vivió en Paraguay (2006-2008)_____ . (Emilio lived in Paraguay from 2006 to 2008.)

3- Beto y María se casan_____ (cuatro meses). (Beto and Maria get married in four months.)

4- Voy a un gimnasio ___ ___ (siete,nueve). (I go to a gym from seven to nine.)

5- Quiero ir a la India_____ (dos meses). (I want to go to India for two months.)

Exercise 4: Complete the sentences using << antes de, durante, después de >>.

1- Camilo estuvo hablando _____ toda la clase. (Camilo was speaking throughout the class.)

2- Estábamos agotados _____ nadar en en mar. (We were exhausted after swimming at the beach.)

3- Cristina estaba muy nerviosa _____ la entrevista. (Cristina was very nervous during the interview.)

4- Me quedé muy relajado _____ de tomar un baño. (I stayed very relaxed after the shower.)

5- Hay que tener los teléfonos apagados_____ los conciertos. (You have to keep your phones off during concerts.)

Exercise 5: Tick the correct answer using << a, hacia, hasta, de, desde >>. In some cases there are two correct possibilities.

1- ¿Usted nos puede llevar ___ la estación?

   a. a   b. de   c. hacia

2- Este camión no llega _____ el centro.

   a. hasta   b. hacia   c. a

3- Para ver esa estrella hay que mirar _____ el este.

   a. de   b. hacia   c. desde

4- El río Amazonas fluye _____ el este.

   a. hacia   b. de   c. desde

5- ¿Cómo se llega ___ el estadio?

   a. hasta   b. a   c. hacia

Exercise 6: Complete the sentences with the correct word from the following: << con, de, a, sobre, en o entre >>.

1- Hay dos fotos ___ el piano. (There are two pictures above the piano.)

2- Esperanza está ___ su padre y su madre. (Esperanza is with his father and mother.)

3- Cartagena está ____ Colombia. (Cartagena is in Colombia.)

4- Gira por la primera ____ la izquierda. (Turn at / take the first left.)

5- Hay unas nubes____ el pueblo. (There are clouds over the village.)

Exercise 7: Reorder the words to form sentences.

1- Te espero/ al hotel/ frente. (I'll wait for you in front of the hotel.)

2- Una estación de metro/ mi casa /hay /cerca de. (There is a metro station near my house.)

3- Debajo de/ el libro/ está/ la mesa. (The book is under the table.)

4- Está / encima/ de la silla/ el teléfono. (The phone is above the chair.)

5- Saturno /lejos /está/ de la tierra. (Saturn is far from Earth.)

Exercise 8: Change these affirmative sentences into negative ones.

1- Hay un banco junto al cine. (There is a bank next to the cinema.)

2- Hay muchos árboles frente al museo. (There are many trees in front of the museum.)

3- Las pantuflas están debajo de la cama. (The slippers are under the bed.)

4- Hay un parque atrás del colegio. (There is a park behind the school.)

5- Hay una mosca dentro de la botella. (There is a fly inside the bottle.)

Exercise 9: Complete the following sentences using <<con, contra or sin>>.

1- Quiero un café_____ leche. (I want a latte.)

2- No puedes irte _____ permiso. (You cannot leave without permission.)

3- Mañana hay una manifestación _____ la pena de muerte. (Tomorrow there is a demonstration against the death penalty.)

4- Es difícil manejar _____lluvia. (It is difficult to drive in rain.)

5- No podrás encender el gas ___ cerillos. (You won't be able to light the gas without matches.)

Exercise 10: Complete the sentences using << por, para, sin, con, contra o según >>.

1- He recibido los documentos ___ correo. (I received the documents by mail.)

2- Es difícil hacer esta traducción ___diccionario. (It is difficult to do this translation without a dictionary.)

3- Necesitamos cortinas ___ la habitación. (We need curtains for the room.)

4- Hace frío, no salgas ___ abrigo. (It's cold, don't go out without a coat.)

5- Están buscando una vacuna _____ el sarampión. (They're looking for a measles vaccine.)

ANSWERS:

Exercise 1

1/ a 2/ por 3/ de 4/ por 5/ a

Exercise 2

1/ Trabajé en una empresa mexicana hasta el año pasado. 2/ Patricio vive en la Ciudad de México desde 2003. 3/ Los bancos abren de ocho a cuatro. 4/ Quiero ir a México dentro de dos meses. 5/ Katia lleva enferma desde el martes.

Exercise 3

1/ Diego estuvo con nosotros desde el principio hasta el final del otoño. 2/ Emilio vivió en Paraguay desde 2006 hasta 2008. 3/ Beto y María se casan dentro de cuatro meses. 4/ Voy a un gimnasio de siete a nueve. 5/ Quiero ir a la India por dos meses.

Exercise 4

1/ Camilo estuvo hablando durante toda la clase. 2/ Estábamos agotados después de nadar en el mar. 3/ Cristina estaba muy nerviosa durante la entrevista. 4/ Me quedé muy relajado después de tomar un baño. 5/ Hay que tener los teléfonos apagados durante los conciertos.

Exercise 5

1/ hacia, a 2/ hasta 3/ hacia 4/ desde 5/ hasta

Exercise 6

1/ Hay dos fotos sobre el piano. 2/ Esperanza está con su padre y su madre. 3/ Cartagena está en Colombia. 4/ Gira por la primera a la izquierda. 5/ Hay unas nubes sobre el pueblo.

Exercise 7

1/ Te espero frente al hotel. 2/ Cerca de mi casa hay una estación de metro. 3/ El libro está debajo de la mesa. 4/ El teléfono está encima de la silla. 5/ Saturno está lejos de la tierra.

Exercise 8

1/ No hay un banco junto al cine. 2/ No hay muchos árboles frente al museo. 3/ Las pantuflas no están debajo de la cama. 4/ No hay un parque atrás del colegio. 5/ No hay una mosca dentro de la botella.

Exercise 9

1/ Quiero un café con leche. 2/ No puedes irte sin permiso. 3/ Mañana hay una manifestación contra la pena de muerte. 4/ Es difícil manejar con lluvia. 5/ No podrás encender el gas sin cerillos.

Exercise 10

1/ He recibido los documentos por correo. 2/ Es difícil hacer esta traducción sin diccionario. 3/ Necesitamos cortinas para la habitación. 4/ Hace frío, no salgas sin abrigo. 5/ Están buscando una vacuna contra el sarampión.

Lesson 15. Por and Para

In the previous lesson, we've touched a little on this topic, but here we'll delve more deeply into *por* and *para*.

Por and *para* both translate into English as 'for,' but they can't be used interchangeably! In this lesson we'll show you when to opt for *por* and when to pick *para*.

The way some people like to look at it is that *por* is used for looking back to the cause or origin of something, and *para* is used for forward-looking things (like purpose or destination). But this is a massive generalization, and we want you to understand the difference in more detail.

When to use *para*

Para is often used in the sense of looking forward towards a goal/deadline/effect. Let's look at *para* first, as it has fewer complicated uses than *por*!

BONUS: Sometimes, in more colloquial speech, you're likely to hear *para* shortened to *pa*. Listen out for it in Spanish movies and songs!

Final goal/destination/purpose/object

One of the main uses of *para* is to talk about the final goal or purpose of something.

Listen to Track 140

—¿Para qué es esto?	What is this for?
—Es para limpiar los platos.	It's for washing dishes.
Una mesa para tres, por favor.	A table for 3 (people), please.
Come verduras para mantenerse sano.	He eats vegetables to stay healthy.
Compré algo para ti.	I bought something for you.

Advantage or disadvantage

When something is good/bad for someone/something.

Listen to Track 141

Beber demasiado alcohol es malo para la salud.	Drinking too much alcohol is bad for the health.
Eres muy importante para mí.	You are very important to/for me.

Deadline

We use *para* to express that something needs to be done by a certain time.

Listen to Track 142

Lo tarea es para el martes.	The homework is for (to be handed in by) Tuesday.
Necesito un vestido para mañana.	I need a dress for/by tomorrow.

Direction after motion verbs

We can use *para* to say where we're headed.

Listen to Track 143

| *Este camión va para las montañas.* | This bus is going to the mountains. |
| *Voy para la casa.* | I'm going/heading home. |

Reaction/response

Use *para* to say that a certain reaction or feeling is being had by a specific person.

Listen to Track 144

| *Para mí, huele a fresa.* | To me, it smells of strawberry. |
| *Para Pedro, Diana es perfecta.* | In Pedro's eyes, Diana is perfect. |

Considering

When we want to say 'for' in the sense of 'considering' or 'given,' we use *para*.

Listen to Track 145

| *Sofía lee bien para su edad.* | Sofía reads well for her age. |

Para + infinitive = in order to

We can use *para* with an infinitive, to mean 'in order to.'

Listen to Track 146

| *Me lo compré para usarlo en la fiesta.* | I bought it to wear to the party. |
| *Marcos estudia para pasar los exámenes.* | Marcos studies (in order) to pass his exams. |

When to use *por*

As we've mentioned, *por* is often used when talking about the root or cause of something, but not always. It's used in various ways, as we explain below. Some of the categories are very similar, and may overlap, but looking at a variety of situations will help you get the picture!

BONUS: After looking at these examples, the phrase *¿por qué?* should now make sense, as it literally means 'for what?'

Cause

The first use we'll look at is cause. When something is the cause of something else, we can use *por* to mean 'because of.'

Listen to Track 147

| *Vengo a Barcelona por su arquitectura.* | I come to Barcelona for/because of its architecture. |
| *Las flores murieron por falta de sol.* | The flowers died for/due to lack of sunlight. |

This can include emotional states. Let's say you're feeling sad because you've just done an exam and you feel it hasn't gone very well.

—¿Por qué estás triste?	Why are you sad?
—Por el examen.	Because of the exam.

How something works

We use *por* to explain how something works or happens, i.e. it happens through/by means of; always writing *medio de* (means of) after *por.* Because, if not, it may not make sense.

Listen to Track 148

El microondas funciona por medio de radiación.	The microwave works by means of radiation.
La estufa funciona por medio de gas	The stove works by means of gas.

Manner of communication or travel

We use *por* to describe the way in which something (e.g. a person or a piece of information) has traveled.

Listen to Track 149

Me lo dijo por teléfono.	S/he told me by phone.
Mi paquete fue enviado por avión	My packet was sent by plain
Lo enviaré por correo.	I'll send it by/in the post.

Behalf

We use *por* when describing things done on someone's behalf.

Listen to Track 150

Llamé a Juan por ti.	I called Juan for you/on your behalf.

For the sake of

Por can be used to refer to doing something for the sake/good of something/someone.

Listen to Track 151

Voy a dejar de beber por mi salud.	I'm going to quit drinking for the sake of my health.

But it can also be used to portray a pointless action:

Pelear por pelear.	To fight for the sake of fighting.
Lo está lavando por lavar.	He's just washing it for the sake of it.

In favor of

Earlier we saw that *estar para* means 'to be about to.'

If we use *por* instead of *para*, we get a completely different phrase. *Estar por* is used to literally say you're for (as opposed to against) something.

Listen to Track 152

Estoy aquí por los derechos humanos.	I'm here for human rights.

Yet to be done

Another way we can use *estar* with *por* is to talk about something that needs to be done, or will be done. Just put an infinitive after the *por*!

Listen to Track 153

El baño está por ser limpiado.	The bathroom is yet to be cleaned.
Laura está por llegar.	Laura is yet to arrive.

Location

Por can be used to describe the general area of that location.

Listen to Track 154

Keith viajó por Perú.	Keith traveled around Peru.

Similarly, if an object moves through another object, use *por*.

El hilo pasó por el ojo de la aguja.	The thread passed through the eye of the needle.

Exchange/price

Use *por* to say that you bought something for a certain amount, or to describe swapping something for something else.

Listen to Track 155

Juan compró el reloj por $3000.	Juan bought the watch for $3000.
Te doy mis papas fritas, por tus galletas,	For your biscuits, I'll give you my chips.

Multiplied by

In math, *por* is used when multiplying numbers. It translates in this case as 'by.'

Listen to Track 156

Tres por tres son nueve.	3x3=9
La hoja de papel mide 6 por 10 cm.	The sheet of paper measures 6 by 10 cm.

'By' in passive constructions

Por is often used in what we call 'passive constructions' when we want to describe something that was done by someone.' Check out these **examples:**

Listen to Track 157

| El libro fue escrito por Cervantes. | The book was written by Cervantes. |
| La mujer fue atacada por el cocodrilo. | The woman was attacked by the crocodile. |

To take for...

To perceive someone or something in a certain way.

Listen to Track 158

| ¡No me tomes por idiota! | Don't take me for an idiot. |
| Lo damos por sentado. | We take him for granted. |

To judge by/going by

This is a situation when you want to make a judgement based on some other information.

Listen to Track 159

| Por lo que me dijo, ... | Going by what she told me, ... |
| Por su voz, creo que estaba feliz. | Judging by his voice, I think he was happy. |

In search of something

This one is a little counterintuitive, but we can use *por* when we are going to get something.

Listen to Track 160

| Fui por mi coche. | I went for (to get) my car. |
| Marco fue a la tienda por fruta. | Marco went to the store for (to buy) fruit. |

However...

We don't mean 'however' in the sense of 'but.' We're using it in the sense of 'however much X happens, Y won't happen.' Check out the **Examples:**

Listen to Track 161

| Por más que te quejes, no cambiará nada. | However much you complain, nothing will change. |
| Por mucho dinero que tenga, no comprará un coche nuevo. | However much money he has, he won't buy a new car. |

Duration

This one is a little complicated. In some situations, *para* (in the case of the duration of something in the future), or maybe even no preposition at all, will be preferable. But here's when you usually use *por*:

When you want to emphasize that something only lasted for a short period of time, use *por*.

Listen to Track 162

Solo estuvo aquí por un momento.	He was only here for a moment.

Use *por* when you want to say how long something lasted in general.

Me quedé en el hotel por dos semanas.	I stayed in the hotel for two weeks.
Vi la serie por tres horas segudias.	I watch the series for three straight hours.

Gracias

When giving thanks for something, we always use *por* not *para*.

Listen to Track 163

Gracias por el anillo.	Thank you for the ring.
Muchas gracias por venir.	Thank you very much for coming.

Workbook Lesson 15: Por and Para

Exercise 1: Select the correct preposition in each case choosing between <<por>> or <<para>>.

1- Te felicito por / para tu trabajo. (Congratulations on your work.)

2- Hay que comprar comida para / por el sábado. (We have to buy food by Saturday.)

3- ¿Por/ para quién es esto? (Who is this for?)

4- No pudimos salir para/ por el frío. (We can't go out in the cold.)

5- Sube el volumen por/ para oír la música mejor. (Turn up the volume to hear the music better.)

Exercise 2: Complete the correct preposition in each case using << por>> or << para>>.

1. *Él vino ___ pedirte un favor.* (He came to ask you a favour.)

2. Javier fue rechazado___ Susana. (Javier was rejected by Susana.)

3. Tienes que haberlo escrito___ el jueves. (You must have written it by Thursday.)

4. Gracias___ ser mi mejor amigo. (Thanks for being my best friend.)

5. *Él me lo vendió ____ $50. (He sold me it for $50.)*

Exercise 3: Transform these affirmative sentences into negative ones.

1. El gato pasa por la casa. (The cat passes by the house.)

2. Pepe es bueno para las matemáticas. (Pepe is good at math.)

3. *Él trabaja los domingos por la mañana.* (He works on Sunday mornings.)

4. El león cruzó por el río. (The lion crossed the river.)

5. Es para limpiar los platos. (It's for cleaning the dishes.)

Exercise 4: Complete the sentences with the correct preposition, using <<por>> or <<para>>.

1. No hay función ___ falta de público. (There is no performance due to a lack of spectators.)

2. Estudio otro idioma____ ser bilingüe. (I study another language to be bilingual.)

3. Iré____ tu fiesta de cumpleaños. (I'll go to your birthday party.)

4. Laura teme hablar____ nerviosismo. (Laura is afraid to speak because of nerves.)

5. Estaré ausente___ una semana. (I will be absent for a week.)

Exercise 5: Translate the following sentences from English to Spanish.

1. What's this for?

2. You're very important to me.

3. I need a dress for the day after tomorrow.

4. For him, it smells like mango.

5. Clara reads well for her age.

Exercise 6: Tick the right answer to complete the sentences.

1- Los jugetes son ____los niños.

  a. por   b. para

2- He decidido cambiar mi departamento ____ una casa.

  a. por   b. para

3- Compré dos pantalones____ el precio de uno.

  a. por   b. para

4- Repartimos dos caramelos ____ niño.

  a. por   b. para

5- Usaré este libro____ estudiar geometría.

  a. para   b. por

Exercise 7: Translate the following sentences from Spanish to English.

1. Mi mamá cambió su vehículo por uno nuevo.

2. Tengo la mañana para caminar.

3. El libro estaba por aquí.

4. Hago ejercicio por las mañanas.

5. No sirve para nada.

Exercise 8: Complete these sentences with <<por>> or <<para>>.

1- Pelear ____ pelear. (Fighting for fighting's sake.)

2- Estoy ____ los derechos humanos. (I am for human rights.)

3- El baño está ____ ser limpiado. (The bathroom will be cleaned.)

4- Lizeth está ____llegar. (Lizeth is coming.)

5- Karen viajó ____ la Guyana. (Karen travelled through Guyana.)

Exercise 9: Complete these sentences with << por>> or <<para>>.

1- Tirar la casa ____ la ventana. (Throw the house out the window.(*idiom*))

2- Mi papá me dio dinero ____ comprarme un vestido. (My dad gave me money to buy myself a dress.)

3- Iremos a ver el espectáculo____ la noche. (We will go to see the show at night.)

4- Me levanto____ las mañanas para ir a la universidad. (I get up in the morning to go to college.)

5- Escucho música____ relajarme. (I listen to music to relax.)

Exercise 10: Complete the paragraph with << por>> or <<para>>.

El viernes mis amigos y yo iremos 1. ____Texas 2. ____ visitar a nuestro amigo Tom. Vamos allá 3.__ descansar también. No tenemos mucho dinero, 4. ____ consiguiente optamos 5.___ ir en coche.

ANSWERS:

Exercise 1

1/ Te felicito por tu trabajo. 2/ Hay que comprar comida para el sábado. 3/ ¿Para quién es esto? 4/ No podemos salir por el frío. 5/ Sube el volumen para oír la música mejor.

Exercise 2

1/ Él vino para pedirte un favor. 2/ Javier fue rechazado por Susana. 3/ Tienes que haberlo escrito para el jueves. 4/ Gracias por ser mi mejor amigo. 5/ *Él me lo vendió por $50.*

Exercise 3

1/ El gato no pasa por la casa. 2/ Pepe no es bueno para las matemáticas. 3/ *Él no trabaja los domingos por la mañana.* 4/ El león no cruzó por el río. 5/ No es para limpiar los platos.

Exercise 4

1/ No hay función por falta de público. 2/ Estudio otro idioma para ser bilingüe. 3/ Iré para tu fiesta de cumpleaños. 4/ Laura teme hablar por nerviosismo. 5/ Estaré ausente por una semana.

Exercise 5

1/ *¿Para qué es esto?* 2/ Tú eres muy importante para mí. 3/ Necesito un vestido para pasado mañana. 4/ Para él, huele a mango. 5/ Clara lee bien para su edad.

Exercise 6

1/ para 2/ por 3/ por 4/ por 5/ para

Exercise 7

1/ My mom traded her vehicle for a new one. 2/ I have the morning to walk. 3/ The book was by here. 4/ I do sport in the morning. 5/ It's useless.

Exercise 8

1/ Pelear por pelear. 2/ Estoy por los derechos humanos. 3/ El baño está por ser limpiado. 4/ Lizeth está por llegar. 5/ Karen viajó por la Guyana.

Exercise 9

1/ Tirar la casa por la ventana. 2/ Mi papá me dio dinero para comprarme un vestido. 3/ Iremos a ver el espectáculo por la noche. 4/ Me levanto por las mañanas para ir a la universidad. 5/ Escucho música para relajarme.

Exercise 10

El viernes mis amigos y yo iremos para Texas para visitar a nuestro amigo Tom. Vamos allá para descansar también. No tenemos mucho dinero, por consiguiente, optamos por ir en coche.

Lesson 16. Perfect Tense

Being able to conjugate verbs in the perfect tense is a great skill to have, as it helps you to describe things that have occurred in the past. All you need to know is how to conjugate one verb (*haber*), and how to form past participles. In today's lesson, we'll learn how to do it.

What is the perfect tense?

You might hear lots of different names for this tense, like 'present perfect,' 'perfect indicative,' or '*pretérito perfecto compuesto*.' Don't be put off by these names, as they all mean the same thing, which we'll call 'the perfect tense' for simplicity!

We use the perfect tense to describe something that has happened. Think of it as the not-too-distant past.

As we said before, it's more commonly used in Spain than in Mexico or Latin America, just as it's more common in the UK than the USA. Here's a table to demonstrate the difference between the perfect tense and the preterite (which is a completely different past tense).

Perfect tense	Preterite tense
I have eaten dinner (already tonight).	I ate dinner (yesterday).
What have you been doing (today, before you came here)?	What did you do (at a specific point in the distant past)?
I've been skating (today).	I went skating (at a specific point in the distant past).
It has been a pleasure to meet you (today).	It was a pleasure to meet her (last week).
I think it has rained (recently, because it's wet now).	I think it rained (last week, but it may well be dry today).

With practice, it will soon become clear when to use which tense. Basically, if you want to say, "I have ...-ed," then you'll need the perfect tense.

How to form it?

The good news is that the perfect tense is pretty easy to form, as it's made of two simple parts.

Haber

This verb means 'to have' when it's used in certain tenses, including the perfect tense (not to be confused with *tener*, which means 'to have' in pretty much all *other* situations).

Past participle

This is the -ed version of the verb, e.g. knitted, played.

Here is the conjugation of *haber* that you'll need:

Yo	he	I have
Tú	has	You have
Él/ella Usted	ha	He/she/it has You (formal) have

Nosotros	hemos	We have
Ustedes	han	You (You plural) have
Ellos/ellas	han	They have

Top tip: remember that in Spanish, the 'h' is silent.

For the perfect tense, this is the only verb you need to know how to conjugate! The past participles don't actually need to be conjugated...

Past participles

Regular formation

The normal formation of past participles is super simple. You take the verb in the infinitive, then:

For -*ar* verbs, remove the -*ar* then add -*ado*.

For -*er* and -*ir* verbs, remove the-*er* or -*ir* then add -*ido*.

For Example:

To play:	jugar	→	jugar	→	jug + ado	→	jugado
To love:	amar	→	amar	→	am + ado	→	amado
To eat:	comer	→	comer	→	com + ido	→	comido
To drink:	beber	→	beber	→	beb + ido	→	bebido
To live:	vivir	→	vivir	→	viv + ido	→	vivido
To pretend:	fingir	→	fingir	→	fing + ido	→	fingido

Irregular past participles

In an unusual twist, the (normally very awkward) verbs *ir*, *ser*, and *estar* actually form their past participles in the regular way!

To go:	ir	→	- ir	→	- + ido	→	ido
To be:	ser	→	ser	→	s + ido	→	sido
To be:	estar	→	estar	→	est + ado	→	estado

However, you're not gonna get away that easily! This is Spanish, so there'll always be some irregular ones sneaking around. The following have irregular past participles which need to be learnt.

Top tip: You might start to spot patterns for how the irregular ones are formed, e.g. things that end in -*cubrir* (*cubrir*, *descubrir*, etc.) have past participles that end in -*cubierto* (*cubierto*, *descubierto*, etc.).

Listen to Track 164

Infinitive	Past participle	English
abrir	abierto	opened
cubrir	cubierto	covered
decir	dicho	said

descubrir	descubierto	discovered
escribir	escrito	written
freír	frito	fried
hacer	hecho	done/made
imprimir	impreso	printed
morir	muerto	died
poner	puesto	put
resolver	resuelto	resolved
romper	roto	broken
satisfacer	satisfecho	satisfied
ver	visto	seen
volver	vuelto	returned

Triggers

A good general rule is that if you're talking about something that's happened in 'this …', e.g. 'today' ('this day'), 'this morning,' 'this week,' 'this month,' 'this year,' then you'll need the perfect tense. It's also useful to recognize other phrases that trigger the perfect tense. Here are some common ones to look out for!

Listen to Track 165

Hoy	Today
Ya	Already
Recientemente	Recently
X veces	X times
Todavía	Still
Nunca/jamás	Never

BONUS LESSON: The Pluperfect Tense

If you're feeling smart, and you got all that, you might want to also think about the pluperfect tense. Instead of talking about things that have happened, it allows you to describe things that had happened.

It's formed in almost the same way as the perfect tense, except that *haber* is conjugated in the imperfect (yet another type of past tense):

Listen to Track 166

Yo	había	I had
Tú	habías	You had
Él/ella	había	He/she/it had
Usted		You (formal) had
Nosotros	habíamos	We had
Ustedes	habían	You (You plural) had
Ellos/ellas	habían	They had

To sum up …

Perfect:	*he* + past participle	I have + past participle
	(*he comido*)	(I have eaten)
Pluperfect:	*había* + past participle	I had + past participle
	(*había comido*)	(I had eaten)

Workbook Lesson 16: Tiempo perfecto - Perfect Tense

Exercise 1: Use the perfect tense to complete the sentences. Use <<Haber>> + the verb in the past participle.

1- Este verano nosotros____ _____(estar) en Alaska. (This summer we went to Alaska.)

2- Este año___ ___ (llover) mucho. (This year it has rained a lot.)

3- Se __ _____ (despertar) a las 10. (He woke up at 10.)

4- ¿Tú ___ ____(leer) algo interesante últimamente? (Have you read anything interesting lately?)

5- Hoy nosotras___ ____(comer) ceviche. (Today we have eaten ceviche.)

Exercise 2: Write the news corresponding to the given headlines. Use the following verbs: << escaparse, acabar, ganar, morir, subir >>.

Example: Sube la gasolina: Ha subido la gasolina. (Gas is on board.)

1- Fuga de 70 presos: _____ . (Escape by 70 prisoners.)

2- Muere el escritor _____. (The writer has died.)

3- Fin de la huelga de transporte _____. (The transport strike has ended.)

4- América, campeón de la liga _____ . (America, league champion.)

5- Suben los impuestos _____. (They raise taxes.)

Exercise 3: Translate the following sentences from Spanish to English.

1- ¿Tú has visto a Eduardo?

2- ¿Qué han hecho ustedes este verano?

3- Hoy hemos trabajado cerca de 10 horas.

4- Él ha jugado a bolos.

5- Ella ha enviado unos correos.

Exercise 4: Choose the right answer.

1- He _____ una vida intense.

   a. tenido   b. teniado

2- Yo ___actriz de Hollywood.

   a. he sido   b. has sido

3- Ella _____ por todo el mundo.

   a. ha viajado   b. has viajado

4- Nosotros _____ en una fábrica.

   a. hemos trabajado b. han trabajado

5- Pedro nunca _____ de México.

   a. ha salido   b. han salido

Exercise 5: Use the perfect tense to complete the sentences. Use <<Haber>> + the verb in the past participle.

1- Pepe_____ _____(estar) en Uruguay. (Pepe has been to Uruguay.)

2- Ellos____ ____(tener) cinco hijos. (They have had five children.)

3- Yo ___ _____ (conocer) personajes famosos. (I have met famous characters.)

4- ¿Tú ____ _____ (comer) paella alguna vez? (Have you ever eaten paella?)

5- Nosotras nunca____ _____(tomar) tequila. (We have never had tequila.)

Exercise 6: Translate the following sentences from Spanish to English.

1- Recientemente he salido con Paula.

2- Ya hemos comido hoy.

3- Todavía no ha llegado la carta.

4- Jamás he estado en Chile.

5- Ellos han descubierto tu secreto.

Exercise 7: Reorder these words to create phrases using the verb *Haber*, with its correct conjugation for each person.

1- Ronaldo/ estar/ nunca / en África. (Ronaldo has never been to Africa.)

2- ¿Ustedes/ comer/ alguna vez/ pozole? (Have you ever eaten pozole?)

3- ¿Ustedes / enamorarse/ alguna vez? (Have you ever fallen in love?)

4- Yo / nunca / ir/ a la ópera. (I've never been to the opera.)

5- Nosotros / usar/ siempre/ el servicio UBER. (We have always used UBER.)

Exercise 8: Form phrases uniting elements from the two columns.

Example: No he podido llamar porque he perdido mi teléfono.

1- No puedo entrar a la casa	1- Trabajar mucho todo el día
2- Juana no ve bien	2- Olvidar la cartera
3- No puedo pagar	3- Perder las llaves
4- Están agotadas	4- Romper los lentes
5- No he podido llamar	5- Tener tiempo

Exercise 9: Write the news corresponding to the given headlines. Use the following verbs: << recoger, reservar, pedir, cambiar, ver >>.

Example: ¿Has visto esa película? Sí, ya la he visto.

1- ¿Has recogido los boletos? (Have you collected the tickets?)

2- ¿Has reservado el hotel? (Have you booked the hotel?)

3- ¿Has pedido la visa? (Did you apply for a visa?)

4- ¿Has cambiado el dinero? (Have you changed the money?)

5- ¿Has visto a Arturo hoy? (Have you seen Arthur today?)

Exercise 10: Write the news corresponding to the given headlines. Use the following verbs: << salir, acabar, haber, cenar, cerrar >>.

Example: **Él** llegó. Salimos de la casa. Cuando salimos de la casa él había llegado.

1- La reunión acabó. Llegué a la oficina. (The meeting is over. I get to the office.)

2- El avión salió. Llegamos al aeropuerto. (The plane went out. We arrived at the airport.)

3- Cerraron las tiendas. Camilo quiso comprar comida. (The shops closed. Camilo wanted to buy food.)

4- Cené. Sofía me llamó. (I had dinner. Sofia called me.)

5- Hubo un accidente. Nos pararon en la Carretera. (There was an accident. They stopped us on the road.)

ANSWERS:

Exercise 1

1/ Este verano hemos estado en Alaska. 2/ Este año ha llovido mucho. 3/ Se ha despertado a las 10. 4/ ¿Tú has leído algo interesante últimamente? 5/ Hoy nosotras hemos comido ceviche.

Exercise 2

1/ Se han fugado setenta presos. 2/ Ha muerto el escritor. 3/ Ha acabado la huelga de transporte. 4/ América ha quedado campeón de la liga. 5/ Han subido los impuestos.

Exercise 3

1/ Have you seen Eduardo? 2/ What have you done this summer? 3/ Today we have worked about 10 hours. 4/ He has been bowling. 5/ She has sent some emails.

Exercise 4

1/ tenido 2/ he sido 3/ ha viajado 4/ hemos trabajado 5/ ha salido

Exercise 5

1/ Pepe ha estado en Uruguay. 2/ Ellos han tenido cinco hijos. 3/ Yo he conocido personajes famosos. 4/ ¿Tú has comido alguna vez paella? 5/ Nosotras nunca hemos tomado tequila.

Exercise 6

1/ I recently dated Paula. 2/ We already ate today. 3/ The letter has not yet arrived. 4/ I've never been to Chile. 5/ They have discovered your secret.

Exercise 7

1/ Ronaldo nunca ha estado en África. 2/ ¿Ustedes han comido alguna vez pozole? 3/ ¿Ustedes se han enamorado alguna vez? 4/ Yo nunca he ido a la ópera. 5/ Nosotros siempre hemos usado el servicio UBER.

Exercise 8

1/ No puedo entrar a la casa porque he perdido las llaves. 2/ Juana no ve bien porque ha roto los lentes. 3/ No puedo pagar porque he olvidado la cartera. 4/ Están agotadas porque han trabajado mucho todo el día. 5/ No he podido llamar porque no he tenido tiempo.

Exercise 9

1/ Sí, los he recogido ya. 2/ Sí, he reservado ya. 3/ Sí, la he pedido ya. 4/ Sí, ya lo he cambiado. 5/ Sí, lo he visto hoy.

Exercise 10

1/Cuando llegué a la oficina la reunión ya había acabado. 2/ Cuando llegamos al aeropuerto, el avión ya había salido. 3/ Cuando Camilo quiso comprar comida ya habían cerrado las tiendas. 4/ Cuando Sofía me llamó ya había cenado. 5/ Nos pararon en la carretera porque había habido un accidente.

Lesson 17. Possessives

What are possessives?

Possessives are used to describe who owns (or possesses) something. We can split possessives into groups:

- Possessive adjectives
- Short form
- Longer form
- Possessive pronouns

We'll look at them bit by bit!

Spanish Possessive adjectives—short form

The short version is the most common form of possessive adjective, and you just stick it in front of the noun.

A really important thing to remember is that the possessive adjective has to agree in number (and gender) with the thing that's possessed, not the person possessing it. We'll show you some examples later.

Here are the short form possessive adjectives:

Listen to Track 168

mi(s)	my
tu(s)	your (familiar singular)
su(s)	his/her/its your (formal singular)
nuestro(s)/nuestra(s)	our
su(s)	Their/your (you plural)

It helps to look at the words in context, and get a bit of practice. Here are some example sentences to start you off:

Listen to Track 169

Estoy buscando mi llave.	I'm looking for my key.
Estoy buscando mis llaves.	I'm looking for my keys.
Toma tu libro.	Take your book.
Toma tus libros.	Take your books.
Alejandra ha perdido sus lentes de contacto.	Alejandra has lost her contact lens.
Alejandra ha perdido sus lentes.	Alejandra has lost her glasses.
Señora, ¿dónde está su perro?	Madam, where is your dog? (formal)

Nosotros/nosotras* estamos en nuestro país.*	We are in our country.
Nosotros/nosotras* estamos en nuestra casa.*	We are in our house.
Estamos con nuestros primos.	We are with our male/mixed group of cousins.
Estamos con nuestras primas.	We are with our female cousins.
¿Quién es su padre?	Who is your father? (familiar plural)
¿Dónde está su madre?	Where is your mother?
¿Quiénes son sus padres?	Who are your parents?
¿Dónde están sus hermanas?	Where are your sisters?
Soy su hija.	I'm their daughter.
Soy su mesero.	I'm your waiter. (you plural)

*Remember, it doesn't matter here what gender we are. What matters is the gender of the object that we own! The same goes for nuestro/a/os/as—it agrees with the thing being possessed, NOT the possessor!

Spanish Possessive adjectives—longer form

These mean pretty much the same as the short form adjectives, but they help to emphasize who is possessing, rather than focusing on the possessed object! We place them after the noun being possessed.

This time, it's not just *nuestro* that have to agree in gender. All the forms have to agree in gender (m/f) AND number (singular/plural) with the thing being possessed.

Listen to Track 170

mío(s)/mía(s)	mine
tuyo(s)/tuya(s)	yours (familiar singular)
suyo(s)/suya(s)	his/hers yours (formal singular)
nuestro(s)/nuestra(s)	ours
suyo(s)/suya(s)	theirs yours (plural)

As you look at the following examples, remember that *suyo(s)/suya(s)* can have various meanings. Context will usually make things clear.

'his' or 'hers'

'yours' (formal singular)

'theirs'

'yours' (plural)

Listen to Track 171

¡Dios mío!	My God!
No sé dónde están tus hermanos, pero veo a los míos por ahí.	I don't know where your brothers are, but I see mines over there.
No llores, hija mía.	Don't cry, my dear (my daughter).
Paula y Claudia son amigas mías.	Paula and Claudia are friends of mine.
Fue un error tuyo.	It was a mistake of yours (it was your mistake).
Fueron errores tuyos.	They were mistakes of yours.
Fue una idea tuya.	It was an idea of yours (it was your idea).
Fueron ideas tuyas.	They were ideas of yours.
Necesito encontrar a Pablo. Tengo que devolverle un documento suyo	I need to find Pablo. I have to give back a document of his.
.Necesito encontrar a Pablo. Tengo que devolverle unos documentos suyos.	I need to find Pablo. I have to give back some documents of his.
Necesito encontrar a Pablo. Tengo que devolverle una corbata suya.	I need to find Pablo. I have to give back a necktie of his.
Necesito encontrar a Pablo. Tengo que devolverle unas corbatas suyas.	I need to find Pablo. I have to give back some neckties of his.
¿Es un conocido suyo?	Is he an acquaintance of yours (formal singular)?
¿Son unos conocidos suyos?	Are they acquaintances of yours?
¿Es una amiga suya?	Is she a friend (female) of yours?
¿Son unas amigas suyas?	Are they friends (females) of yours?
Es un traje nuestro.	It's a suit of ours.
Son trajes nuestros.	They're suits of ours.
Es hermana nuestra.	She's a sister of ours.
Son algunas de nuestras hermanas.	They're some of our sisters.
Chicos, es un logro suyo.	Guys, it's an achievement of yours (familiar plural).
Chicos, todos son logros suyos.	Guys, they're all achievements of yours.
Chicos, ¿fue esto una broma suya?	Guys, was this a prank of yours?
Chicos, ¿fueron bromas suyas?	Guys, were they pranks of yours?
Juan es un compañero suyo.	Juan is a colleague of theirs.
Juan y Pol son compañeros suyos.	Juan and Pol are colleagues of theirs.
Ana es prima suya.	Ana is a cousin (female) of theirs.
Ana y Andrea son primas suyas.	Ana and Andrea are cousins (female) of theirs.
Señores, ya hemos escuchado un discurso suyo.	Gentlemen, we have already heard a speech of yours (you plural).

Señores, ya hemos escuchado algunos discursos suyos.	Gentlemen, we have already heard speeches of yours.
Señores, leí una carta suya.	Gentlemen, I read a letter of yours.
Señores, leí unas cartas suyas.	Gentlemen, I read some letters of yours.

Spanish Possessive Pronouns

Sometimes the longer form is used with the definite article (*el/la/los/las*).

The difference is that in these cases, the possessive is acting as a pronoun, meaning that it replaces the noun rather than modifying it.

The possessive pronouns are the same as the longer form possessives as mentioned above. Here's a reminder:

Listen to Track 172

mío(s)/mía(s)	Mine
tuyo(s)/tuya(s)	yours (familiar)
suyo(s)/suya(s)	his/hers yours (formal)
nuestro(s)/nuestra(s)	ours
suyo(s)/suya(s)	Theirs/yours (plural)

Again, remember that *suyo(s)/suya(s)* can have various meanings.

Listen to Track 173 – 179

Este plátano es el mío.	This banana is mine (my one).
Estos plátanos son los míos.	These bananas are mine (my ones).
Esa fresa es la mía.	That strawberry is mine (my one).
Esas fresas son las mías.	Those strawberries are mine (my ones).
Vi el tuyo.	I saw yours (your one).
Vi los tuyos.	I saw yours (your ones).
Vi la tuya.	I saw yours (your one).
Vi las tuyas.	I saw yours (your ones).
¿Cuál perro?	Which dog?
—El suyo.	Hers (her one).
¿Cuáles perros?	Which dogs?
—Los suyos.	Hers (her ones).
¿De cuál falda hablamos?	Which skirt are we talking about?
—(De) La suya.	Hers (her one).
¿De cuáles faldas hablamos?	Which skirts are we talking about?
—(De) Las suyas.	Hers (her ones).
Este libro es el suyo.	This book is yours (formal singular) (your one).
Estos libros son los suyos.	These books are yours (your ones).

Creo que esta bebida es la suya.	I think this drink is yours (your one).
Creo que estas bebidas son las suyas.	I think these drinks are yours (your ones).
Ese es el nuestro.	This one is ours (our one).
Esos son los nuestros.	These ones are ours (our ones).
Esa es la nuestra.	That one is ours (our one).
Esas son las nuestras.	Those ones are ours (our ones).
Mi deseo es aprender. ¿Y el suyo?	My desire is to learn. And yours (familiar plural) (your one)?
Mis planes son claros. ¿Y los suyos?	My plans are clear. And yours (your ones)?
La idea de ellos es impresionante. ¿Cuál es la suya?	Their idea is impressive. What is yours (your one)?
Las ideas de ellos son impresionantes. ¿Ya tienen las suyas?	Their ideas are impressive. Do you have yours (your ones) already?
Juan y Ángel viven en la esquina. El edificio café es el suyo.	Juan and Ángel live on the corner. The brown building is theirs (their one).
Juan y Ángel se estacionaron ahí. Los coches azules son los suyos.	Juan and Ángel parked over there. The blue cars are theirs (their ones).
Juan y Ángel viven en la esquina. La casa verde es la suya.	Juan and Ángel live on the corner. The green house is theirs (their one).
Juan y Ángel se estacionaron ahí. Las motos negras son las suyas.	Juan and Ángel parked over there. The black motorcycles are theirs (their ones).
Señores y señoras, este mesero es el suyo.	Ladies and gentlemen, this waiter is yours (your one).
Señores y señoras, estos meseros son los suyos.	Ladies and gentlemen, these waiters are yours (your ones).
Señores y señoras, esta mesa es la suya.	Ladies and gentlemen, this table is yours (your one).
Señores y señoras, estas mesas son las suyas.	Ladies and gentlemen, these tables are yours (your ones).

Cool extra stuff

You can also use a long form possessive with *lo* to refer to some unnamed business, or to say that you're in your element:

Listen to Track 180

¡Mi novio sabe de lo nuestro!	My boyfriend knows about us!
Lo suyo es fascinante.	That stuff with you guys is fascinating.
Eso es el mío.	This is my thing/I'm in my element.

We have lots of phrases in English where we use a possessive with body parts. In Spanish, we actually don't use the possessive in these cases:

Me duele la cabeza.	My head hurts.
Dame la mano.	Give me your hand.
Cierra la boca.	Shut your mouth.

Workbook Lesson 17: Posesivos – Possessives

Exercise 1: Complete the phrases with possessive pronouns.

1- ¿Cuál es ___ color preferido? (What is your favorite color?)

2- Mi hermano y yo jugamos mucho al tenis, es ____ deporte favorito. (My brother and I play tennis a lot, it's our favorite sport.)

3- La señora Marta y ___ hijos son muy agradables. (Mrs. Martha and her children are very nice.)

4- Anoche fui al cine con ____ padre y ____ hermanos. (Last night I went to the movies with my father and my brothers.)

5- Juan, Pedro, ¿dónde están ___ libros? (Juan, Pedro, where are your books?)

Exercise 2: Translate the following sentences from Spanish to English.

1- Rodrigo trabaja con su padre.

2- Su abuela tiene 86 años.

3- Dame tu chaqueta.

4- ¿Quién es tu profesor?

5- Abel, es su mujer.

Exercise 3: Complete sentences as in the example: << mías, nuestros, suyas, tuyo, suyo >>

Example: ¿De quién es este libro? Es mío.

1- ¿De quién son estas llaves? Son ____. (Whose keys are these? They are mine.)

2- ¿Son ____ estas maletas? (Are these suitcases yours?)

3- ¿De quién son estos CDs? Son ____. (Whose are these CDs? They're ours.)

4- ¿Es ____ este reloj? (Is this watch yours?)

5- ¿De quién es este paraguas? Es ____. (Whose umbrella is this? It's yours.)

Exercise 4: Tick the right answer.

1- ¿Es ese su coche? No ___ es más grande.

  a. el mío   b. mío

2- Este abrigo no es de Pedro. ____ es negro.

  a. El suyo   b. Tuyo

3- ¿Ese es nuestro profesor? No_____ es más joven.

  a. el suyo   b. el nuestro

4- Mi profesora es peruana. ____ es colombiana.

  a. La mía   b. La mío

5- Un amigo___ es pintor.

  a. mío   b. el mío

Exercise 5: Complete the sentences as in the example: <<mío, tuyo, suyo, ustedes, nuestro, (un, una, unas, unas)>>

Example: (amiga, yo) _____es piloto - Una amiga mía es piloto

1- (Amiga, yo) _____ ha ganado un premio. (A friend of mine has won a prize.)

2- Ayer estuve con (primo, ustedes) _____. (Yesterday I was with a cousin of yours.)

3- Raquel es (prima, nosotros) _____ . (Rachel is our cousin.)

4- El sábado conocimos a (familiares, ustedes) _____ . (On Saturday, we met some of your relatives.)

5- ¿Es Susana (tía, tu)? _____ . (Is Susana your aunty?)

Exercise 6: Translate the following sentences from Spanish to English.

1- Estos lápices no son míos.

2- ¿Es tuya esa bolsa?

3- Una tía nuestra vive en Londres.

4- ¿De quién es esto? Es suyo.

5- Ésta no es la patineta de Germán, la suya es pequeña.

Exercise 7: Sort the following words to create sentences.

1- mi coche/ es / el tuyo /caro /pero / es más. (My car is expensive, but yours is more.)

2- ha / perdido /equipo / nuestro. (Our team has lost.)

3- abuelos / se llaman / tus / Pedro y Ana. (Your grandparents are called Peter and Ana.)

4- hijos / son / mis / muy inteligentes. (My children are very intelligent.)

5- perro/ tu / es / muy cariñoso. (Your dog is very sweet.)

Exercise 8: Change these affirmative sentences into negative ones.

1- Este dinero es tuyo. (This money is yours.)

2- Nuestro abuelo ha muerto. (Our grandfather is dead.)

3- Su cabello es negro, el suyo es café. (His hair is black, hers is brown.)

4- Mi casa es grande, pero tu casa es enorme. (My house is big but your house is huge.)

5- Tus gallinas comen muy bien. (Your chickens eat very well.)

Exercise 9: Translate the following sentences from Spanish to English.

1- Me gustan mucho sus pinturas.

2- Conozco a una amiga tuya.

3- ¿Cuándo celebra Mateo su cumpleaños?

4- Pepe no encuentra sus llaves.

5- Una prima suya vive en Nueva York.

Exercise 10: Complete the statements below using possessive pronouns.

¿Quieres saber algo de ____ familia? Pues mira, ___familia no es muy grande, pero vivimos en diferentes ciudades de México. ___ padres están jubilados y viven en ___ casa que está en Ajijic. ___ hermana se llama Claudia y ella y ___ marido Fernando viven en Cancún. (You want to know about our family? Look, my family's not very big, but we live in different cities in Mexico. My parents are retired and live in their home in Ajijic. Mysister's name is Claudia, and she and her husband Fernando live in Cancún.)

ANSWERS:

Exercise 1

1/ ¿Cuál es tu color preferido? 2/ Mi hermano y yo jugamos mucho al tenis, es nuestro deporte favorito. 3/ La señora Marta y sus hijos son muy agradables. 4/ Anoche fui al cine con mi padre y mis hermanos. 5/ Juan, Pedro, ¿dónde están sus libros?

Exercise 2

1/ Rodrigo works with his father. 2/ His grandmother is 86 years old. 3/ Give me your jacket. 4/ Who's your teacher? 5/ Abel, it's his wife.

Exercise 3

1/ ¿De quién son estas llaves? Son mías. 2/ ¿Son suyas estas maletas? 3/ ¿De quién son estos CDs? Son nuestros. 4/ ¿Es tuyo este reloj? 5/ ¿De quién es este paraguas? Es suyo.

Exercise 4

1/ El mío 2/ El suyo 3/ El nuestro 4/ La mía 5/ Mío

Exercise 5

1/ Una amiga mía ha ganado un premio. 2/ Ayer estuve con un primo de ustedes. 3/ Raquel es prima nuestra. 4/ El sábado conocimos a unos familiares de ustedes. 5/ ¿Es Susana tía tuya?

Exercise 6

1/ These pencils are not mine. 2/ Is that bag yours? 3/ One of our aunts lives in London. 4/ Whose is this? It's yours. 5/ This is not German's skateboard, his is small.

Exercise 7

1/ Mi coche es caro, pero el tuyo es más. 2/ Nuestro equipo ha perdido. 3/ Tus abuelos se llaman Pedro y Ana. 4/ Mis hijos son muy inteligentes. 5/ Tu perro es muy cariñoso.

Exercise 8

1/ Este dinero no es tuyo. 2/ Nuestro abuelo no ha muerto. 3/ Su cabello no es negro, el suyo es café. 4/ Mi casa no es grande, pero su casa es enorme. 5/ Tus gallinas no comen muy bien.

Exercise 9

1/ I like his paintings very much. 2/ I know a friend of yours. 3/ When does Matthew celebrate his birthday? 4/ Pepe can't find his keys. 5/ A cousin of yours lives in New York.

Exercise 10

¿Quieres saber algo de nuestra familia? Pues mira, mi familia no es muy grande, pero vivimos en diferentes ciudades de México. Mis padres están jubilados y viven en su casa que está en Ajijic. Mi hermana se llama Claudia y ella y su marido Fernando viven en Cancún.

Lesson 18. Demonstrative Adjectives and Demonstrative Pronouns

Demonstrative adjectives and demonstrative pronouns are slightly different, so let's start by looking at the adjectives and then move on to the pronouns.

What is a demonstrative adjective?

Demonstrative adjectives demonstrate which thing is being talked about. Adjectives are words that modify nouns. So basically, a demonstrative adjective is a word that you put before a noun, and it specifies which noun you're referring to if there's any ambiguity (e.g. 'this egg' vs. 'that egg').

In English, we distinguish between 'this' and 'that.' In Spanish, there's one additional level. Spanish-speakers differentiate between 'that which isn't right next to me but isn't too far away' and 'that all the way over there.' In other words, there are two different versions of 'that' depending on how far away the object is (more on that later)!

So, the Spanish demonstrative adjectives are these:

Listen to Track 181

este __	this __ (masculine)
esta __	this __ (feminine)
estos __	these __ (masculine plural)
estas __	these __ (feminine plural)
ese __	that __ (masculine)
esa __	that __ (feminine)
esos __	those __ (masculine plural)
esas __	those __ (feminine plural)
aquel __	that __ over there (masculine)
aquella __	that __ over there (feminine)
aquellos __	those __ over there (masculine plural)
aquellas __	those __ over there (feminine plural)

How they work

Because they're adjectives, we put them before nouns, just like in English. The demonstrative adjective that you use has to agree in gender (masculine or feminine) and number (singular or plural) with the noun it's modifying. We've listed all the gender and number options above.

Here are some examples for you to read, to help give you some context and understand how to use demonstrative adjectives.

Listen to Track 182

Este anillo es de oro.	This ring is made of gold.
Compré este libro ayer.	I bought this book yesterday.
Esta mañana fui al mercado.	This morning I went to the market.
Me encanta esta falda.	I love this skirt.
Estos perros son míos.	These dogs are mine.
Vendrá uno de estos días.	He will come one of these days.
Estas máquinas están rotas.	These machines are broken.
Quiero comprar estas chaquetas.	I want to buy these jackets.

Ese camión va al centro.	That bus goes to the city center.
Dame ese lápiz.	Pass me that pen.
Esa mochila es de Beatriz.	That backpack belongs to Beatriz.
Me gusta esa foto.	I like that photo.
Esos zapatos son de muy buena calidad.	Those shoes are really good quality.
¿Estás cómodo usando esos pantalones?	Are you comfortable wearing those jeans?
Esas arañas me dan miedo.	Those spiders frighten me.
La señora robó una de esas manzanas.	The lady stole one of those apples.

Aquel edificio es donde trabaja mi madre.	That office over there is where my mother works.
Me gusta mucho aquel chico.	I really like that guy over there.
Aquella chica no deja de mirarme.	That girl over there won't stop staring at me.
No nos conocíamos en aquella época.	We didn't know each other back then (far away in time, in the distant past).
Aquellos hombres son artistas.	Those men over there are artists.
No he estado en aquellos países.	I haven't been to those (faraway) countries.
Aquellas mujeres son muy inteligentes.	Those women over there are very intelligent.
Me gustaría caminar por aquellas montañas.	I'd like to walk around those mountains over there.

For native English speakers, correctly differentiating between *ese* (that) and *aquel* (that over there) can take a while to master. Here are some sentences that make use of 'this,' 'that,' and 'that over there' so you can see the difference.

Listen to Track 183

Carlos, no me basta esta hoja de papel. ¿Me pasas ese cuaderno? Si no, mejor voy a usar aquella computadora.	Carlos, this sheet of paper isn't big enough. Would you pass me that notebook? Otherwise I'll go use that computer.
Rafael quiere entrar en esta iglesia y Nerea quiere visitar ese museo en la próxima calle. Yo quiero caminar hasta aquella torre afuera del pueblo.	Rafael wants to go into this church, and Nerea wants to visit that museum in the next street. I want to walk to that tower outside the village.
Este hombre es mi marido, ese señor a tu lado es su padre y aquellos niños jugando afuera son nuestros hijos.	This man is my husband. That man next to you is his father. Those children playing outside are our children.
No toques esta pluma, es mía. Ese lápiz es tuyo, o puedes buscar aquellos colores que te compró mamá ayer.	Don't touch this pen. It's mine. That pencil is yours. Or you can look for those crayons that Mommy bought you yesterday.

What is a demonstrative pronoun?

Now we're done with adjectives, let's look at pronouns. As we said earlier, demonstratives demonstrate which thing someone is talking about. Pronouns are words that replace nouns. So basically, a demonstrative pronoun is a word that you use instead of a noun, and it specifies which noun you're referring to.

Demonstrative pronouns are useful when we don't have to give as much context. If we already know we're talking about cars, we don't need to say 'this car' and 'that car.' Instead, we can just say 'this one' and 'that one.'

So, the Spanish demonstrative pronouns are these:

Listen to Track 184

este	this one (masculine)
esta	this one (feminine)
estos	these ones (masculine plural)
estas	these ones (feminine plural)
ese	that one (masculine)
esa	that one (feminine)
esos	those ones (masculine plural)
esas	those ones (feminine plural)
aquel	that one over there (masculine)
aquella	that one over there (feminine)
aquellos	those ones over there (masculine plural)
aquellas	those ones over there (feminine plural)

An important note on spelling...

Until recently, demonstrative pronouns (except the neuter ones, mentioned below) had an accent on them. This was to differentiate between demonstrative adjectives and demonstrative pronouns, and you used to have to remember which ones took accents. It looked something like this:

Me gusta esta casa. (I like this house.) vs. *Me gusta ésta.* (I like this one.)

Aquel gato es mío. (That cat is mine.) vs. *Aquél es mío.* (That one is mine.)

It's good for you to be aware of this, because a heap of what you read will still use the old rules. But what's the new rule? <u>Leave out the accents altogether</u>!

How they work

Because they're pronouns, they're used to replace nouns. The demonstrative pronoun that you choose has to agree in gender and number with the noun it's replacing. And don't forget to differentiate between 'that' and 'that over there'!

Demonstrative pronouns are a little different from demonstrative adjectives, because, as well as masculine and feminine forms, you have a kind of genderless form, called the 'neuter' form.

It's used when we're not referring to a particular noun. It can be used to refer to ideas, statements, or sometimes objects, but not living things (if we're talking about a person or animal, we need to figure out its gender and use the corresponding masculine or feminine pronoun).

The neuter ones:

Listen to Track 185

esto	this
eso	that
aquello	that (more distant)

Examples

Look through these sentences and see if they make sense!

Este es mi coche.	This one is my car.
Dame otra pluma. Esta no escribe.	Give me another pen. This one doesn't work.
Esta es mi falda favorita.	This skirt is my favorite one.
En una oficina como esta, hay que trabajar duro.	In an office like this one, you have to work hard.
Estos dos son los míos.	These two are my ones (mine).
A ver si estos funcionan.	Let's see if these ones work.
Estas son mejores que aquellas.	These ones are better than those ones over there.
Me encantaría tener calificaciones como estas.	I'd love to have grades like these ones.
(NEUTER) Esto me hace feliz.	This (situation/environment) makes me happy.
(NEUTER) ¿Quién ha hecho esto?	Who's done this?

Ese es mejor que este.	That one is better than this one.
No me gusta este hombre. Prefiero ese.	I don't like this man. I prefer that one.
Esa es la mía.	That one is my one.
No quiero esta vela. Quiero esa, la rosa.	I don't want this candle. I want that one, the pink one.
Esos son los mejores.	Those ones are the best.
Nos gustan estos libros, pero nos gustan también esos.	We like these books, but we also like those ones.
Esas sí que son valientes.	Now those ones—they're brave.
¿Que cuáles flores me gustan? ¡Me encantan esas!	Which flowers do I like? I love those ones!
(NEUTER) ¡Eso es, campeón! ¡Muy bien!	That's it, buddy! Well done!
(NEUTER) Quiero que pare todo eso.	I want all that to stop.

Aquel sería el mejor.	That one over there would be the best one.
No me gusta este traje. Voy a comprar aquel.	I don't like this suit. I'm going to buy that one over there.
Aquella fue la época más violenta.	That was the most violent era.
¿Cuál? —Aquella.	Which one? —That one.
Aquellos son tuyos. Esos son míos.	Those ones over there are yours. Those ones (a bit closer) are mine.

¿Aquellos son tus zapatos?	Are those ones your shoes?
Aquellas viven fuera de la ciudad.	Those ones live outside the city.
Mis películas favoritas son aquellas con actores poco conocidos.	My favorite movies are those with unknown actors.
(NEUTER) Aquello es lo que te espera.	That's what awaits you.
(NEUTER) No me meto en todo aquello.	I'm not getting involved in all that.

¡Muy bien!

Hopefully this lesson has shown you the difference between adjectives and pronouns and taught you how to use the demonstrative forms of each. Try and spot them when you're reading in Spanish and think about whether you think they're adjectives or pronouns.

Workbook Lesson 18: Adjetivos demostrativos y Pronombres Demostrativos – Demonstrative Adjectives and Demonstrative Pronouns

Exercise 1: Complete the phrases with demonstrative pronouns.

1- _____ chica es amiga de Ana. (That girl is Ana's friend.)

2- _____ zapatos son muy caros. (These shoes are very expensive.)

3- _____ es Juan, mi novio. (This is John, my boyfriend.)

4- ¿De quién es _____? (Whose is that?)

Exercise 2: Translate the following phrases from Spanish to English.

1- estas llaves

2- aquella maleta

3- esa revista

4- este verano

5- este es tu paraguas

Exercise 3: Complete the sentences, as in the example.

Example: ¿De quién es ___ libro?: – ¿De quién es este libro? (Whose book is this?)

1- Me gusta mucho _____ amionant. (I really like this restaurant.)

2- ___ vaso está sucio. (This glass is dirty.)

3- ¿Conoces a ___ chico? (You know this guy?)

4- Mira, ___ es el padre de Carlos. (Look, that's Charles's father)

5- ¿A dónde va ___ amion? (Where does this bus go?)

Exercise 4: Tick the right answer.

1- _____ verano vamos a ir a París.

  a. Este   b. Estos

2- Nací en 1989. _____ mismo año nació mi primo.

  a. Ese   b. Este

3- ¿Qué haces _____ noche?

  a. esa   b. esta

4- _____ mes ha sido fabuloso.

  a. Este   b. Aquel

5- _____ tarde tengo un examen.

  a. Esta   b. Esa

Exercise 5: Complete sentences as in the example. Use the following demonstratives: << este, estos, eso, esos, aquellos >>.

1- Mi amigo Juan dice que ___ bar es el mejor de la ciudad. (My friend Juan says this bar is the best in the city.)

2- ¿Ustedes conocen a _____ chicas? Son hermosas. (You know those girls? They are beautiful.)

3- ___ es la casa de Ramón, la blanca. (That's Ramon's house, the white one.)

4- ¿Cuánto cuesta ___ moto? (How much is this bike?)

5- ____ día llovió sin parar. (That day it rained non-stop.)

Exercise 6: Translate the following sentences from English to Spanish.

1- Give me those papers, please.

2- Do you like that lamp for the house?

3- How much is this computer?

4- Where do I put this picture?

5- That's not what I said.

Exercise 7: Sort the following words to create a correct sentence.

1- Compañía / esta / es / muy segura. (This company is very safe.)

2- Relojes / estos/ son / muy baratos. (These watches are very cheap.)

3- Raqueta / cuánto / cuesta/ esta? (How much is this racket?)

4- Dame / plato/ ese / de allí. (Give me that plate over there.)

5- Jardín / no entres/ este / es privado. (Do not enter, this garden is private.)

Exercise 8: Change these affirmative sentences into negative ones.

1- Aquel perro está jugando con su dueño. (That dog is playing with his master.)

2- Esa azafata es rubia. (That stewardess is blonde.)

3- Eso es cierto. (That is true.)

4- Esta silla es muy cómoda. (This chair is very comfortable.)

5- Necesitan unos pantalones de mezclilla como estos. (They need jeans like these.)

Exercise 9: Complete the following dialogue with the corresponding demonstrative pronouns.

___ es mi familia. Mi madre se llama Rebeca y mi papá Alberto. Tengo dos hermanos. ___ que está sentado se llama David, y el que ____ jugando es el menor, Pedro. ____ que están en el jardín son mis primos Diego y Camila. ____ que están en el patio son nuestros perros, Lancer y Claudio. Bueno, ____ es toda mi familia. ¡Que tengas un buen día!

(This is my family. My mother's name is Rebecca and my dad is Alberto. I have two brothers. The one sitting here is called David. And that one playing is the younger one, Peter. Those in the garden are my cousins, Diego and Camila. Those in the yard are our dogs, Lancer and Claudio. Well this is my whole family. Have a good day!)

Exercise 10: Translate the following sentences from Spanish to English.

1- Estas camisas cuestan 30 dólares.

2- ¿Cómo está esa pizza? Deliciosa.

3- ¿Hay alguien en esa casa?

4- ¿Quieres algo de aquella tienda?

5- Esas son las nuevas estudiantes.

ANSWERS:

Exercise 1

1/ Esa chica es amiga de Ana. 2/ Estos zapatos son muy caros. 3/ Este es Juan, mi novio. 4/ ¿De quién es eso?

Exercise 2

1/ these keys 2/ that suitcase 3/ that magazine 4/ this summer 5/ this is your umbrella

Exercise 3

1/ Me gusta mucho este restaurante. 2/ Este vaso está sucio. 3/ ¿Conoces a ese chico? 4/ Mira, ese es el padre de Carlos. 5/ ¿A dónde va este camión?

Exercise 4

1/ Este verano vamos a ir a París. 2/ Nací en 1989. Ese mismo año nació mi primo. 3/ ¿Qué haces esta noche? 4/ Este mes ha sido fabuloso. 5/ Esta tarde tengo un examen.

Exercise 5

1/ Mi amigo Juan dice que este bar es el mejor de la ciudad. 2/ ¿Ustedes conocen a esas chicas? Son hermosas. 3/ Esa es la casa de Ramón, la blanca. 4/ ¿Cuánto cuesta esta moto? 5/ Aquel día llovió sin parar.

Exercise 6

1/ Dame esos papeles, por favour. 2/ ¿Te gusta esa lámpara para la casa? 3/ ¿Cuánto cuesta esta computadora? 4/ ¿Dónde pongo este cuadro? 5/ Eso no es lo que yo dije.

Exercise 7

1/ Esta compañía es muy segura. 2/ Estos relojes son muy baratos. 3/ ¿Cuánto cuesta esta raqueta? 4/ Dame ese plato de allí. 5/ No entres, este jardín es privado.

Exercise 8

1/ Aquel perro no está jugando con su dueño. 2/ Esa azafata no es rubia. 3/ Eso no es cierto. 4/ Esta silla no es muy cómoda. 5/ No necesitan unos pantalones de mezclilla como estos.

Exercise 9

Esta es mi familia. Mi madre se llama Rebeca y mi papá Alberto. Tengo dos hermanos. Ese que está sentado se llama David y el que está jugando es el menor, Pedro. Aquellos que están en el jardín son mis primos Diego y Camila. Esos que están en el patio son nuestros perros, Lancer y Claudio. Bueno, esta es toda mi familia. ¡Que tengas un buen día!

Exercise 10

1/ These shirts cost $30. 2/ How is that pizza? Delicious. 3/ Is anyone in that house? 4/ Do you want anything from that store? 5/ Those are the new students.

Lesson 19. Making Comparisons

In this lesson, we'll look at comparatives and superlatives, and some handy phrases that can be slipped into conversation or writing!

A comparative compares two things, while a superlative describes something to the highest possible degree.

For Example:

Adjective	Comparative	Superlative
Bright	Brighter	Brightest
Happy	Happier	Happiest
Expensive	More expensive	Most expensive

Comparatives

Let's start with comparatives—those are the words which often end in –er in English. We need to know how to say that A is 'more + adjective' or 'less + adjective' than B. The formula is pretty simple. The words for 'more' and 'less' are these:

More	*Más*
Less	*Menos*

All you have to do is stick *más* or *menos* before the adjective (that's the word which describes a noun), then add *que*, meaning 'than.' Let's look at some examples:

Listen to Track 186

Maria is more elegant than Juan.	*María es más elegante que Juan.*
Ana is less greedy than Ignacio.	*Ana es menos golosa que Ignacio.*
Your mental health is more important than this exam.	*Tu salud mental es más importante que este examen.*
The UK is less humid than Thailand.	*El Reino Unido es menos húmedo que Tailandia.*
The book is funnier (more funny) than the film.	*El libro es más gracioso que la película.*
Jorge is less grumpy than his twin brother.	*Jorge es menos gruñón que su gemelo.*

This formula also works for adverbs (words which describe verbs), as you can see here:

Marta fights more bravely than her brother.	*Marta lucha más valientemente que su hermano.*
Today, they spoke less confidently than yesterday.	*Hoy hablaron menos confiadamente que ayer.*

Superlatives

Superlatives allow us to say that something is 'the most + adjective' or 'the least + adjective.' All you have to do is add *el/la/los/las* before *más* or *menos*. You choose whichever one matches the noun and remember to make sure the adjective also agrees with the noun. Some examples will make it clearer.

Listen to Track 187

Jason is the funniest (the most funny).	Jason es el más gracioso.
Caitlyn is the least tall.	Caitlyn es la menos alta.
My shoes are the shiniest.	Mis zapatos son los más brillantes.
My female cousins are the least annoying.	Mis primas son las menos molestas.

Top tip: to make something plural, you'll need to add –s or –es.

Irregular Stuff

As usual, you won't get away with learning Spanish without learning exceptions to the rules! There aren't too many to learn, but they are really common, so it's worth taking time to practice them.

Don't forget, we have these irregularities in English, too! You wouldn't describe something as 'gooder' or 'badder' than something else, you'd say 'better' or 'worse.' The same kinds of words are irregular in Spanish.

Listen to Track 188

Good (/well*)	Bueno/a (/bien*)
Better	Mejor
Best	El/la mejor

Bad (/badly*)	Malo/a (/mal*)
Worse	Peor
Worst	El/la peor

*As well as adjectives, you may want to use comparatives and superlatives with adverbs. It's the difference between "you did a good job" and "you did the job well."

Big (in the sense of 'old,' e.g. when talking about siblings)	Grande
Bigger (older)	Mayor
Biggest (oldest)	El/la mayor

Small (in the sense of 'young,' e.g. when talking about siblings)	Pequeño/a
Smaller (younger)	Menor
Smallest (youngest)	El/la menor

Más de/Menos de

Listen to Track 189

So far, we've looked at *más* and *menos* with *que*. There are some occasions when you'll need to use *más de* or *menos de*. This is for when you're using numbers or quantities.

| There will be more than 30 people. | Habrá más de 30 personas. |
| There will be fewer than 30 chairs. | Habrá menos de 30 sillas. |

Phrases that use comparatives

There are several phrases that are super useful to know, and they all involve some form of comparison. Let's take a look:

Listen to Track 190

As ... as ...	Tan ... como ...
Victoria is as kind as Nacho.	Victoria es tan amable como Nacho.

The more ... , the more ...	Cuanto más ... , más ...
The more I work, the more money I earn.	Cuanto más trabajo, más dinero gano.

More and more	Cada vez más
I'm getting more and more excited.	Me pongo cada vez más emocionada.

As ... as possible	Lo más ... posible
Dress as smartly as possible.	Vístase lo más arreglado posible.

More than anything (mainly)	Más que nada
I mainly like rock music.	Más que nada, me gusta la música rock.

More or less	Más o menos
- How old are you? Like 40?	- ¿Cuántos años tienes? ¿40 o así?
- Haha, more or less!	- ¡Jaja*, más o menos!

*This is legit for how Spanish speakers write 'haha,' which makes sense, because the Spanish 'j' sound is quite like the English 'h' sound! Jajaja.

What a	¡Qué ... tan ...!
What a beautiful dog!	¡Qué perro tan bonito!

To go from bad to worse	Ir de mal en peor
The situation has gone from bad to worse.	La situación ha ido de mal en peor

To go from bad to worse / from the fire into the frying pan	Salir de Guatemala para entrar en Guatepeor
You're going from bad to worse with your grades!	¡Con estas notas, sales de Guatemala para entrar en Guatepeor!

Quiz time!

What ~better~ way to finish off than to have a little practice?! Use the lesson above to help you translate the following sentences from Spanish into English. If you're feeling daring, try and translate the English phrases into Spanish, too!

In case you need it, this glossary has some of the words used in the context of the quiz!

Listen to Track 191

there is/there are	hay
adults	los adultos

children	los niños
I have	tengo
money	dinero
than you	que tú
dances	baila
skillfully	habilidosamente
I go out	salgo
frequently/frequency	frecuentemente/frecuencia
brave	valiente
selfish	egoísta
but	pero
husband	marido/esposo
was	fue
a day	un día
I sing	yo canto
than her	que ella
my brother	mi hermano
than me	que yo
I want	quiero
to see you	verte
I saw	vi
cars	coches/carros
stubborn	terco/a
your dad	tu papá
house	la casa
ready	listo/a
exam	examen

1. *Tengo menos dinero que tú.*

2. *Carolina baila más habilidosamente que Juana.*

3. *Salgo menos frecuencia que mi gemelo.*

4. *Clara es la más valiente.*

5. *Miguel es el menos egoísta.*

6. *Soy una persona buena, pero mi marido es mejor.*

7. *Ayer fue un día malo. Hoy fue peor.*

8. *Yo canto mejor que ella.*

9. *Mi hermano es mayor que yo.*

10. *Más que otra cosa, quiero verte.*

11. *Vi más de 150 coches.*

12. *Juanca es menor que yo.*

13. Eres tan terco como tu papá.

14. Se pone cada vez más y más difícil.

15. La casa está más o menos lista.

16. ¡Qué examen tan más difícil!

BONUS QUESTIONS:

1. Pedro dances more often than Laura.

2. I want to spend as much as possible.

3. Cristina is more important than him.

4. I understand Spanish better

Well done for getting through the quiz; there were some tough ones in there!

Here are the answers to the quiz:

1. I have less money than you.

2. Carolina dances more skillfully than Juana.

3. I go out less frequently than my twin.

4. Clara is the bravest.

5. Miguel is the least selfish.

6. I am a good person, but my husband is better.

7. Yesterday was a bad day. Today was worse.

8. I sing better than her.

9. My brother is older than me.

10. More than anything else, I want to see you.

11. I saw more than 150 cars.

12. Juanca is younger than me.

13. You're as stubborn as your dad.

14. It gets more and more difficult.

15. The house is more or less ready.

16. What a difficult exam!

17. Pedro baila más seguido que Laura.

18. Quiero gastar lo más posible.

19. Cristina es más importante que él.

20. Entiendo mejor el español.

Hopefully this has given you a solid basis for making comparisons in Spanish. Remember to make a daily learning habit—practice a little every day, and you should see your Spanish going *de bien en mejor*!

Workbook Lesson 19: Hacer comparaciones

– **Making Comparisons**

Exercise 1: Complete the sentences with comparative adjectives.

1- Mis hermanas son _____ (+ alto) que yo. (My sisters are taller than me.)

2- Yo bailo (+ bueno)_____ que ella. (I dance better than her)

3- ¿Que país está (- poblado)___ que la India? (Which country is less populated than India?)

4- ¿Qué es (- malo) _____, estar enfermo o sin dinero? (What is worse, to be sick or without money?)

5- ¿Qué deporte es (- peligroso) _____ , el esquí o el alpinismo? (Which sport is less dangerous, skiing or mountaineering?)

Exercise 2: Translate the following phrases from Spanish to English.

1- la más inteligente

2- el más gordo

3- el más potente

4- el menos viejo

5- el menos caro

Exercise 3: Complete the sentences, as in the example: << viejo, caro, rápido, potente, largo>>

Example: Camilo mide 1,67, Pedro mide 1,70 (alto): Pedro es más alto que Camilo

1- Luisa tiene 19 años, María tiene 24 años: María es ___ _____ que Luisa. (Louisa is 19 years old, Mary is 24 years old: Mary is older than Louisa.)

2- Fresas 20 pesos el kilo, peras 15 pesos el kilo: las fresas son ___ _____ que las peras. (Strawberries 20 pesos per kilo, pears 15 pesos per kilo: strawberries are more expensive than pears.)

3- León 80 k/h, canguro 50 k/h: el león es _____ _____ que el canguro. (Lion 80 k / h, kangaroo 50 k / h: the lion is faster than kangaroo)

4- Río Amazonas 6788 km, Río Danubio 2800 km: el río Amazonas es ___ ___ que el Danubio. (Amazon river 6788 km, Danube river 2800 km: the Amazon River is longer than the Danube.)

5- Toshiba 200 GB, Apple 300 GB: Apple es ___ _____ que Toshiba. (Toshiba 200 GB, Apple 300 GB: Apple is more powerful than Toshiba.)

Exercise 4: Tick the right answer.

1- Soy más fuerte _____ tú.

   a. que   b. quien

2- Este departamento es muy _____.

   a. antiguo   b. antigua

3- Esta casa es muy _____.

   a. baratas   b. barata

4- Esta falda es muy _____.

   a. corto   b. corta

5- Este libro es aburrido, prefiero uno _____ _____.

   a. menos entretenido   b. más entretenido

Exercise 5: Complete the sentences. Use the following demonstratives: << tan, igual de >>.

1- Ana y María son _____ de altas. (Ana and Mary are equally tal.)

2- Margarita y Pedro son _____ de inteligentes. (Margaret and Peter are just as intelligent.)

3- Soy _____ alto como tú. (I am as tall as you.)

4- Sofía es simpática, pero Loli es _____ de simpática. (Sofia is nice, but Loli is just as nice.)

5- Sus hermanos no son _____ trabajadores. (His brothers are not as hardworking.)

Exercise 6: Translate the following sentences from English to Spanish to.

1- My mother is younger than my father.

2- What's the best movie you've ever seen?

3- Clara's hair clearly is not as long as Claudia's.

4- Elon Musk is as smart as Bill Gates.

5- This show is not so entertaining.

Exercise 7: Sort the following words to create a correct sentence.

1- La más alta / Carla / es / de sus hermanas. (Carla is the tallest of her sisters.)

2- Los mas cómodos / los/ son / mis zapatos. (My shoes are the most comfortable.)

3- De su familia/ Soraya/ Es / la más cariñosa. (Soraya is the most loving of her family.)

4- Las mejores / de la ciudad/ son / estas naranjas. (These oranges are the best in town.)

5- El peor/ libro/ que he/ leído / este es. (This is the worst book I've ever read.)

Exercise 8: Change these affirmative sentences into negative ones.

1- Este televisor es el más caro. (This TV is the most expensive.)

2- Laura es la más bajita/chaparra. (Laura is the shortest.)

3- El Nilo es el río más largo del mundo. (The Nile is the longest river in the world.)

4- Esta bebida es la más refrescante. (This drink is the most refreshing.)

5- Dormir es lo mejor para descansar. (Sleeping is the best way to rest.)

Exercise 9: Change these sentences, like in the example.

Pedro (chico + simpático): Pedro es el chico más simpático.

1- Julia (chica + alegre)_____ . (Julia is the happiest girl.)

2- Regina (reloj + caro)_____ . (Regina is the most expensive watch.)

3- Para mí, el café de Colombia (+ bueno)_____del mundo. (For me, Colombian coffee is the best in the world.)

4- ¿Cuál es el país (+ interesante) _____ que has visitado? (Which is the most interesting country you've ever visited?)

5- El día de mi boda fue el (+ feliz) _____ de mi vida. (My wedding day was the happiest day of my life.)

Exercise 10: Complete these phrases with comparatives.

1- Mi perro es _____(+ grande) que el tuyo. (My dog is bigger than yours.)

2- Emilio no bebe ni fuma, dice que es (+ sano)_____ para él. (Emilio does not drink or smoke, he says it is healthier for him.)

3- ¿Viajar a China es (+ económico) ____ que viajar a Japón? (Is traveling to China cheaper than traveling to Japan?)

4- ¿Cuál es la ciudad (- contaminado) _____ de América Latina? (Which is the least polluted city in Latin America?)

5- ¿Qué país es el (- poblado) _____ del mundo? (Which country is the least populated in the world?)

ANSWERS:

Exercise 1

1/ más altas 2/ mejor 3/ menos poblado 4/ peor 5/ menos peligroso

Exercise 2

1/ The smartest 2/ The fattest 3/ The most powerful 4/ The least old 5/ The least expensive

Exercise 3

1/ más vieja/grande 2/ más caras 3/ más rápido 4/ más largo 5/ más potente

Exercise 4

1/ que 2/ antiguo 3/ barata 4/ corta 5/ más entretenido

Exercise 5

1/ Ana y María son igual de altas. 2/ Margarita y Pedro son igual de inteligentes. 3/ Soy tan alto como tú. 4/ Sofía es simpática, pero Loli es igual de simpática. 5/ Sus hermanos no son tan trabajadores.

Exercise 6

1/ Mi madre es más joven que mi padre. 2/ ¿Cuál es la mejor película que has visto? 3/ Claramente, el cabello de Clara no es tan largo como el de Claudia. 4/ Elon Musk es tan inteligente como Bill Gates. 5/ Este espectáculo no es tan entretenido.

Exercise 7

1/ Carla es la más alta de sus hermanas. 2/ Mis zapatos son los más cómodos. 3/ Soraya es la más cariñosa de su familia. 4/ Estas naranjas son las mejores de la ciudad. 5/ Este es el peor libro que he leído.

Exercise 8

1/ Este televisor no es el más caro. 2/ Laura no es la más bajita/chaparra. 3/ El Nilo no es el río más largo del mundo. 4/ Esta bebida no es la más refrescante. 5/ Dormir no es lo mejor para descansar.

Exercise 9

1/ Julia es la chica más alegre. 2/ Regina es el reloj más caro. 3/ Para mí, el café de Colombia es el mejor del mundo. 4/ ¿Cuál es el país más interesante que has visitado? 5/ El día de mi boda fue el más feliz de mi vida.

Exercise 10

1/ Mi perro es más grande que el tuyo. 2/ Emilio no bebe ni fuma, dice que es más sano para él. 3/ ¿Viajar a China es más económico que viajar a Japón? 4/ ¿Cuál es la ciudad menos contaminada de América Latina? 5/ ¿Qué país es el menos poblado del mundo?

Lesson 20. Direct and Indirect Object Pronouns

You might have seen little words in Spanish like *me, te, lo, nos*, etc. These words are called object pronouns (*los pronombres personales de complemento*) which can be split into three types:

- direct
- indirect
- reflexive

In this lesson, we aim to show you how to use direct and indirect object pronouns, and not to confuse them with reflexive ones!

To make things clearer, we've color-coded things for you!

Key:

Scarlet: Subject

Dark green: Direct Object

Indigo: Indirect Object

Spanish Direct Object Pronouns

Direct object pronouns are used to refer to the object of the sentence, i.e. the thing that's having something done to it. For example, the direct object in this example is 'the car':

- David admires the car.

This can be translated as:

- *David admira el coche.*

But sometimes we don't want to keep repeating 'the car'—we prefer to say 'it.'

- David admires it.
- *David lo admira.*

In this case, *lo* is the direct object pronoun.

Table

This table shows you all the direct object pronouns, as you might want to say that David washes me, you, him, her, us, you, them, etc.

me	*Me*	us	*nos*
you (informal)	*Te*	you (plural)	*los/las*
him/it/you (formal)	*Lo*	them (formal masc.)	*los*
her/it/you (formal)	*La*	them (formal fem.)	*las*

All you have to do is find your subject and your verb, and ask **who** or **what** is being ~verbed~ by David.

Who/what is David admiring?

Listen to Track 192

Who/What is being admired by David?

David admires me.	*David me admira.*	→	¿A quién admira David?	*A mí*
David admires you.	*David te admira.*	→	¿A quién admira David?	*A ti*
David admires Moorish architecture.	*David la admira.*	→	¿Qué admira David?	*La arquitectura mora.*
David admires us.	*David nos admira.*	→	¿A quién admira David?	*A nosotros.*
David admires you all.	*David los admira.*	→	¿A quién admira David?	*A todos ustedes*
David admires the trees.	*David los admira.*	→	¿Qué admira David?	*Los árboles.*

Spanish Indirect Object Pronouns

In contrast, **in**direct object pronouns are when you do something **to** someone or something. For example, the direct object here is the gift (*el regalo*) and the **indirect** object is Irina.

- José gives the gift **to** Irina.

This can be translated as:

- *José da el regalo **a** Irina.*

Sometimes, if we know for a fact that the interaction is between José and Irina, we'll quit repeating her name.

- José gives the gift to her/José gives her the gift.
- *José le da el regalo.*

Check out this table. It shows you all the indirect object pronouns, as you might want to say that José gives the gift to me, to you, to him, to her, to us, to you, to them, etc.

me	*Me*	us	*nos*
you (informal)	*Te*	you (plural)	*les*
him/it/you (formal)	*Le*	them/you (formal masc.)	*les*
her/it/you (formal)	*Le*	them/you (formal fem.)	*les*

All you have to do is find **who** or **what** is on the receiving end of the verb.

Who is José giving the gift **to**? In other words, **who** is receiving the gift?

Listen to Track 193

Who is receiving the gift?

José gives the gift to me.	*José me da el regalo.*	→	*¿ A quién le da José el regalo?*	A mí
José gives the gift to you.	*José te da el regalo.*	→	*¿ A quién le da José el regalo?*	A ti
José gives the gift to him/her/you (formal).	*José le da el regalo.*	→	*¿ A quién le da José el regalo?*	A él / a ella / a usted.

José gives the gift to us.	*José nos da* el regalo.	→	*¿ A quiénes les da José* el regalo?	A nosotros
José gives the gift to you (plural).	*José les da* el regalo.	→	*¿ A quiénes les da José* el regalo?	A ustedes
José gives the gift to them	*José les da* el regalo.	→	*¿ A quiénes les da José* el regalo?	A ellos / a ellas.

This is how the verb *gustar* works! '*Me gusta*' doesn't technically mean 'I like.' It means 'it is pleasing TO me.' There's no direct object in this case.

- I like apples. → Apples please me.
- *Me gustan las manzanas.*
- I like you. → You please me.
- *Me gustas (tú).*
- Do you like me? → Do I please you?
- *¿Te gusto (yo)?*

FYI: it doesn't sound as creepy as 'do I please you?' once you put it in Spanish.)

Difference between direct and indirect object pronouns

Sometimes it can be difficult to identify whether an object is direct or indirect. Think of it like this:

Direct: who/what is being verbed?

Indirect: who/what is that object being verbed TO?

If that's not clear yet, don't worry!

Most of the time, you don't even have to be certain which one you're using. The only ones that differ are *lo/la/los/las* vs. *le/le/les*.

Direct	Indirect
Me	*me*
Te	*te*
lo/la	*le*
Nos	*nos*
Los/las	*les*
los/las	*les*

When *le* becomes *se*

When combining a direct object pronoun and an indirect object pronoun, **the indirect one will come first**. This will lead to instances of *le lo* and *les lo*, or *le la* and *les la*. Although they make logical sense, these are actually wrong.

They're kind of a mouthful to say (try saying '*Laura les la dio*' three times fast) so we change the *le* or *les* to a *se*. This does NOT mean we're dealing with reflexive verbs or anything like that. Just makes it easier to pronounce. Easy peasy!

Listen to Track 194

- Laura gave the fruit to her grandparents.
  - *Laura les dio la fruta a sus abuelos.*
- Laura gave them the fruit.
  - *Laura les dio la fruta.*
- Laura gave them it.
  - *Laura ~~les~~ la dio. → Laura se la dio.*

Order

As you know, word order in Spanish can be different from how it is in English. There are a few rules when it comes to word order of pronouns in different situations.

Order of a Spanish direct object pronoun and indirect object pronoun

If you've got one of each, stick the indirect one first.

Listen to Track 195

- Pablo gave the flowers to Carolina.
  - *Pablo le dio las flores a Carolina.*
- Pablo gave them to her.
  - *Pablo ~~le~~ las dio → Pablo se las dio.*

Order with infinitives—either before or after

You can whack object pronouns straight onto the ends of infinitives.

Listen to Track 196

- I want to donate the money.
  - *Quiero donar el dinero.*
- I want to donate it.
  - *Quiero donarlo.*
- I want to donate it to the homeless lady.
  - *Quiero donarlo a la señora sin casa.*
- I want to donate it to her.
  - *Quiero donár~~te~~lo. → Quiero donárselo.*

But you have other options, too! You can stick them before the infinitive and the verb that triggers the infinitive.

- I want to donate the money.
  - *Quiero donar el dinero.*
- I want to donate it.
  - *Lo quiero donar.*

- I want to donate it to the homeless lady.
  - › *Lo quiero donar a la señora sin casa.*
- I want to donate it to her.
  - › ~~*Le*~~ *lo quiero donar.* → *Se lo quiero donar.*

Order with the gerund

This works the same as it does with the infinitive. You can choose where to put the object pronoun(s).

Listen to Track 197

- I'm sending the email to you.
  - › *Estoy enviandote el correo electrónico.*
- I'm sending it to you.
  - › *Te lo estoy enviando.* (Pronouns at the beginning)
  - › *Estoy enviándotelo.* (Pronouns at the end)

Order with the present tense

With the present tense, both direct and indirect object pronouns go before the verb (the indirect comes first).

Listen to Track 198

- Marina sends the letters to me.
  - › *Marina me envía las cartas a mí.*
- Marina sends me the letters.
  - › *Marina me envía las cartas.*
- Marina sends me them.
  - › *Marina me las envía.*

Order with the perfect tense

The same rule applies to the perfect tense—indirect then direct then verbs!

Listen to Track 199

- Carlos has told the story to his friends.
  - › *Carlos ha contado la historia a sus amigos.*
- Carlos has told them the story.
  - › *Carlos les ha contado la historia.*
- Carlos has told it to them.
  - › *Carlos ~~les~~ la ha contado.* → *Carlos se las ha contado.*

Order with the preterite

The rule is the same again for this version of the past tense!

Listen to Track 200

- Enrique sold the shoes to you.
  - › *Enrique **te vendió** los zapatos **a ti**.*
- Enrique sold you the shoes.
  - › *Enrique **te vendió** los zapatos.*
- Enrique sold you them.
  - › *Enrique **te los vendió**.*

Order with future

You won't believe your luck ... same rule again.

Listen to Track 201

- We'll sing the song to her.
  - › *Le cantaremos la canción a ella.*
- We'll sing her the song.
  - › *Le cantaremos la canción.*
- We'll sing it to her.
  - › *~~Le~~ la cantaremos. → Se la cantaremos.*

Order with affirmative imperatives

When you're telling someone to do something, just stick the object pronouns on the end of the verb. Indirect then direct.

Listen to Track 202

- Bring the food to me.
  - › *Tráeme la comida a mí.*
- Bring me the food.
  - › *Tráeme la comida.*
- Bring it to me.
  - › *Tráemela.*

Order with negative imperatives

When you have to tell someone NOT to do something, the object pronouns go between the *no* and the verb.

Listen to Track 203

- Don't bring the food to me.
  - › *No me traigas la comida a mí.*
- Don't bring me the food.
  - › *No me traigas la comida.*
- Don't bring it to me.
  - › *No me la traigas.*

Don't confuse them with reflexive pronouns!

Reflexive pronouns are tiny words which look very similar to object pronouns, so try not to get them confused. Reflexive pronouns tell us a verb is reflexive, i.e. it's something that you do to yourself, e.g. *lavarse las manos* (to wash one's own hands). They are:

Listen to Track 204

me	nos
te	os
se	se

When a reflexive pronoun is thrown into the mix, just make sure you put it before any object pronouns.

Here's an example. We put it before the direct object pronoun:

- I wash my hands.
  - › *Me lavo las manos.*
- I wash them.
  - › *Me las lavo.*

Watch out for *se*, as it could be reflexive OR it could just be the easier-to-pronounce-object-pronoun-combo that we looked at earlier!

We know that's a lot to take in ...

... but we hope this has given you a solid foundation for using direct and indirect object pronouns in all kinds of different situations. *¡Hasta la próxima!*

Workbook Lesson 20. Direct and Indirect Object Pronouns

Exercise 1: Rewrite the following sentences using the correct indirect object pronoun.

1- José le escribió una carta a su mamá.

2- Carolina le ha pedido un favor a María.

3- Jesús le abrió la puerta a su perro.

4- Alejandro trajo comida para ti.

5- El gato le gruñó al niño.

Exercise 2: Rewrite the following sentences using the correct direct object pronoun.

1- Alberto ha comprado un celular (a ti.)

2- Lina escucha a la profesora.

3- Helena tomó las pastillas para el dolor de cabeza.

4- Raquel está haciendo la tarea.

5- Viviana te está enviando el correo electrónico (a ti).

Exercise 3: Complete the following sentences with the correct direct or indirect object pronoun.

1- Yo ___(él) di el libro.

2- Mi mamá ___(ella) lo entregó ayer.

3- Carla ___ (yo) escribió ayer.

4- Ángel ____ (ellos) admira.

5- Valeria _____ (nosotros) odia.

Exercise 4: Complete the following sentences using the correct word, 'les' or 'se'.

1- Laura ____ dio la fruta.

2- Pablo ____ las comió.

3- Javier ____ los probó.

4- Ellos ____ abrieron la puerta.

5- Valentina ____ borró el pizarrón.

Exercise 5: Change the sentence from having the pronoun at the end to having the pronoun at the beginning.

Example: Estoy escribiéndotelo -> Te lo estoy escribiendo.

1- Estoy enviándotelo.

2- Está operándolo.

3- Estamos completándolo.

4- Están comprándolo.

5- Estás moviéndolo.

Exercise 6: Change the sentence from having the pronoun at the end to having the pronoun at the beginning.

Example: Te lo estoy cocinando -> Estoy cocinándotelo.

1- Te lo acabo de enviar.

2- Maria se los está archivando.

3- Claudia y María te lo acaban de decir.

4- Leonardo te está moviendo la ropa.

5- Viviana te lo acaba de pedir.

Exercise 7: Choose the correct option to complete the following sentences.

1- ___ ____ exijo.
  a. Te lo   b. Lo te   c. Acabo de

2- (Ella) ___ ____ piensa quitar mañana.
  a. Se lo   b. Te está   c. Va a

3- Carlos __ __ __(nosotros) premiar por el buen trabajo.
  a. los va   b. nos va a   c. va a

4- _____ escribiéndotelo.
  a. Estoy   b. Acabo   c. Voy a

5- Yo ___ ____ estoy poniendo al perro.
  a. se lo   b. te lo   c. me lo

Exercise 8: Underline the indirect object pronoun in the following the sentences.

1- Mi papá me está manejando las finanzas.

2- Los estudiantes están viéndolo en sus libros.

3- Las mujeres se lo quieren donar.

4- Su novio le trae las galletas.

Exercise 9: Rewrite the following sentences using the indirect object pronoun.

1. Mi hermana va a conducir la camioneta.

2. Los maestros fueron a ver a su director.

3. Las mujeres quieren regalar perfumes a sus amigas.

4. La chica quiere llevar galletas a su novio.

Exercise 10: Rewrite the following sentences using the direct object pronoun.

1- Alejandro va a comérselo. (El helado)

2- Los tripulantes van a hacerlo. (El servicio)

3- Ángela quiere terminarlo. (El libro)

4- La gerente acaba de mencionárnosla. (La política)

ANSWERS:

Exercise 1

1/ José se la escribió. 2/ Carolina se lo ha pedido. 3/ Jesús se la abrió. 4/ Alejandro te la trajo. 5/ El gato le gruñó.

Exercise 2

1/ Alberto te lo ha comprado. 2/ Lina la escucha. 3/ Helena las tomó. 4/ Raquel la está haciendo. 5/ Viviana te lo está enviando.

Exercise 3

1/ Yo le di el libro. 2/ Mi mamá se lo entregó ayer. 3/ Carla me escribió ayer. 4/ Ángel los admira. 5/ Valeria nos odia.

Exercise 4

1/ Les 2/ Se 3/ Se 4/ Les 5/ Les

Exercise 5

1/ Te lo estoy enviando. 2/ Lo está operando. 3/ Nosotros lo estamos completando. 4/ Ellos lo están comprando. 5/ Tú lo estás moviendo.

Exercise 6

1/ Estoy enviándotelo. 2/ Está archivándoselos. 3/ Acaban de decírtelo. 4/ Está moviéndotela. 5/ Acaba de pedírtelo.

Exercise 7

1/ Te lo 2/ Se lo 3/ Nos va a 4/ Estoy 5/ Se lo

Exercise 8

1/ Mi papá me está manejando las finanzas. 2/ Los estudiantes están viéndolo en sus libros. 3/ Las mujeres se lo quieren donar. 4/ Su novio le trae las galletas.

Exercise 9

1/ Mi hermana va a conducirla. 2/ Los maestros fueron a verlo. 3/ Las mujeres quieren regalarles perfumes. 4/ La chica quiere llevarle galletas.

Exercise 10

1/ Alejandro va a comerse el helado. 2/ Los tripulantes van a hacer el servicio. 3/ Ángela quiere terminar el libro. 4/ La gerente acaba de mencionarnos la política.

Lesson 21. Shortcut to Tenses

Spanish tenses can be complicated and cause countless headaches to any learner. While learning the complicated ins and outs of each of the different tenses is necessary to really take your Spanish to a more fluent level, there are a few shortcuts you can use to help you get there!

It is possible to use just three different verbs to express the recent past, the ongoing present, and the near future. If you are able to express these three things, you'll be able to get the conversational ball rolling more easily and gain the confidence you need to dive deeper into the dreaded world of Spanish tenses!

Past Tenses

The past in Spanish is one of the most complicated things for English speakers. Since Spanish actually has—not one, not two but— three ways to refer to things that took place in the past, knowing when to use which one can be very difficult.

Preterite- This is used when the action in the past happened one time or within a specified period of time.

Listen to Track 205

i.e.- I lived in Argentina for six months. *Viví en Argentina durante 6 meses.*

Imperfect- This is used for actions in the past that took place multiple times or during a period of time that isn't specified.

i.e.- He always went to this cafe. *Siempre iba a este café.*

Present Perfect- This conjugation is a combination of the verb *haber* and the past participle of the verb (ending in -ado or -ido). This is the one we've previously called the Perfect tense. Its use differs throughout the Spanish-speaking world and in Mexico is not very common. However, the general rule for using this tense is when the event in the past being referenced still has an impact on the present.

i.e. I have paid the bill- *He pagado la cuenta.*

While the three tenses mentioned above seem relatively cut and dried on the surface, they regularly trip up the non-native Spanish speaker. With practice, though, you'll find yourself becoming more familiar with them.

There is, however, one little shortcut you can use to refer to something that happened in the near past. This is using the verb *acabar*. It's like the English equivalent of saying "just".

Using *acabar* to talk about the near past

To use this verb to talk about the near past you will use the following pattern

Acabar + de + verb in infinitive

This is referring to something that you "just" did, or that was "just" done by someone else. *Acabar* is an -ar verb conjugated regularly.

Listen to Track 206

Yo acabo de

Tú acabas de

Él/ Ella/ Usted acaba de

Nosotros acabamos de

Ustedes acaban de

Ellos/ Ellas/ acaban de

Some examples of this verb used for near past are:

First person singular: *Acabo de leer ese libro.* (I just read that book.)

Second person singular: *Acabas de regresar de la tienda.* (You just came from the store.)

Third person singular: *Acaba de hacer la cena.* (He/she just made dinner.)

First person plural: *Acabamos de comer.* (We just ate.)

Second person plural: *Acaban de volver de vacaciones.* (You (plural) just returned from vacation.)

Third person plural: *Acaban de comprar los boletos.* (They just bought the tickets.)

Future Tenses

Learning to talk about the future in Spanish is pretty easy for the native English speaker. This is simply because, generally speaking, the different options available are similar to their English equivalents.

Using the present- This is used for events that will happen in the near future. To use this conjugation to refer to the future in Spanish, you <u>have</u> to specify the time in which it will happen.

i.e. We leave tomorrow. *Nos vamos mañana*

Future conjugation- This is like saying "will" in English. The use is similar to that of the "will" future in English, although in spoken Spanish it isn't as common.

i.e. I will go to the store later - *Más tarde iré a la tienda.*

The last way that you can use to speak about the future in Spanish is probably the most common, and, conveniently enough, the easiest to learn! This is with the verb *ir*.

Ir a to talk about the future

Using the verb *ir*, meaning to go, to talk about the future is extremely common, especially in everyday, colloquial speech. It's like the English "going to…"

To use this verb, you will use the following pattern:

Ir + a + verb in infinitive

Ir is irregularly conjugated. The conjugations are the following:

Listen to Track 207

Yo voy a

Tú vas a

Él/ Ella/ Usted va a

Nosotros vamos a

Ustedes van a

Ellos/ Ellas van a

Some examples of using these constructions are:

First person singular: *Voy a ir a la fiesta.* (I'm going to go to the party.)

Second person singular: *Vas a tener que estudiar mucho.* (You're going to need to study a lot.)

Third person singular: *Va a comprar el pan.* (He/she is going to buy the bread.)

First person plural: *Vamos a viajar a Grecia.* (We're going to travel to Greece.)

Second person plural: *Van a comer en la casa.* (You (plural) are going to eat at home.)

Third person plural: *Van a sacar al perro.* (They are going to walk the dog.)

The present

Talking about the present in Spanish is pretty easy. The hardest part is simply familiarizing yourself with the conjugations themselves.

The present tense in Spanish is very versatile. It can be used to talk about the simple present, a continuous action taking place in the present, and the future.

Estudio español- I study Spanish.

Leo el libro.- I am reading the book.

Luego te llamo.- I'll call you then.

There is, however, a Spanish equivalent to the English present progressive that can be used to talk about something going on at the current moment. It is very useful to be familiar with it, and it will help you a lot when speaking to a native Spanish speaker!

The Present Progressive in Spanish

The present progressive is, like in English, saying "to be doing X".

It is formed using the verb *estar* and has the following construction:

Estar + verb ending in -ing

The conjugation of the verb *estar* is:

Listen to Track 208

Yo estoy

Tú estás

Él/ Ella/ Usted está

Nosotros estamos

Ustedes están

Ellos/ Ellas están

The -ing ending in Spanish is pretty simple to learn. With *-ar* verbs, you will simply remove the ending and add *-ando*. With *-er/-ir* verbs, you will do the same, but add the ending *-iendo*.

-ar	-er/-ir
Hablar- hablando	Comer- comiendo
Estudiar- estudiando	Vivir- viviendo
Andar- andando	Hacer- haciendo

If you have a stem-changing verb, you will change the appropriate vowel, and add the ending.

e:i	o:u
Decir- diciendo	Dormir- durmiendo
Servir- sirviendo	Poder- pudiendo

And, there are some instances when the spelling needs to change so as not to change the pronunciation:

Caer- Cayendo

Leer- Leyendo

Ir- Yendo

Creer- Creyendo

Some examples of using this construction to talk about events taking place in the present are:

Listen to Track 209

First person singular: *Estoy hablando con mi madre.* (I am talking to my mom.)

Second person singular: *Estás yendo muy despacio.* (You're going very slowly.)

Third person singular: *Está estudiando biología.* (He/she is studying biology.)

First person plural: *Estamos viviendo en Guadalajara.* (We are living in Guadalajara.)

Second person plural: *Están viendo la tele.* (You (plural) are watching TV.)

Third person plural: *Están durmiendo.* (They are sleeping.)

The constructions mentioned above are all commonly used in everyday speech, and are simple, easy-to-remember ways of talking about the (near) past, the future, and the present progressive.

While it is important to learn the different tenses in Spanish in order to take your language to the next level, using the shortcuts taught to you in this lesson will help give you the level of confidence you need to engage in a large variety of conversations.

Workbook Lesson 21. Shortcut to tenses

Exercise 1: Complete the following statements with the correct word conjugation for the pronoun in brackets.

1- (Ella) _____ de terminar la cena.

2- (Ellos)_____ de correr 10 kilómetros.

3- (Yo) _____ a competir en el próximo campeonato.

4- (Él) _____ a terminar el libro mañana.

5- (Ustedes) _____ a comenzar la tarea.

Exercise 2: Complete the following form of the verb in brackets as a tense shortcut, according to the pronoun.

1- (Ella) (vivir) _____ en México en el 2006.

2- (Ellos) (correr) _____ 10 kilómetros todos los domingos.

3- (Yo) (comer) _____ frijoles y arroz a la hora de la comida.

4- (Él) (leer) _____ 'Romeo y Julieta' todos los años

5- (Ustedes) (cocinar) _____ la comida de mañana.

Exercise 3: Use the correct form of the future tense shortcut with the following sentences.

1- (Ir) _____ a Rio de Janeiro el próximo año.

2- (Comprar) _____ un nuevo celular.

3- Más tarde, (Llamar) _____ a mi mamá.

4- (Ver) _____ a mis padres el próximo mes.

5- El próximo año, (Tener) _____ un mejor trabajo.

Exercise 4: Use the correct form of the past tense shortcut with the following sentences.

1- Ayer por la mañana (ir) _____ a una cafetería muy buena.

2- Anoche (salir y tomar) _____ unas copas de vino.

3- Anoche no (dormir) _____ nada.

4- (Completar) _____ la tarea hace un momento.

5- (Trabajar) _____ en esa compañía por 3 años.

Exercise 5: Use the correct form of the present tense shortcut with the following sentences.

1- (Ella) (cepillar) _____ los dientes todos los días.

2- (Él) (entrenar) _____ dos horas al día.

3- (Nosotros) (desayunar) _____ a las 9:00 a.m.

4- (Ellos) (tomar) _____ jugo de naranja en el desayuno.

5- (Yo) (escribir) _____ historias diferentes todas las semanas.

Exercise 6: Use the correct form of the present progressive tense shortcut with the following sentences.

1- (Yo) (hablar) _____ con mi mamá.

2- (Ella) (limpiar)_____ la casa.

3- (Él) (organizar) _____ los zapatos.

4- (Nosotros) (vivir) _____ en Bogotá.

5- (Él) (entrenar) _____ en este momento.

Exercise 7: Identify the correct tense for each sentence.

1- Iré a tomar una siesta.

2- Mi papá come plátano todos los días.

3- Los estudiantes rompieron la silla.

4- Hemos vivido en Colombia por 5 años.

5- El perro está ladrando.

Exercise 8: Decide if the following sentences are correct or incorrect.

1- Acabo de comido una hamburguesa.

2- Voy a terminar mi trabajo mañana.

3- He comer mucho el día de hoy.

4- Mantengamos el secreto.

5- Completaré el trabajo ayer.

Exercise 9: Rewrite the sentences by using 'acabo de' and 'voy a' depending on the case.

1- Me comí una hamburguesa hace un momento.

2- Comeré huevos mañana.

3- Viajo a Orlando el próximo mes.

4- Terminé de limpiar hace un minuto.

5- Llegué hace 30 segundos.

ANSWERS:

Exercise 1

1/ Acaba de terminar la cena. 2/ Acaban de correr 10 kilómetros. 3/ Voy a competir en el próximo campeonato. 4/ Va a terminar el libro mañana. 5/ Van a comenzar la tarea.

Exercise 2

1/ Vivió en México en el 2006. 2/ Corren 10 kilómetros todos los domingos. 3/ Voy a comer/Comeré frijoles y arroz a la hora de la comida. 4/ Lee 'Romeo y Julieta' todos los años. 5/ Cocinarán la comida de mañana.

Exercise 3

1/ Iré 2/ Compraré 3/ Llamaré 4/ Veré 5/ Tendré

Exercise 4

1/ Fui 2/ Salí y tomé 3/ Dormí 4/ He completado/Completé 5/ Trabajé

Exercise 5

1/ Se cepilla 2/ Entrena 3/ Desayunamos 4/ Toman 5/ Escribo

Exercise 6

1/ Estoy hablando 2/ Está limpiando 3/ Está organizando 4/ Estamos viviendo 5/ Está entrenando

Exercise 7

1/ Future tense 2/ Present tense 3/ Past tense 4/ Present perfect tense 5/ Present progressive tense

Exercise 8

1/ Incorrect 2/Correct 3/ Incorrect 4/ Correct 5/ Incorrect

Exercise 9

1/ Acabo de comer una hamburguesa hace un momento. 2/ Voy a comer huevos mañana. 3/ Voy a viajar a Orlando el próximo mes. 4/ Acabo de terminar de limpiar hace un minuto. 5/ Acabo de llegar hace 30 segundos.

Lesson 22. Imperfect tense

The imperfect tense, also known as the *pretérito imperfecto*, is super useful for talking about the past. Luckily, it's not too complicated, either! Read on to learn how it works.

What is it?

The imperfect tense is a type of past tense. It's used to talk about something that used to happen or was happening.

When do I use it?

There are a few ways to use the imperfect tense. Here are the main ones:

Describing continuing states/events/feelings in the past

Let's say you're telling a story set in the past, and you want to describe the weather, someone's actions, and their mood:

Listen to Track 210

Llovía mucho y Claudia lloraba. Estaba triste porque tenía el corazón roto.

(It was raining a lot, and Claudia was crying. She was sad because she had a broken heart.)

Talking about repeated actions in the past

This is when you want to talk about something that used to happen, like something you used to do when you were younger, or something that used to happen over a period of time:

Listen to Track 211

Cuando era pequeño, iba al parque cada semana.

(When I was little, I went to the park every week.)

Setting the scene of what was happening when something else interrupted it

This one is really useful when you're telling a story where an event occurs (preterite), and it interrupts another ongoing event or situation (imperfect).

Listen to Track 212

Mientras estudiaba, mi perro entró en mi cuarto y me distrajo.

(While I was studying, my dog came into my room and distracted me.)

When you're using the imperfect in this way, you might want to use it with the gerund. You'd use the imperfect progressive (*estar* + gerund) for the action that was ongoing, and the preterite for the interrupting verb:

Estaba viendo la tele cuando, de repente, sonó el teléfono.

(He was watching TV when, all of a sudden, the phone rang.)

When using reported speech

Sometimes, you want to report what someone else said, but you don't want to use a direct quote. Here's the difference:

Direct speech: Carlos said, "I'm happy."

Indirect/reported speech: Carlos said that he was happy.

Notice that we use "was" in the past tense. This would be the same in Spanish.

Direct speech: *Carlos dijo: «Estoy feliz»*.

Indirect/reported speech: *Carlos dijo que estaba feliz.*

How do I form it?

The imperfect tense is pretty simple to form.

For *-ar* verbs, you remove the ending (*-ar*) from the infinitive, then add the following endings to the stem:

yo	-aba	nosotros/as	-ábamos
tú	-abas	ustedes	-aban
él/ella/usted	-aba	ellos/ellas	-aban

Check out these example sentences to help give you a feel of when this tense is used:

Listen to Track 213

Yo salía mucho cuando era más joven.	I used to go out a lot when I was younger.
¿Estabas en la casa cuando llamé a la puerta?	Were you in the house when I knocked on the door?
Juan hablaba como si fuera un experto.	Juan spoke as if he were an expert.
Nadábamos aquí cada viernes.	We used to swim here every Friday.
Mandaban cartas.	You (plural) used to send letters.
Estaban bailando cuando Pedro los interrumpió.	They were dancing when Pedro interrupted them.

For *-er* and *-ir* verbs, remove the stem (the *-er* or the *-ir*) from the infinitive, then add:

yo	-ía	nosotros/as	-íamos
tú	-ías	ustedes	-ían
él/ella/usted	-ía	ellos/ellas/	-ían

Take a look at some examples:

Listen to Track 214

Dije que tenía miedo.	I said that I was scared.
Hacía calor.	It was hot (weather).
¿Con padres tan tolerantes, podías hacer lo que te diera la gana cuando eras joven?	With such relaxed parents, could you do whatever you wanted when you were growing up?
Irina y yo salíamos hasta que apareció su ex.	Irina and I were going out until her ex showed up.
Volvían a casa tarde todos los días.	You (plural) used to return home late every day.
Tomaban demasiado antes de asistir a Alcohólicos Anónimos.	They used to drink too much before they went to AA.

Irregular verbs

Good news! Not many verbs are irregular in the imperfect. The only ones that are irregular are *ir*, *ser*, and *ver* (and certain words that are connected to *ver*, like *prever*).

Ir (to go)

Listen to Track 215

iba	íbamos
iba	Iban

Examples:

Iba a decirte algo.	I was going to tell you something.
¿Ibas para la casa cuando me llamaste?	Were you going (on your way) home when you called me?
Ernesto iba al centro comercial frecuentemente.	Ernesto used to go to the mall frequently.
Antes de que falleciera, mi abuela y yo íbamos de vacaciones cada año.	Before she passed away, my grandma and I used to go on holiday every year.
Cuando eran pequeños, iban al mercado con su mamá cada fin de semana.	When you (plural, informal) were little, you used to go to the market with your mom every weekend.
Los chicos iban a clase cuando Pedro se desmayó.	The boys were going to (on the way to) class when Pedro passed out.

Ser (to be)

Listen to Track 216

era	éramos
era	eran

Cuando yo era joven, me gustaban los peluches.	When I was young, I liked cuddly toys.
Eras la chica más amable del grupo.	You were the nicest girl in the group.
María dijo que su marido era guapo.	María said that her husband was handsome.
Éramos valientes en esa época.	We were brave in that period.
Miguel y tú eran una pareja bonita, pero ya se acabó.	Miguel and you were a lovely couple but it's over now.
Eran las ocho de la mañana.	It was eight o'clock in the morning.

Ver (to see)

Listen to Track 217

veía	veíamos
veía	veían

Veía dos películas cada noche.	I used to watch two films a night.
¿Veías a menudo a Juan?	Did you used to see Juan often?
La luz estaba apagada. Marco no veía nada.	The light was switched off. Marco couldn't see anything.
Mi ex y yo nos veíamos cada día.	My ex and I used to see each other every day.
¿Veín caricaturas cuando eran niños?	Did you guys watch cartoons when you were kids?
Veían la tele todos los días.	They used to watch TV every day.

Workbook Lesson 22. Imperfect tense

Exercise 1: Write the correct imperfect tense conjugation for the following verbs.

1- (Él) Vivir _____

2- (Ustedes) Comer _____

3- (Yo) Escribir _____

4- (Ellos) Jugar _____

5- (Yo) Mover _____

Exercise 2: Choose the correct imperfect tense conjugation for the following verbs.

1- Las trabajadoras:	a. llaman	b. llamaban	c. llamaba
2- El vigilante:	a. dormía	b. dormían	c. dormíais
3- Los perros:	a. corrían	b. corría	c. corríamos
4- Tú:	a. hablabas	b. hablaban	c. hablaba

Exercise 3: Write five sentences. In each sentence, use a different verb in the imperfect tense from the following list.

1- Cepillar

2- Arreglar

3- Contar

4- Planificar

5- Viajar

Exercise 4: Complete the sentences with the correct form of the verb in brackets.

1- When I was a little boy, I cried a lot. = Cuando _____(ser) niño, _____ (llorar) mucho.

2- When you were coming from the store... = Cuando _____ (venir) de la tienda...

3- We used to play a lot = _____ (jugar) mucho.

4- We used to go to that gym when we were teenagers = _____ a ese gimnasio cuando éramos adolescentes.

5- They used to see him a lot. = Lo _____ (ver) mucho.

Exercise 5: Complete the sentences with the correct form of the verb in parenthesis.

1- When we were a couple... = Cuando _____ (ser) novios…

2- You used to go to this bar. = (Tú) _____ (ir) a ese bar.

3- We used to see each other a lot. = Nos _____ (ver) mucho.

4- My brother used to be slim. = Mi hermano _____ (ser) delgado.

5- I used to see her all the time. = La _____ (ver) todo el tiempo.

Exercise 6: Choose the correct option to complete the sentences.

1- _____ a mi tía todos los días.

   a. visité   b. visitaba

2- _____ el vestido verde para el evento.

   a. llevó   b. llevaba

3- Carlota _____ la cena cuando el timbre sonó.

   a. preparó   b. preparaba

4- Juan _____ 7 kilómetros cada semana.

   a. corrió   b. corría

5- Pablo _____ dos libros al año cuando era adolescente.

   a. leyó   b. leía

Exercise 7: Complete the sentences with the correct form of the verb in brackets.

Durante nuestras vacaciones…

1- Mis hermanas _____ (jugar) a las cartas.

2- Mi tía _____ (mandar) mensajes.

3- Mi primo _____ (escuchar) música.

4- Mis primos _____ (platicar).

5- Mis papás _____ (ver) muchas películas.

Exercise 8: Complete the following text with the correct form of the verbs in brackets.

Antes de terminar la universidad, yo _____ (vivir) en Medellín con mis amigos Paula y Manuel. Los fines de semana mis amigos y yo _____ (tomar) cerveza y después _____ (salir) a bailar. Además, nosotros también _____ (ir) al cine y a los bolos. Lo que más me _____ (gustar) de esos tiempos _____ (ser) ir a la playa.

Exercise 9: Use the correct form of the verb to complete the sentences.

1- Ser:

   _____ las cinco de la mañana.

2- Estudiar:

   Juan siempre _____ antes de una prueba.

3- Comer:

   Yo _____ en el restaurante con frecuencia.

4- Limpiar:

   Tú _____ las ventanas cada dos meses.

5- Enviar:

   De vez en cuando, Juan y Pedro les _____ dinero a sus padres.

Exercise 10: Complete the sentences with the correct form of *one* of the verbs in brackets.

Cuando era pequeño, _____ (ser / tener) un niño muy deportista. Me _____ (prestar / gustar) ir al patio a jugar en los columpios y en el sube y baja. Mientras yo jugaba, mi papá _____ (comer / leer) el periódico o _____ (comer / leer) empanadas.

ANSWERS:

Exercise 1

1/ Vivía 2/ Comían 3/ Escribía 4/ Jugaban 5/ Movía

Exercise 2

1/ llamaban 2/ dormía 3/ corrían 4/ hablabas

Exercise 3

Answers: may vary.

Exercise 4

1/ era, lloraba 2/ venías 3/ jugábamos 4/ íbamos 5/ veían

Exercise 5

1/ éramos 2/ Ibas 3/ veíamos 4/ era 5/ veía

Exercise 6

1/ visitaba 2/ llevó 3/ preparaba 4/ corría 5/ leía

Exercise 7

1/ Jugaban 2/ Mandaba 3/ Escuchaba 4/ Platicaban 5/ Veían

Exercise 8

Antes de terminar la universidad, yo vivía en Medellín con mis amigos Paula y Manuel. Los fines de semana mis amigos y yo tomábamos cerveza y después salíamos a bailar. Además, nosotros también íbamos al cine y a los bolos. Lo que más me gustaba de esos tiempos era ir a la playa.

Exercise 9

1/ Eran 2/ Estudiaba 3/ Comía 4/ Limpiabas 5/ Enviaban

Exercise 10

Cuando era pequeño, era un niño muy deportista. Me gustaba ir al patio a jugar en los columpios y en el sube y baja. Mientras yo jugaba, mi papá leía el periódico o comía empanadas.

Lesson 23. Direct vs Indirect Speech

The difference between direct and indirect speech (also called reported speech) is easy to understand, but not very easy to apply when speaking in a foreign language. It is a very important part of communicating, however, and plays a major role in most conversations.

So, what's the difference?

That's a very good question! Before we get too far ahead of ourselves with all the little technicalities, let's make sure that we understand what we're dealing with here.

In order to do this, take the following conversation:

Pedro: Where are you going?

Jose: To the store.

Pedro: Will you get milk?

Jose: Sure, no problem.

Now, let's say Pedro later goes on to have a conversation with someone else, about the above-mentioned interaction. There are some options for how they could go about doing this. Let's just say it looked something like this:

Pedro: I asked Jose where he was going. He said, "To the store." So, I asked if he would get some milk, and he said "Sure, no problem."

The above recounting of a previous event or exchange with another person is what we're going to look at. You have two options when doing this.

The first, is by using quotation marks. This is direct speech. This means that the words are being repeated exactly like they were said.

He said, "To the store."

...and he said, "Sure, no problem."

The second way of recounting a conversation is through indirect speech. In the example above, this is done through changing the verb tense, although that isn't always required (we will look at that more later).

Original: Where are you going

Reported: I asked him where <u>he was going</u>.

Original: Will you get some milk?

Reported: I asked if he <u>would get</u> some milk.

Basically, there are <u>3 important rules</u> to keep in mind when using indirect (reported) speech. They are:

You will <u>not</u> use quotation marks

Since you're not quoting, you <u>don't need to say word-for-word</u> what the person said

When reporting what someone said, you generally change the verb tense.

Reporting Verbs

There are still a few things we need to talk about before getting into everyone's favorite part about grammar–the technicalities.

In order to identify that something is being "reported" or to communicate that you are repeating something that someone said previously, you'll use a reporting verb. We have them in English as well.

The most common are:

Listen to Track 218

Spanish	English meaning	Example (in indirect/ reported speech)
Decir*	Say	*Me dijo que tenía que estudiar-* He told me he had to study.
Preguntar*	Ask	*Le preguntó si podía ir a la fiesta-* She asked if she could go to the party.
Querer saber*	Want to know	*Juan quiso saber si lo podía llevar al cine-* Juan wanted to know if I could take him to the movies.
Querer*	Want	*María quería que José hablara con ella-* Maria wanted José to talk with her.
Pedir*	To ask for	*Me pidió que le trajera las llaves-* He asked me to bring him the keys.
Anunciar	Announce	*El profesor anunció que tendremos un examen el martes-* The teacher announced that we will have an exam on Tuesday.
Comentar	Comment	*Me comentó que no había podido dormir mucho la semana pasada-* He told me he couldn't sleep much last week.
Confesar	Confess	*Alicia le confesó a su novio que había salido con otro-* Alicia confessed to her boyfriend that she had gone out with another man.
Contestar	Answer	*Le contestamos a Pablo que sí iríamos a la fiesta-* We answered Pablo that yes, we would go to the party.
Prometer	Promise	*Me prometiste que lavarías la ropa-* You promised me you would do the laundry.
Quejarse	Complain	*Los niños se quejaron de que no tenían juguetes-* The children complained that they didn't have toys.
Recordar	Remind	*Nos recordaron que la cena empezaba a las 20.00-* They reminded us that the party started at 8:00pm.

*Most common of the most common

"Que"–your new best friend

You'll notice that (almost) all of the examples above in the chart using reported speech include the little word "que." This is not a coincidence.

When speaking in reported speech you will always use the "que" (meaning "that"). Even if in English we can and would omit the "that", you still need it in Spanish.

"She said <u>that</u> she was tired."- Here, in English the "that" is optional. This is not the case in Spanish.

"He asked <u>that</u> I go to the store." (He asked me to go to the store.) - This is one of the examples where "that" wouldn't be used in English, but it would in Spanish.

But wait… the questions…

If you're reporting a question, you have a few options available as they don't always need the "que".

Yes and No Questions

If the answer to the question being reported can be "yes" or "no" you <u>don't need the "que."</u> In these situations we would use "si" like in English (if).

"He asked me if I could go to the store."- *Me preguntó si podía ir a la tienda.*

Questions with question words

If you are reporting a question that contains question words (where, who, when, etc.), you will not need the "que" but stick with the question word used in the original context.

Listen to Track 219

María: Where is Sara? (*¿Dónde está Sara?*)

Reported speech: Maria wanted to know where Sara was. (*María quería saber dónde estaba Sara.*)

Let's get a little more technical.

We'll try to ease you into all of this grammatical stuff. It seems like a lot to remember. But, a lot of it is very common in English as well, so try to not to feel too overwhelmed!

Personal pronouns and Possessive pronouns

Again, let's start with an **Example:**

Listen to Track 220

María: Can you tell my brother that I need to talk to him? *¿Puedes decirle a mi hermano que necesito hablar con él ?*

Here, obviously a few things need to change if you want to report this statement. For one, he's not your brother and for another you're not the one that needs to speak to him.

In this situation, the personal pronouns (you, I) need to change, as well as the possessive (my). Here's how this statement would sound when repeating it later on to someone else:

Direct speech: Maria asked me, "Can you tell my brother that I need to talk to him?" *María me pidió, "Puedes (tú) decirle a mi hermano que (yo) necesito hablar con él?*

The pronouns remain the same.

Indirect/ Reported speech: Maria asked me to tell her brother that she needed to talk to him. *María me pidió que (yo) le dijera a su hermano que (ella) necesita hablar con él.*

Here, you can see that the pronouns did change.

So far so good, right? It's pretty basic stuff up to this point. Just like in English, we need to change the subject and the pronouns.

Time phrases

Obviously, more often than not, if you're reporting something that happened, it's because the person you're recounting the event to wasn't there when it took place–i.e. it was in the past.

So, here's how you would change around your time phrases, so they line up with what you're saying:

Listen to Track 221

Time used in direct speech	Time used in reported speech	Example in direct speech	Example in reported speech
Hoy (today)	*Ese día/ Aquel día* (that day)	*Juan dijo, "hoy es mi cumpleaños."*- Juan said, "Today is my birthday."	*Juan dijo que aquel día era su cumpleaños.*- Juan said that that day was his birthday.
Ahora (now)	*Entonces* (then)	*Mis padres me dijeron, "tienes que volver a casa ahora."*- My parents told me, "You have to come home now."	*Mis padres me dijeron que tenía que volver a casa entonces.*- My parents told me I had to go home then.
Ayer (yesterday)	*El día anterior* (the day before)	*Martín dijo, "fui a la fiesta ayer."*- Martin said, "I went to the party yesterday."	*Martín dijo que había ido a la fiesta el día anterior.*- Martin said he went to the party the day before.
Mañana (tomorrow)	*El día siguiente* (the next day)	*Me contó, "iré a trabajar mañana."* He told me, "I'll go to work tomorrow."	*Me dijo que iría a trabajar al día siguiente*- He told me he would go to work the next day.
La semana/el mes/ el año que viene (next week, next month, next year)	*A la semana siguiente/ Al mes siguiente/ Al año siguiente* (the following week/month/year)	*Clara me dijo "lo haré la semana que viene."* Claire said to me, "I'll do it next week."	*Clara dijo que lo haría a la semana siguiente*- Claire said she'd do it the following week.
La semana pasada/el mes pasado/ el año pasado (last week, last month and last year)	*La semana anterior/el mes anterior/ el año anterior* (the previous week/ month/ year)	*Ana dijo " lo vi el año pasado"* Ana said, "I saw him last year."	*Ana dijo que lo había visto el año anterior*- Ana said that she had seen him the previous year.
Hace + period of time (period of time+ago)	*Hacía*+period of time (period of time + before)/ period of time + ante	*Me dijo, "hace seis meses que rompimos."*- She said, "We broke up six months ago."	*Me dijo que habían roto hace seis meses*- She told me that they broke up six months ago.
Aquí (here)	*Ahí* (there)	*Jesús me dijo "nací aquí."*- Jesus told me, "I was born here."	*Jesús me dijo que había nacido ahí*- Jesus told me he was born there.
Este/ Esta (this)	*Ese/ Esa* (that)/ *Aquel/ aquella* (that)	*Alejandro dijo, "me gusta mucho este libro."* Alejandro told me, "I really like this book."	*Alejandro dijo que le gustó mucho ese libro*- Alejandro told me he really liked that book.
Estos/ Estas (these)	*Eses/ Esas* (those)/ *Aquellos/ aquellas* (those)	*Me dijo el profesor, "a los niños les encantan estas películas."*- The teacher told me, "The children love these movies."	*Me dijo el profesor que a los niños les encantaban esas películas*- The teacher told me that the children loved those movies.

As you'll notice above, all of the examples are written in the past. This is also something important to pay attention to, and probably one of the most important grammatical points of reported speech. So, let's go ahead and dive right into that!

Verb tenses in indirect (reported) speech.

The tense of the reporting verb (present, past, future) will have a big impact on the rest of the sentence.

Not only will you need to pay attention to the tense, but also to what is being said.

Command/Request vs information

Depending on the context of the conversation being reported, you'll need to use different ways of repeating it.

This is where things can start to get a little tricky. We do have similar rules in English as in Spanish, but in English they are a little more flexible, and followed less frequently.

Here are some good rules to keep in mind when using indirect speech in Spanish:

If the reporting verb is in the present or present perfect tense you do not need to change the verb tense–unless it's a command (we'll talk more about this in a minute).

If the reporting verb is in the preterite, imperfect, or the past perfect tense, you do need to change the verb tense.

Let's look at a short scenario and see what we have:

Scenario: Let's say you're texting with someone, and your friend (who you're with physically) wants to know what the person texting you is saying.

Person 1: What did he say?

Person 2: He asked if we are free tonight. (Reporting information)

Person 1: Why? What does he want?

Person 2: He wants us to help him move. (Reporting a request)

Here, we can see that in the first part, Person 2 is simply repeating the information. He asked a question, and this is what it is. The reporting verb "want to know" is in the present, so the second verb is in the present as well.

In the second part of the exchange, the reporting verb is in the present, so in English, we keep it in the present as well. In Spanish, however, if we are reporting a request or command, we need to use the subjunctive. In this case it will be the present subjunctive because the reporting verb is in present.

In Spanish, the conversation would go like this:

Listen to Track 222

Person 1: *¿Qué dijo?"*

Person 2: *Quiere saber si estamos libres esta noche.* (Present-present)

Person 1: *¿Por qué? ¿Qué quiere?*

Person 2: *Quiere que le ayudemos a mudarse.* (Present-present subjunctive)

Note: This change to the subjunctive only happens with certain verbs: Decir, Pedir, Querer. An easy way to remember to do this is if the verb will be followed by "si" or "que."

If it's followed by "si", you will <u>not</u> use the subjunctive.

Quiere saber si podemos salir esta noche. (He wants to know if we can go out tonight.)

Me pregunta si quiero verlo mañana. (He's asking if I can meet up tomorrow.)

Again, in this situation you're not necessarily relaying the request or the command, but merely the information contained in the request itself.

When followed by "*que*" and reporting a request or command:

Listen to Track 223

Fernando dice, "Ten cuidado." (Fernando says, "Be careful.")

Me dice que tenga cuidado. (He tells me to be careful.)

Fernando pide, "¿Me puedes ayudar con los deberes?" (Fernando asks, "Can you help me with my homework?")

Fernando me pide que le ayude con los deberes. (Fernando asks me to help him with the homework.)

But NOT: *Fernando me dice, "tienes que ir a clase mañana"* (This is <u>not</u> a command.)

Fernando me dice que tengo que ir a clase mañana.

Verb Tense Changes

So, if you feel like all of that has settled into your mind and it's not going to explode just yet, let's keep chugging along!

As mentioned above, if the reporting verb is in the present tense, it will only change (to present subjunctive) if the thing being reported is a command/ request.

When the reporting verb is in the past, however, the rest of the information being reported will need to change tense. Here's how it's going to work:

Listen to Track 224

Present Simple–Imperfect

Direct speech: *Angela dijo, "No puedo ir."* (Angela said, "I can't go.")

Indirect/ Reported speech: *Angela dijo que no podía ir.* (Angela said that she couldn't go.)

Listen to Track 225

Preterite–Pluscuamperfecto (past perfect)

Direct speech: *Sergio dijo, "Ayer compré un celular nuevo."* (Sergio said, "Yesterday I bought a new cell phone.")

Indirect/ Reported speech: *Sergio dijo que el día anterior había comprado un móvil nuevo.* (Sergio said that the day before he had bought a new phone.)

Future simple (will)–Conditional simple (would)

Listen to Track 226

Direct speech: *Candela dijo, "Llegaré tarde."*- (Candela said, "I'll arrive late.")

Indirect/ Reported speech: *Candela dijo que llegaría tarde.* - (Candela said that she would arrive late.)

Imperfect/Conditional/Past Perfect

With these, you will not change second verb tense. Yay!

Imperfect:

Listen to Track 227

Direct speech: *Juan dijo, "la playa era muy bonita."* (Juan said, "The beach was very pretty.")

Indirect/ Reported speech: *Juan dijo que la playa era muy bonita.* (Juan said that beach was very pretty.)

Conditional:

Listen to Track 228

Direct speech: *María dijo, "Me gustaría vivir en Nueva York."* (Maria said, "I would like to live in New York."

Indirect/ Reported speech: *María dijo que le gustaría vivir en Nueva York.* (Maria said she would like to live in New York.

Past Perfect

Listen to Track 229

Direct speech: *Mi padre me dijo, "a las 5 ya había llegado."* (My dad told me, "At 5 I had already arrived.")

Indirect/ Reported speech: *Mi padre me dijo que a las 5 ya había llegado.* (My dad told me that at 5 he had already arrived.)

Just one more thing... I promise!

One last thing to remember: like we saw with the present tense, is that if the verb in the past is a reporting verb, and what is being reported is a command or request, you will use the subjunctive–past subjunctive this time!

Listen to Track 230

Direct speech: *Mis padres me dijeron, "vuelve a casa a las 23.00."* (My parents told me, "Be home by 11:00pm.)

Indirect/ Reported speech: *Mis padres me dijeron que volviera a casa a las 23.00.* (My parents told me to be home by 11:00 pm.)

¡Madre Mía! That was a lot of information!

Let's see if we can condense it down just a little bit.

Important rules to remember. If you are using reported speech:

You will <u>not</u> use quotation marks

Since you're not quoting, you <u>don't need to say word-for-word</u> what the person said

When reporting what someone said, you generally change the verb tense.

If you do need to change the verb tense, this is why and when:

If the reporting verb is in the present or present perfect tense, you <u>do not need to change</u> the verb tense–unless <u>it's a command.</u>

Commands or requests with a present tense reporting verb will take the present subjunctive conjugation in the following verb.

If the reporting verb is in the preterite, imperfect, or the past perfect tense, <u>you do need to change the verb tense.</u>

Again, commands or requests with a past tense reporting verb will need to take the past subjunctive conjugation in the following verb.

If the reporting verb is in the past, these are the changes you'll make:

Present simple–imperfect

Preterite–Past Perfect (Pluscuamperfecto)

'Will' future–simple continual (would)

Verb tenses that will not change the tense of the other verbs:

Imperfect

Conditional

Past Perfect

Things to keep in mind:

- Remember your reporting verbs
- Remember to change the personal and possessive pronouns
- Remember your time phrases

In reality, it's not as complicated as it looks. It may take a little practice to get used to, but after a while, you'll find that it's pretty similar to what we do in English.

Workbook Lesson 23. Direct vs Indirect Speech

Exercise 1: Complete the sentences with the correct form of the verb in the original statements.

1- Estoy cansadísimo - Me dijo que _____ cansadísimo.

2- Quiero ir al parque contigo - Me dijo que _____ ir al parque conmigo.

3- Te espero en la esquina a las 7 - Me dijo que me _____ en la esquina a las 7.

4- Mañana te llevaré de excursión - Me dijo que al día siguiente me _____ de excursión.

5- La semana que viene veremos una película mexicana - Me dijo que la semana siguiente _____ una película mexicana.

Exercise 2: Decide if the following sentences are correct or incorrect.

1- Me dijo que estábamos cansadísimo.

2- Me dijeron que iríamos a dormir temprano.

3- Me comentó que no pudo dormir mucho mañana.

4- Le prometí que no lo hará de nuevo.

Exercise 3: Now, rewrite the incorrect sentences from exercise 2 in their correct form.

1- _____.

2- _____.

3- _____.

Exercise 4: Rewrite the following sentences in indirect speech.

1- Julia afirmó: "Soy buena memorizando."

- Julia afirmó _____.

2- Nosotros confirmamos: "El camión de la basura pasó a las 9."

- Nosotros confirmamos _____ a las 9.

3- La profesora contó: "Antes tenía un pez."

- La profesora contó _____.

4- El alcalde explica: "La ciudad está en perfecto estado."

- El alcalde explicó _____.

5- Los niños se han quejado: "No nos gusta el jugo de pera."

- Los niños se han quejado de _____.

Exercise 5: Rewrite these questions in indirect speech.

1- La mamá pregunta a su hijo: "¿Te has bañado?"

- La mamá pregunta a su hijo _____.

2- El profesor preguntó: "¿Cuándo murió Cleopatra?"

- El profesor preguntó _____.

3- Verónica preguntó a su mejor amiga: "¿Por qué lloras?"

  - Verónica preguntó a su mejor amiga _____.

4- Mi hermana me pregunta todos los días: "¿Quieres jugar Monopoly?"

  - Mi hermana me pregunta todos los días _____.

5- La policía preguntó al viajero: "¿En qué estación se baja usted?"

  - La policía preguntó al viajero _____.

Exercise 6: Decide whether the sentences are direct or indirect speech:

1- Sara dijo que no toleraría esto ni un minuto más.

2- "Pedro es nuestro supervisor," dijo Juan.

3- José y María preguntaron si estábamos listos.

4- Ana mencionó que irían al museo.

5- "Ken tomará café con Claudia," contó Caterina.

Exercise 7: Now, convert the previous sentences into the opposite speech, meaning direct into indirect and indirect into direct.

1- _____

2- _____

3- _____

4- _____

5- _____

Exercise 8: Report the following text

"El coche estaba estacionado al lado del parque" dijo Jesús, pero su mamá le respondió, "El coche ya no está ahí."

"Llamemos a la policía, entonces," exclamó Jesús. "Y, ¿nos ayudarán?" se preguntó su mamá.

Exercise 9: Rewrite the following commands/requests in indirect speech.

1- "Ponlo aquí" - Él me dijo que _____.

2- "No lo olvides" - Ella me recordó _____.

3- "Estaciona tu coche detrás de la casa" - Él me pidió _____ detrás de la casa.

4- "No lo dudes." - Ellos me dijeron _____.

5- "Por favor, comunícate con ellos hoy." - Ella me pidió _____.

Exercise 10: Rewrite the following indirect speech sentences as direct speech sentences.

1- Renata dijo que ella compraría la cena.

2- Pablo preguntó si íbamos a la fiesta.

3- Laura comentó que había comido pizza con su novio anoche.

4- Isabel y Natalia dijeron que estaban enfermas.

5- Julián indicó que había terminado su turno.

ANSWERS:

Exercise 1

1/ estaba 2/ quería 3/ esperaba 4/ llevaría 5/ veríamos

Exercise 2

1/ Incorrect 2/ Correct 3/ Incorrect 4/ Incorrect

Exercise 3

1/ Me dijo que estaba cansadísimo. 2/ Me comentó que no pudo dormir mucho ayer. 3/ Le prometí que no lo haría de nuevo.

Exercise 4

1/ Julia afirmó que era buena memorizando. 2/ Nosotros confirmamos que el camión había pasado a las 9. 3/ La profesora contó que antes había tenido un pez. 4/ El alcalde explicó que la ciudad estaba en perfecto estado. 5/ Los niños se han quejado de que no les gustaba el jugo de pera.

Exercise 5

1/ La mamá pregunta a su hijo si se ha bañado. 2/ El profesor preguntó que cuándo había muerto Cleopatra. 3/ Verónica preguntó a su mejor amiga por qué lloraba. 4/ Mi hermana me pregunta todos los días si quiero jugar Monopoly. 5/ La policía la preguntó al viajero en qué estación se bajaba él.

Exercise 6

1/ Indirect speech 2/ Direct speech 3/ Indirect speech 4/ Indirect speech 5/ Direct speech

Exercise 7

1/ Sara dijo: "No toleraré esto un minuto más." 2 / Juan dijo que Pedro era su supervisor. 3/ José y María preguntaron: "¿Están listos?" 4/ Ana mencionó: "Iremos al museo." 5/ Caterina dijo que Ken tomaría un café con Claudia.

Exercise 8

Jesús dijo que el coche estaba estacionado al lado del parque, pero su mamá le respondió que el coche ya no estaba ahí. Jesús exclamó que llamaran a la policía y su mamá le preguntó si los ayudarían.

Exercise 9

1/ Él me dijo que lo pusiera ahí. 2/ Ella me recordó que no lo olvidara. 3/ Él me pidió que estacionara mi coche detrás de la casa. 4/ Ellos me dijeron que no lo dudara. 5/ Ella me pidió que, por favor, me comunicara con ellos hoy.

Exercise 10

1/ Renata dijo: "Yo compraré la cena." 2/ Pablo preguntó: "¿Van a la fiesta?" 3/ Laura comentó: "Comí pizza con mi novio anoche." 4/ Isabel y Natalia dijeron: "Estamos enfermas." 5/ Julián indicó: "He terminado mi turno."/ "Terminé mi turno."

Lesson 24. Imperative

Giving commands is an important part of speaking a language. In Spanish, commands are very important and frequently used in daily speech.

Read on for a quick introduction to this very useful element of the language!

Before We Dive in Too Deep...

Obviously, everyone knows what a command is. In English, forming the commands is pretty straightforward and relies more on your intonation than anything. When we hear the term "command" we usually think about a harsh, scolding tone or being told to do something by an authority figure. "Clean your room!", "Turn in that report!", "Don't be late!"

In Spanish, however, this isn't always the case. There are a few different ways to give "commands" and some of them would even be considered polite.

Depending on where in the Spanish speaking world you are, you will find that the use of commands may differ. In Spain, for example, the informal command form is used all the time and there is nothing strange about someone you don't know speaking to you in the "tú" command form; but in some Latin American countries, as in Mexico, this would be extremely rude and the formal command form would be used.

Either way, the use of commands in Spanish is much more common and not quite as harsh as we as English speakers may be used to.

Usted (The Formal "You") and Ustedes Commands

The "usted" conjugation is the formal, respectful "you." So, this first way of forming the command will be used in any situation where you may feel you aren't comfortable with the person you're speaking to.

However, the "ustedes" is the plural You. "Ustedes" is the personal pronoun needed for communicating directly with a group of people (*Ustedes son muy responsables* – **You** are very responsible.) Not to confuse with the "ustedes" (plural form of the formal you) from Spain that is utilize when you're speaking to a group of **people you would want to show respect to**.

*"*Ustedes*" in Mexico is literally the plural "You" but in Spanish, both are used in either a formal or an informal situation. Don't forget it!

The Affirmative Usted Commands

To form the "affirmative" usted command, you'll need to go through a few different steps. These will be the same as forming the present subjunctive conjugation of the "usted" and "ustedes" forms.

Go to the Yo!

Put the verb in the "yo" (first person singular) form

(The reason for this will be clearer when we look at the examples)

Drop the "o" and add the appropriate ending:

For "ar" verbs,

Usted- add an "e"

Ustedes- add an "en"

For "er" and "ir" verbs,

Usted- add an "a"

Ustedes- add an "an"

Here are some Examples:

Listen to Track 231

Verb	Meaning	Yo Form	(Formal You) "Usted" Form	(Second Person Plural) "Ustedes" Form
hablar*	to talk	hablo	hable	hablen
decir**	to speak/ tell	digo	diga	digan
comer	to eat	como	coma	coman
venir	to come	vengo	venga	vengan
comprar	to buy	compro	compre	compren

*Here, conjugating to the "yo" form may not seem completely necessary, since there is no spelling/ pronunciation change.

**Here, however, we see the importance of going to the "yo" form. If not, the spelling/ pronunciation change will not carry over, and the command will be formed incorrectly.

Irregular Formal Commands

There aren't many irregular "usted/ ustedes" commands. They are:

Listen to Track 232

Verb	Meaning	"Usted" Command	"Ustedes" Command
dar	to give	dé	den
ir	to go	vaya	vayan
ser	to be	sea	sean
estar	to be	esté	estén
saber	to know	sepa	sepan

The Negative Formal Commands

Unlike the informal commands which we will see in a moment, there is no change in conjugation when forming the negative formal commands. Simply add a "no" and there you have it!

Listen to Track 233

Affirmative Formal Command Form	Negative Formal Command Form
Hable/ Hablen	*No hable/ No hablen*
Diga/ Digan	*No diga/ No digan*
Coma/ Coman	*No coma/ No coman*
Venga/ Vengan	*No venga/ No vengan*
Compre/ Compren	*No compre/ No compren*

Tú Command (The Informal "You")

The "tú" form of conjugating verbs is the informal, familiar "you." This is used with people you are comfortable with.

In Mexico it will only be used with friends or close family members.

Affirmative "Tú" Commands

To form the affirmative "tú" command, you will simply conjugate the verb in the 3rd person present conjugation (i.e. the "usted, él, ella") form.

Verb	Meaning	Tú Command Form
Hablar	To talk	*Habla*
Comer	To eat	*Come*
Escribir	To write	*Escribe*

Irregular "Tú" Commands

There are 8 irregular "tú" commands. They are:

Listen to Track 234

Verb	Meaning	Tú Command Form
Decir	To say/ tell	*Di*
Salir	To leave/ go out	*Sal*
Hacer	To do/ make	*Haz*
Ser	To be	*Sé*
Ir	To go	*Ve*
Tener	To have	*Ten*
Poner	To put/ place	*Pon*
Venir	To come	*Ven*

Negative "Tú" Commands

To form the negative "tú" command, you will need to follow just a few simple steps.

These steps will be the same as for forming the present subjunctive in the "tú" form.

Go to the Yo!

Drop the "o"

Add the appropriate ending

"-ar" verbs take an "es"

"-er" and "-ir" verbs take an "as"

Listen to Track 235

Verb	Yo Form	Negative "Tú" Command
Hablar	Hablo	No hables
Comer	Como	No comas
Escribir	Escribo	No escribas

Negative Irregular "Tú" Commands

To form the negative form of the irregular "tú" commands, you will follow the same pattern as the present subjunctive "tú" conjugations.

Listen to Track 236

Verb	Yo Form	Tú Negative Command Form
Decir	Digo	No digas
Salir	Salgo	No salgas
Hacer	Hago	No hagas
Ser	Soy*	No seas
Ir	Voy**	No vayas
Tener	Tengo	No tengas
Poner	Pongo	No pongas
Venir	Vengo	No vengas

*For this verb, the -oy gets dropped, not just the -o. The same would happen with the verb "estar" (Estoy- Estés)

** This verb is still somewhat irregular in the negative command form, as simply dropping the -oy and adding the -as ending would result in the 3rd person singular present conjugation ("vas").

At first glance, the imperative form in Spanish can seem a little overwhelming. The best way to get familiar with it is simply to practice!

Workbook Lesson 24. Imperative

Exercise 1: Use the pronoun in brackets and give commands using the verb in brackets.

1- (tú/correr dos kilómetros) _____.

2- (ella/tomar las pastillas) _____.

3- (ustedes/hacer la tarea) _____.

4- (ellos/comer el desayuno) _____.

5- (él/escucha la canción) _____.

Exercise 2: Complete the table

Infinitive	positive imperative	negative imperative
cantar/tú		
hablar/usted		
abrazar/ustedes		
saltar/nosotros		
decir/ustedes		

Exercise 3: Construct the positive imperative.

1- Por favor, ¡(mirar/ustedes) _____ atentamente!

2- ¡(Hacer/tú) _____ tus deberes!

3- ¡Por lo menos (alegrarse/nosotros) _____ un poco!

4- ¡(Lavar/tú) _____ ropa!

5- ¡(Venir/tú) _____ aquí!

Exercise 4: Construct the negative imperative.

1- ¡Hoy tú (cocina) _____ la cena!

2- ¡Por favor, (ir/nosotros) _____ a ese restaurante!

3- ¡(jugar/ellos) _____ Monopoly!

4- ¡(hablar/ustedes) _____ todos al mismo tiempo!

5- ¡(creerse/tú) _____ tan importante!

Exercise 5: Answer the questions following the example.

Example: ¿Guardo la leche en el refri? (Tú). Sí, guárdala.

¿Guardo las manzanas en el refri? (Usted). Sí, guárdelas.

1- ¿Abro la ventana de tu habitación? (Tú) Sí, _____.

2- ¿Compro las frutas en el mercado? (Usted) Sí, _____.

3- ¿Apago la luz del baño? (Usted) Sí, _____.

4- ¿Compro unos libros en la librería? (Tú) Sí, _____.

5- ¿Vendo los departamentos del centro de la ciudad? (Usted) Sí, _____.

Exercise 6: Write the imperative, as shown in the example.

Example: (Darme su pasaporte). Usted → Deme su pasaporte.

1- (Ayudar a las estudiantes). Tú→

2- (Venderle su casa). Usted→

3- (Salir por allá). Ustedes. →

4- (Escribir más rápido). Ustedes. →

5- (Estudiar menos horas.) Tú. →

Exercise 7: Write the negative imperative as shown in the example.

Example: (Abrir la puerta). Usted → No abra la puerta.

1- (Bajar volumen). Usted. →

2- (Comer más hamburguesas). Ustedes. →

3- (Pagar la factura). Ustedes. →

4- (Dejar el libro). Tú. →

5- (Pasar la basura). Nosotros. →

Exercise 8: Form the second person affirmative, as shown in the example.

Example: ¿Por qué no tomas un taxi? → *__Toma__* el taxi.

1- ¿Por qué no tomas el refresco? →

2- ¿Por qué no rompen las revistas? →

3- ¿Por qué no abres la ventana? →

4- ¿Por qué no traes la tarea? →

5- ¿Por qué no haces el trabajo? →

Exercise 9: Now, form the second person negative as shown in the example.

Example: ¿Por qué no traes a la bebé? → No *__la__* traigas.

1- ¿Por qué no escribes el número? →

2- ¿Por qué no haces la lasaña? →

3- ¿Por qué no ordenas tu ropa? →

4- ¿Por qué no ponen la música? →

5- ¿Por qué no escribes el libro? →

Exercise 10: Transform the affirmative sentence into a negative one.

1- Camine rápido.

2- Mueva el coche.

3- Tira basura en la calle.

4- Suba las escaleras por el lado izquierdo.

5- Deje las maletas en el pasillo.

ANSWERS:

Exercise 1

1/ Corre dos kilómetros 2/ Tómate las pastillas 3/ Hagan la tarea 4/ Coman el desayuno 5/ Escucha la canción

Exercise 2

infinitive	positive imperative	negative imperative
cantar/tú	Canta	No cantes
hablar/usted	Hable	No hable
abrazar/ustedes	Abrácense	No se abracen
saltar/nosotros	Saltemos	No saltemos
decir/ustedes	Digan	No digan

Exercise 3

1/ Por favor, ¡miren atentamente! 2/ ¡Haz tus deberes! 3/ ¡Por lo menos alegrémonos un poco! 4/ ¡Lava tu ropa! 5/ ¡Ven aquí!

Exercise 4

1/ ¡Hoy tú no cocinas la cena! 2/ ¡Por favor, no vayamos a ese restaurante!/ ¡Por favor, no hay que ir a ese restaurante! 3/ ¡No jueguen Monopoly! 4/ ¡No hablen todos al mismo tiempo! 5/ ¡No te creas tan importante!

Exercise 5

1/ Sí, ábrela. 2/ Sí, cómprelas. 3/ Sí, apáguela. 4/ Sí, cómpralos. 5/ Sí, véndalos.

Exercise 6

1/ Ayuda a las estudiantes. 2/ Véndale su casa. 3/ Salgan por allá. 4/ Escriban más rápido. 5/ Estudia menos horas.

Exercise 7

1/ No baje el volumen. 2/ No coman más hamburguesas. 3/ No paguen la factura. 4/ No dejes el libro. 5/ No pasemos la basura.

Exercise 8

1/ Toma el refresco. 2/ Rompan las revistas. 3/ Abre la ventana. 4/ Trae la tarea. 5/ Haz el trabajo.

Exercise 9

1/ No lo escribas. 2/ No la hagas. 3/ No la ordenes. 4/ No la pongan. 5/ No lo escribas.

Exercise 10

1/ No camine rápido. 2/ No mueva el coche. 3/ No tires la basura. 4/ No suba las escaleras por el lado izquierdo. 5/ No deje las maletas en el pasillo.

Lesson 25. Conditional Tense

The conditional tense is used to describe what would happen. You can use it when talking about hypothetical situations, e.g. 'I would buy the dress.'

How to form it

If you know the rules for the future tense and the imperfect tense, then forming the conditional is really simple! Don't worry if you don't know them; we'll break it down.

The conditional tense is formed by joining the future tense stem with the imperfect endings of -er and -ir verbs.

For regular verbs, the stem will simply be the infinitive.

The imperfect endings we need to stick onto the stems are:

-ía	-íamos
-ías	-ían
-ía	-ían

Let's look at some examples to make things clearer:

Ir- + -ía → iría.	I would go.
Jugar- + -ías → jugarías.	You would play.
Comer- + -ía → Pablo comería.	Pablo would eat.
Luchar- + -íamos → lucharíamos.	We would fight.
Correr- + -ían → correrían.	You (You plural) would run.
Cantar- + -ían → cantarían.	They would sing.

So usually, you just take the infinitive, and add one of the endings given above. Read through these example sentences, and you'll see that it works the same for -ar, -er, and -ir verbs!

Listen to Track 238

-ar	
Yo bailaría toda la noche.	I would dance all night.
Caminaría a casa.	She would walk home.
¿No ayudarían a su hijo?	Would you (You plural) not help your son?
-er	
Romperías el columpio.	You would break the swing.
Rosa vendería su reloj.	Rosa would sell her watch.
Margarita dijo que traerían bebidas.	Margarita said that you (You plural) would bring drinks.

-ir	
Viviríamos en una mansión.	We would live in a mansion.
Perder heriría su orgullo.	Losing would hurt his pride.
Carlos, escribirías buenas novelas.	Carlos, you'd write good novels.

Irregular stems

If you've looked at the future tense, you'll know that some verbs have irregular stems. They need to be learnt, but luckily there aren't too many. Here are the most common ones:

Infinitive	**Conditional stem**
caber (to fit)	*cabr-*
decir (to say)	*dir-*
haber (to have/to be/to exist)*	*habr-*
hacer (to do/to make)	*har-*
poder (to be able to)	*podr-*
poner (to put)	*pondr-*
querer (to want)	*querr-*
saber (to know/to taste)	*sabr-*
salir (to leave)	*saldr-*
tener (to have)	*tendr-*
valer (to be worth)	*valdr-*
venir (to come)	*vendr-*

*Haber is most commonly used in one of two ways. The first is 'there is'/'there are.'

For Example:

Listen to Track 239

Hay un coche ahí. (There is a car there.)

Habría un coche ahí. (There would be a car there.)

The second is 'to have' in compound tenses.

He comido. (I have had dinner.)

Habría comido. (I would have had dinner.)

Another irregularity to remember with stems is that if a stem has an accent, the accent moves to the ending, e.g.

Reír → Reiría

When to use the conditional

Often, the conditional tense is used with a condition, i.e. I would do something if certain conditions were met.

These conditions are conjugated in the imperfect subjunctive. There's no need to go into the imperfect subjunctive in detail right now, but it's helpful to be able to recognise it, so here are the common endings. Each person has two different forms for you to choose from, but I suggest the *-ra* form, as it's more common than the *-se* form.

In each case, you take off the infinitive ending, and add the new endings to the stem. There are exceptions (this is Spanish, after all!) but let's not go into those right now!

-ar verbs

Listen to Track 240

yo	hablara/hablase
tú	hablaras/hablases
él/ella/usted	hablara/hablase
nosotros	habláramos/hablásemos
ustedes	hablaran/hablasen
ellos/ellas	hablaran/hablasen

-er/-ir

Listen to Track 241

yo	vendiera/vendiese
tú	vendieras/vendieses
él/ella/usted	vendiera/vendiese
nosotros	vendiéramos/vendiésemos
ustedes	vendieran/vendiesen
ellos/ellas	vendieran/vendiesen

So, one way we can use the conditional is using the word *si* ('if') in one of these formulae:

Si [imperfect subjunctive], [conditional].

[Conditional] *si* [imperfect subjunctive].

Listen to Track 242

Si tuviera la oportunidad, iría a Francia.	If I had the opportunity, I would go to France.
Iría a Francia si tuviera la oportunidad.	I would go to France if I had the opportunity.
Si viniera Juan, me alegraría mucho.	If Juan came, I'd be really happy.
Me alegraría mucho si viniera Juan.	I'd be really happy if Juan came.
Si no dañara la salud, bebería.	If it weren't bad for one's health, I'd drink.
Bebería si no dañara la salud.	I'd drink if it weren't bad for one's health.

Here are some more example sentences. Try to identify the conditional and the imperfect subjunctive in each case.

Listen to Track 243

Si tuviera un profe interesante, estudiaría más.	If I had an interesting teacher, I would study more.
Si mis alumnos mostraran más interés, les enseñaría cosas más variadas.	If my students showed more interest, I'd teach them a greater variety of stuff.
Si perdiera todo mi dinero, ¿me amarías igual?	If I lost my money, would you still love me?
Conocerías a sus padres si salieras con él.	You'd meet his parents if you dated him.
Sandra leería más si tuviera tiempo.	Sandra would read more if she had the time.
Todo sería mejor si Miguel regresara a la casa.	Everything would be better if Miguel came home.
Hijo, si nos hicieras caso, te permitiríamos más libertad.	Son, if you did as we tell you, we would allow you more freedom.
Si tuviéramos la oportunidad, abriríamos una panadería.	If we had the opportunity, we'd open a bakery.
Si lo intentaran, conseguirían más.	If they tried, they would achieve more.

If I were you...

Another cool way of using the conditional is in the phrase 'if I were you.' There are a couple of ways to say this in Spanish:

Listen to Track 244

Si yo fuera tú...	If I were you...
Si yo fuera tú, llamaría a Humberto.	If I were you, I'd call Humberto.
Yo que tú...	If I were you...
Yo que tú, compraría la camisa.	If I were you, I'd buy the shirt.

Workbook Lesson 25. Conditional Tense

Exercise 1: Write the conditional tense of the verbs for the pronouns shown.

Verbs	Tú	Ella	Nosotros
Hablar	hablarías	hablaría	hablaríamos
Mover			
Querer			
Tener			
Venir			
Jugar			

Exercise 2: Complete the sentences with the conditional tense of the verb in brackets.

1- Para Año Nuevo (desear, yo) _____ hacer un viaje.

2- Yo me (venir) _____ a vivir a la capital y (preferir, tú) _____ vivir en la playa.

3- ¿Te (recoger) _____ Jesús y Alberto en caso de ser necesario?

4- ¿Te (gustar) _____ tomar un té?

5- No sé qué (tomar) _____ tu hermano. No había nada en el refri.

Exercise 3: Rewrite the infinitive in the conditional tense.

Alejandro no sabe qué hacer; dale tus sugerencias...

Example: No sabe si puede pedir un préstamo al banco. → Yo que tú, pediría un préstamo al banco.

1- No quiere presentarse a una entrevista de trabajo.

2- No sabe si comprar un coche o no.

3- No quiere hacer el curso de francés.

4- No quiere salir con Claudia.

5- No sabe si examinarse antes o después del invierno.

Exercise 4: What would you do in these situations? Write sentences using the conditional tense.

1- En el cine: la película está a punto de empezar, pero la persona de al lado responde una llamada. _____ _____.

2- En la alberca para adultos: dos chicas toman bebidas en vasos de vidrio. _____ _____.

3- En casa de una amiga que te hospeda: necesitas usar la lavadora, pero las instrucciones están en holandés y no sabes cómo funciona. _____.

4- En la calle: alguien ha estacionado su moto justo delante de tu puerta y tú no puedes pasar con las bolsas del súper. _____.

5- Por la radio local: escuchas un anuncio de trabajo que te interesa. _____.

Exercise 5: Use the following verbs in the correct form of the conditional tense to complete the sentences: << planchar, comer, gustar, permitir, tener, decir >>.

1- Yo que tú no _____ esa camisa.

2- (a mí) No me _____ vivir en un departamento cerca del centro.

3- Yo no _____ una relación con alguien así.

4- ¿Señorita, (usted) me _____ su identificación por favor?

5- Yo en tu lugar, le _____ una pequeña mentira.

Exercise 6: Match the following situations/problems with their corresponding solutions.

Problems:

1- Esta tarde tengo que pagar a mi arrendador la renta de mi departamento pero no me pagaron en mi trabajo.

2- Mañana tengo un examen muy importante pero no he estudiado nada porque tuve muchísimas tareas que entregar para otras materias.

3- He perdido el camión y necesito llegar a tiempo al aeropuerto, ya que no puedo cancelar el boleto de avión.

4- Mi padre tiene 60 años y lo han despedido después de llevar trabajando más de 25 años en la misma empresa.

5- Estoy enamorado de la novia de mi hermano. ¿Qué hago?

Solutions:

A. Tomar un taxi o llamar a un amigo.

B. Hablar con tu amigo, y si no lo entiende, alejarte.

C. Ayudarle a buscar un nuevo trabajo urgentemente.

D. Tomar 6 cafés y estudiar toda la noche.

E. Hablar con él y pagarle en cuanto te paguen en el trabajo.

Exercise 7: Complete the following dialogue with the correct from of the verbs in brackets.

María: ¿A dónde (viajar) _____ para pasar las vacaciones?

Carlos: Yo (querer) _____ pasar las vacaciones en las montañas. (dormir) _____ hasta tarde, (prender) _____ la calefacción y tú (preparar) _____ el desayuno. Después del desayuno, (ir) _____ todos los días a caminar un rato y me (meterse) _____ en las aguas termales.

Exercise 8: Read the following text and complete it with the correct verb from the table.

Carolina era fotógrafa y tenía que ir a la Ciudad de México para hacer una sesión de fotos a un modelo internacional famoso. El caso es que cuando se **1** hacia el aeropuerto de Medellín encontró un tráfico muy intenso: el embotellaje empezó a complicarse tanto, que ella pensó que **2** el vuelo, y que ya no **3** a su trabajo. Así que llamó desde su celular al aeropuerto para saber si **4** más vuelos a la Ciudad de México ese mismo día. Afortunadamente desde el aeropuerto salía un vuelo más ese día y Carolina se **5** en ese vuelo.

1	movía	dirija	dirigía
2	perdió	perdería	perderá
3	llegaría	llegará	llegaba

4	habría	habrá	habrían
5	iría	volaría	irá

Exercise 9: Decide if the following sentences are correct.

1. Si yo fuera tú, hará la tarea más temprano.

2. Yo comería mucho antes de salir si fuera a viajar por 12 horas.

3. Yo que tú, cerraré todas mis redes sociales por un tiempo.

4. Si tuviera fiebre, Pedro irá a comprarme alguna de medicina.

5. Mi mamá me cocinaría si está aquí.

Exercise 10: Now, rewrite the incorrect sentences in Exercise 9 correctly.

_____

_____

_____

_____

ANSWERS:

Exercise 1

Verbs	Tú	Ella	Nosotros
Hablar	hablarías	hablaría	hablaríamos
Mover	moverías	movería	moveríamos
Querer	querrías	querría	querríamos
Tener	tendrías	tendría	tendríamos
Venir	vendrías	vendría	vendríamos
Jugar	jugarías	jugaría	jugaríamos

Exercise 2

1/ desearía 2/ vendría - preferirías 3/ recogerían 4/ gustaría 5/ tomaría

Exercise 3

1/ Yo que tú, me presentaría a la entrevista de trabajo. 2/ Yo que tú, compraría un coche. 3/ Yo que tú, haría el curso de francés. 4/ Yo que tú, saldría con Claudia. 5/ Yo que tú, me examinaría antes/después del invierno.

Exercise 4

Answers: may vary.

Exercise 5

1/ plancharía 2/ gustaría 3/ tendría 4/ permitiría 5/ diría

Exercise 6

1/ E 2/ D 3/ A 4/ C 5/ B

Exercise 7

María: ¿A dónde viajarías para pasar las vacaciones?

Carlos: Yo querría pasar las vacaciones en las montañas. Dormiría hasta tarde, prendería la calefacción y tú prepararías el desayuno. Después del desayuno, iría todos los días a caminar un rato y me metería en las aguas termales.

Exercise 8

1/ dirigía 2/ perdería 3/ llegaría 4/ habrían 5/ iría

Exercise 9

1/ Incorrect 2/ Correct 3/ Incorrect 4/ Incorrect 5/ Incorrect

Exercise 10

1/ Si yo fuera tú, haría la tarea más temprano. 2/ Yo que tú, cerraría todas mis redes sociales por un tiempo. 3/ Si tuviera fiebre, Pedro iría a comprarme alguna medicina. 4/ Mi mamá me cocinaría si estuviera aquí.

Conclusion

Learning grammar is not a walk in the park. So, if you were able to finish all of that by consistently learning every day, hats off to you! What an amazing, amazing job you did and you should be very proud.

If you were not able to follow the daily plan as suggested, don't despair. The important thing is you made use of this book to build a solid foundation in your Spanish grammar.

We at My Daily Spanish hope that you will continue to keep learning every day. Even just a few minutes of daily study go a long way. It could be just listening to a 30-minute Spanish podcast, watching a Spanish movie or TV series, writing to a friend in Spanish, talking to a native Spanish speaker or reading the news in Spanish… the list goes on.

We have other available books at the My Daily Spanish store and on Amazon. Feel free to browse the different titles. They will help you solidify your knowledge of Spanish grammar.

If you have comments, questions or suggestions about this book, you may reach us at contact@mydaiyspanish.com. We'd be happy to hear from you.

You can also follow My Daily Spanish in social media where we aim to give you fun and useful contents to help you keep learning Spanish daily.

- Facebook (facebook.com/mydailyspanish)
- Instagram (@holamydailyspanish)
- Twitter (@mydailyspanish), and
- Pinterest (pinterest.com/mydailyspanish)

And so with this, we say goodbye. It has been an awesome 30 days (or more!) with you. Keep learning Spanish!

My Daily Spanish team

AUDIO DOWNLOAD INSTRUCTIONS

- Copy and paste this link into your browser:
  - › https://mydailyspanish.com/mexican-spanish-grammar/
- Click on the book cover. It will take you to a Dropbox folder containing each individual file. (If you're not familiar with what Dropbox is or how it works, don't panic, it just a storage facility.)
- Click the download button in the Dropbox folder located in the upper right portion of your screen. A box may pop up asking you to sign in to Dropbox. Simply click, "No thanks, continue to download" under the sign in boxes. (If you have a Dropbox account, you can choose to save it to your own Dropbox so you have access anywhere via the internet.)
- The files you have downloaded will be saved in a .zip file. Note: This is large file. Don't try opening it until your browser tells you that it has completed the download successfully (usually a few minutes on a broadband connection but if your connection is unreliable, it could take 10 to 20 minutes).
- The files will be in your "downloads" folder unless you have changed your settings. Extract them from the folder and save them to your computer or copy to your preferred devices, *et voilà* ! You can now listen to the audio anytime, anywhere.
- In case you have questions. Don't hesitate to contact us at contact@mydailyspanish.com

About My Daily Spanish

Mydailyspanish.com is a website created to help busy learners learn Spanish. It is designed to provide a fun and fresh take on learning Spanish through:

- Helping you create a daily learning habit that you will stick to until you reach fluency, and
- Making learning Spanish as enjoyable as possible for people of all ages.

With the help of awesome content and tried-and-tested language learning methods, My Daily Spanish aims to be the best place on the web to learn Spanish.

The website is continuously updated with free resources and useful materials to help you learn Spanish. This includes grammar and vocabulary lessons plus culture topics to help you thrive in a Spanish-speaking location–perfect not only for those who wish to learn Spanish, but also for travellers planning to visit Spanish-speaking destinations.

For any questions, please email contact@mydailyspanish.com.

✓   11 fun and engaging Spanish stories

✓   1,500+ Spanish words and expressions

✓   Practice your listening and pronunciation skills with the FREE audio narrated by a native Spanish speaker

LEARN MORE